Selected Political Writings

A reprint of the Cambridge University Press edition, with new editorial preface, re-vised introduction, and updated bibliography by Melvin Richter.

Original ISBN 0–521–21156–5 (cloth)
Original ISBN 0–521–29061–9 (paper)
Original Library of Congress Catalog Card Number 76–4753

MONTESQUIEU

Selected Political Writings

Translated and Edited by

MELVIN RICHTER

HACKETT PUBLISHING COMPANY

Indianapolis/Cambridge

For Micha

Montesquieu: 1689–1755

Copyright © 1990 by Hackett Publishing Company, Inc.
All rights reserved
Printed in the United States of America

99 98 97 96 95 94 93 92 91 90   1 2 3 4 5

For further information, please address

Hackett Publishing Company, Inc.
P.O. Box 44937
Indianapolis, Indiana 46244-0937

Library of Congress Cataloging-in-Publication Data

Montesquieu, Charles de Secondat, baron de, 1689–1755.
  [Selections. English. 1990]
  Selected political writings/Montesquieu; edited, with new
introduction and preface by Melvin Richter.
      p.   cm.
  Rev. ed. of: The political theory of Montesquieu. 1977.
  Includes bibliographical references.
  ISBN 0-87220-091-4—ISBN 0-87220-090-6 (pbk.)
  1. Political science—Early works to 1800. 2. State, The—Early
works to 1800. I. Richter, Melvin, 1921–   . II. Title.
JC179.M6813   1990
320—dc20   89-29578
                                                       CIP

Contents

EDITORIAL PREFACE

This volume makes available in modern English the most significant parts of Montesquieu's political, social, and legal theory. They have been translated by me from the best editions of his *Persian Letters* (1721), *Considerations on the Causes of the Greatness of the Romans and Their Decline* (1734), and the *Spirit of the Laws* (1st ed. 1748; revised ed., 1757).[1] So far as I know, this book is the only modern translation in English of selections from all three major political texts. First published in my *Political Theory of Montesquieu*, they are reproduced here without modification in order to provide students with as inexpensive an edition as possible.[2] My Introduction has been much shortened. The list of suggested readings at the end of this volume includes work on Montesquieu done since 1977.

Something ought to be said about how these translations are related to Montesquieu's original texts in French. The *Persian Letters* and the *Considerations* have long been recognized as masterpieces of French style, as well as works so original in their matter that they helped create new genres throughout Europe. Although *The Spirit of the Laws* is ostensibly the least literary of Montesquieu's great works, anyone presumptuous enough to attempt its translation must hesitate before the delicate structures of meaning, images, and rhythms created in such passages as those celebrating the distinctive spirit of the French people (IX, 7; XIX, 5), the chapter satirizing apologists of Negro slavery (XV, 5), and in the same tone (that of the *Persian Letters*), the inimitable set piece on the Inquisition's persecution of the Jews (XXV, 13). Confronted with such writing, the translator can aspire to little more than avoiding disgrace.

These selections from Montesquieu have a modest set of objectives in view: to make available his theories in accurate translations that present the fewest possible obstacles to modern students. When read in French today, Montesquieu does not appear quaint, despite constant references to governments and societies long since vanished. I have tried to render Montesquieu's meaning in a simple style that avoids archaism and anomaly. While seeking to find English terms that convey his ideas and style, I have had to depart from his sentence structure. Even had I wished to do so, I could not have produced the complex and beautifully balanced sentences he sometimes wrote. Nor have I retained Montesquieu's style in the titles of books and chapters. In *The Spirit of the Laws*, these often began with *De* ("Concerning"). Although such headings indicate Montesquieu's sympathy for the essayistic style of Montaigne and Bacon, to maintain this form is to set up an unnecessary barrier between Montesquieu and his potential modern readers. For the same reason I have omitted the italics Montesquieu often employed.

Montesquieu understood himself to be an intellectual innovator who needed new categories, concepts, and distinctions. Some of these he expressed by the use of familiar terms in new senses; others, by words and phrases of his own creation. To emphasize Montesquieu's terms of art, those special concepts he used to convey his theoretical intentions, I have employed a limited number of French words, the specialized meanings of which are given at the end of my Introduction. Thus when a term is given in French, it may be helpful to consult the section on *French Terms Used in the Translation*. Montesquieu's own notes in his texts, as well as my own, are given separately. A glossary of references follows the notes at the back of the book.

While doing my translations, I used no dictionaries Montesquieu himself could not have consulted. For the most part I depended upon the 1740 edition of the *Dictionnaire de l'Académie Française*.[3] A most useful eighteenth-century French-English and English-French dictionary based on that of the French Academy is the *Dictionnaire Royal François-Anglois et Anglois-François* of Abel Boyer. Montesquieu owned its first edition. On occasion, as when Montesquieu himself used English words, it is necessary to know their meaning in eighteenth-century usage. The best guide is Samuel Johnson's *Dictionary of the English Language*, published in 1755, the year of Montesquieu's death. Another source of great value for finding English equivalents is the correspondence of Montesquieu's friend, Lord Chesterfield. In his letters to his son and godson, Chesterfield, who knew France well, often compared and contrasted French and English linguistic usage, politics, and history.

I should like to acknowledge with gratitude the support of the American Council of Learned Societies, The National Endowment for the Humanities, The Social Science Research Council, and the PSC/CUNY Research Award Program, City University of New York. I have been much aided over the years by friends, colleagues, and students: Raymond Aron, Evelyn Barish, Samuel H. Beer, Jean Ehrard, Brenda Forman, Nannerl Keohane, David Lowenthal, Robert Loy, Allen Mandelbaum, Robert Shackelton, Susan Tenenbaum. Of all my debts, the greatest I owe are to my wife, Michaela Wenninger Richter, for her editorial skill and for her encouragement. My sons, Anthony and Giles, have provided invaluable support. This book is dedicated to Micha and to them.

M.R.

Paris
July 1989

INTRODUCTION

I
Montesquieu's Mind and Influence

Charles de Secondat, Baron de la Brède et de Montesquieu (1689–1755), made original contributions to political and social theory in his three major books: the *Persian Letters* (*Lettres persanes.* 1st ed. , Amsterdam, 1721), *Considerations on the Causes of the Greatness of the Romans and their Decline* (*Considérations sur les causes de la grandeur des Romains et leur décadence.* 1st ed. , Amsterdam, 1734), and *The Spirit of the Laws* (*De l'Esprit des loix.* 1st ed. , Geneva 1748).

At the time of the American Revolution, few other theorists could rival Montesquieu's prestige in the English-speaking world. In England, the most widely accepted interpretation of its law and constitution was that of Blackstone, of whom it has been said that his plagiarism of Montesquieu "would be nauseating if it were not comic."[1] To the brilliant thinkers of the Scottish Enlightenment who sought to establish a historical science based on successive modes of production through which mankind moved, "Montesquieu was the Bacon of this branch of philosophy, Dr. [Adam] Smith is the Newton."[2]

During the debate about adopting the American Constitution, both federalists and anti-federalists argued their cases on the basis of their respective interpretations of Montesquieu. Thus Hamilton, defending the feasibility of the federal system, wrote: "Opponents . . . have with great assiduity cited and circulated the observations of Montesquieu on the necessity of a contracted territory for a republican government. But they seem not to have been apprised on the sentiments of that great man in another part of his work. . . ."[3] Madison phrased his theory of the constitutional separation of powers as a gloss upon Montesquieu: "The oracle who is always consulted and cited upon this point is the celebrated Montesquieu. . . . Let us endeavor in the first place to ascertain his meaning on this point."[4]

Two centuries after the American and French Revolutions, Montesquieu is once again becoming accessible to students of political theory. A new edition of Montesquieu in French has been projected in honor of the three-hundredth anniversary of his birth.[5] Books such as *The Spirit of the Laws* have been retranslated into English for the first time since the eighteenth century.[6] Other important works by Montesquieu, such as his methodological "Essay on the Causes That May Affect Men's Minds and Characters," which turned up only after his death, have now made their way into English.[7] The decline of Marxism as an intellectually compelling force in France has been accompanied by a revival of

1

French interest in liberalism. This has made Montesquieu and his spiritual descendants, Benjamin Constant, Madame de Staël, Alexis de Tocqueville, and most recently, Raymond Aron, into crucial figures in that long-neglected tradition.

Just a few years ago it could be said that of Montesquieu's once unrivaled reputation, there remained only two traces: the belief that Montesquieu was a crude determinist who held climate to be the unique and unmediated cause of human action and institutions; the impression that Montesquieu's theory of politics was mechanical and narrowly legal, separated, that is, from any adequate view of the ways in which government actually operates and is affected by its social setting. Both of these views are demonstrably inaccurate. Careful students of *The Spirit of the Laws* who have read as far as Book XIX know that Montesquieu was not a crude geographical determinist. As for the alleged legalism of Montesquieu, there is little doubt that, for better or worse, his treatment of law and politics emphasized the character of the society within which such arrangements function. Montesquieu was among the creators of what are now known as political sociology and comparative politics. In the eighteenth century, he was regarded as a political theorist second to none in the attention he attracted from Virginia to St. Petersburg.

Montesquieu contributed much to what are now called the social sciences. Comte and Durkheim declared him to be the precursor of sociology. Ernst Cassirer and Franz Neumann found him to have been the inventor of that style of ideal-type analysis that culminated in Max Weber. Sir Frederick Pollock thought Montesquieu to be "the father of modern historical research" and of a "comparative theory of politics and law based on wide observations of actual systems." He has been called the first modern practitioner of comparative law and the founder of sociological jurisprudence. To Friedrich Meinecke, Montesquieu was among the founders of that view of the past known as *Historismus* ("historicism" or "historism"), a distinctly modern perspective characterized by its relativism, holism, emphasis upon the positive value of the irrational and customary, as well as the uniqueness of every case and period. John Millar and Adam Ferguson, speaking for the Scottish Enlightenment, viewed Montesquieu as the founder of a philosophical history that aspired to the discovery of the basic lawsgoverning human development. As for Montesquieu's explanation of laws, institutions, and political attitudes by reference to the social system in which they functioned, Hegel judged *The Spirit of the Laws* to be the first notable use of that method, the perfection of which he considered to be his own greatest contribution to the study of man. Lord Keynes called Montesquieu the greatest French economist, "the real French equivalent of Adam Smith . . . head and shoulders above the Physiocrats in penetration, clear-headedness and good sense (which are the qualities a good economist should have)." Montesquieu's contributions to penal law, with his attacks upon cruel penalties as unjustifiable, have been called the "Magna Carta of the citizen" and helped inspire the work of Marquis Beccaria. Montesquieu's concept of a society as having a general spirit pervading all its aspects clearly anticipates modern cultural anthropology. Jean Ehrard has ascribed to Montesquieu some of the discoveries claimed for Marxism and the sociology of knowledge: that "the real history of men in society does not coincide with their consciousness; their actual springs of action differ from their avowed motives." Raymond Aron and W. G. Runciman have discerned in Montesquieu the first practitioner of political sociology.[8]

Yet Montesquieu's place in the history of political theory has been obscured by this tendency to treat him as the founder of one or another of the modern social sciences. The most perceptive proponents of this view, such as Durkheim, noted with regret that Montesquieu remained in critical respects a political philosopher. To what extent was this true? And if so, does it not add to Montesquieu's value as a thinker rather than detract from it?

Montesquieu's relationship to his predecessors is complex, as is his relationship to the quarrel about the value of the political philosophies of the ancients and moderns. On the one hand, he believed that he had developed a novel method to formulate a theory for a novel situation. Modern European states of his time differed in significant respects, such as their commerce and international relations, he thought, from anything previously known. Modern science, knowledge, and *moeurs* in many respects surpassed those of the ancients. For example, he finds that the modern law of nations is far gentler than that of the Romans: ". . . in respect to which I leave the reader to judge how much we have improved upon them. Here we must render homage to our modern age (*nos temps modernes*), to reason, religion, philosophy, and *moeurs* at the present time."[9] Montesquieu implied that anyone in the mid-eighteenth century who sought the best state then attainable should study England, the model for combining political liberty, commerce, and religion.

Yet Montesquieu never gave up his lifelong dialogue with past political philosophers. Although he held that monarchy was the government uniquely suited to modern commercial states, Montesquieu stopped for a chapter of *The Spirit of the Laws* (XI, 9) to explain why the ancients, and especially Aristotle, had never understood it. His *Pensées*, written for his private use, is full of imaginary conversations with his predecessors. One early passage gives the flavor of Montesquieu's great admiration for what he regarded as the very core of classical political life and thought: "It is the love of *patrie* that gives to the histories of Greece and Rome that nobility lacking in our own. There it was always the spring of all actions. . . . Ever since these two great peoples passed from the scene, men seem to have been greatly reduced in stature."[10]

Montesquieu maintained the tension between knowledge, virtue, and liberty in their ancient and modern forms by positing the love of *patrie*, the self-sacrificing pursuit of the common good, as the principle of republics, morally superior to monarchies but unattainable for moderns. Although monarchy, as he defined it stipulatively, was thus the best possible modern state, nevertheless Montesquieu lavished so much praise upon ancient republics that the classical ideal exerts at least as much allure as the modern opulent and free commercial society. The third type of government, despotism, served as a negative model. As such, it was a means of condemning those absolutist French institutions he thought menaced liberty. In his *Pensées*, he reproached Machiavelli for having counseled European rulers to use despotic means to deal with subjects qualitatively different from those of Asiatic states where such methods had originated.[11]

If we shift from the consideration of how Montesquieu should be classified as a thinker to assessing his influence, what emerges is a pattern of extraordinary effects upon otherwise discrepant theorists from the middle of the eighteenth century through the American and French Revolutions, the Terror, First Empire, and Restoration, well into the nineteenth century. A great scholar of European political thought during Montesquieu's lifetime has written:

> [E]ven Diderot and Rousseau were completely unknown at the
> beginning of the forties. . . . In these years, Montesquieu
> negotiated and discussed with church and state, almost as if he were
> a political force. Sometimes he conceded and sometimes he did not,
> according to the circumstances. He was the real arbiter and lord of
> the political thought of his time.[12]

After his death, Montesquieu was honored by an addition to the fifth volume of the *l'Encyclopédie*, the eulogy of him written by d'Alembert, the co-editor with Diderot of that notable collective work of the *philosophes*. Many of the political articles were written by disciples of Montesquieu, such as the Chevalier de Jaucourt. But Montesquieu was almost as much used by the aristocratic *parlements*, which opposed reform of the kind sought by many of the *philosophes*. After the French Revolution began, he was among the principal sources for its critics, both liberal like Constant, and counter-revolutionary like De Maistre. Yet during the Terror, Montesquieu was much cited by the members of the Committee of Public Safety headed by Robespierre. To catalogue Montesquieu's admirers in the century after his death is to chart appeals to his authority by theorists and political movements violently opposed to one other. Among them were Malesherbes, Blackstone, and Madison; Rousseau, Marat, and Robespierre; Hume, Burke, Chateaubriand, and De Maistre; Mme de Staël, Constant, and Tocqueville. Because Montesquieu appealed to such discrepant schools of thought, it may safely be assumed that his political thought was profoundly ambivalent, and that his position both in intellectual and class terms was complex, full of tensions, and abounding with paradoxes. On the basis of what has been said about Montesquieu and the almost unprecedented diversity of his influences, what should be concluded about him? What sort of a theorist was he? Certainly he ought to be distinguished from two other types of thinkers: the first, perhaps best exemplified by Kant, whose greatest philosophical contributions stem in large part from their application of a rigorous method; the second, a type which, like Hegel, aspires to an encyclopedic and systematic view of the world within which politics is carefully located.

Montesquieu claimed to have devised a new and rigorous method, just as he claimed unity, if not system, for his sprawling *Spirit of the Laws*. Yet in practice, he refused to choose among mutually exclusive intellectual options. By loose definitions, by availing himself to the full of his extraordinary intellectual imagination, he generated tensions among a plurality of overlapping and often contradictory explanations and perspectives. It was in this way that he kept open his intellectual universe and his power to suggest intellectual and political strategies to men and groups otherwise antagonistic.

Montesquieu was a daring and brilliant theorist, remarkably fertile both in general conceptual schemes and in individual explanatory hypotheses. It is nevertheless true that he frequently became impatient with his own insights. Often he phrased them in short, underdeveloped passages that might and sometimes did serve as the organizing conception of another man's treatise or book. As he wrote in a number of places, his purpose was to make men think and to do so in new ways. To tell his readers everything would be pedantic and so would risk boring them. Even though he himself was willing to make his way through enormous quantities of materials at a time when he was losing his sight, he never ceased to believe that the essence of intellectual life is tact, delicacy of touch, and the capacity to communicate the excitement of ideas, and to amuse while doing so.

Thus Montesquieu's milieu left him an amateur in many respects, although he was ultimately ambivalent about accepting the judgment and style of the salons. Like Tocqueville, perhaps the greatest of his followers, Montesquieu was an aristocrat trained as a magistrate in the tradition of comparative law rather than as a middle-class specialist with an advanced degree in a departmental specialty of the social sciences. Both Tocqueville and Montesquieu were great theorists of politics and society. Both merit their status as authors of genuine classics which still retain their power to stimulate despite changes in the world neither could have anticipated.

There is another point essential to the understanding of Montesquieu. His thought is so often fresh, flexible, and immediately applicable that his readers today may forget his precise position in the history of thought and the development of politics and society. The fact is that many distinctions that seem obvious or irresistible to us simply had not been established or recognized in his time. "Law" was a term that could be applied to the acts of legislators, to the causes alleged to explain human behavior, or to the principles of physics or biology. Some critics, therefore, summarily dismiss his work as muddled or ill-informed, and indeed Montesquieu's definitions of liberty and law now are more often used as targets than as models by political philosophers. Similarly, we are apt to assume that no theorist couldpossibly merit attention today if he thought that aristocracies should and could play a significant part in maintaining free modern regimes. But such intellectual judgments on our part would be anachronistic, for we would not be taking into account the intellectual and political universes which defined Montesquieu's perception of alternatives. Nor should we be complacent about the distinctions we oppose to Montesquieu's.

Raymond Aron has pointed out that no one since Montesquieu has resolved his distinctive dilemma: how to explain the causes of legal, political, and social phenomena and yet retain a rational basis for condemning some governments and their actions (such as the Spanish conquest of the Americas), or certain practices that are social or religious (slavery, the Inquisition, or the burning to death of widows in India after their husbands' deaths). Can we both explain why someone acts as he does and condemn him morally for not having acted otherwise? Is the distinction between fact and value one that accounts for the types of moral, political, and legal evaluations we make?

One school of Montesquieu's critics has attempted to reduce his work to an ideology that rationalized the interests and prejudices of his class as it existed in the middle of the eighteenth century. Some of these criticisms are of sufficient weight so that students ought to know about them and to make up their own minds about their validity. But in order to do so, it is necessary to learn something about the society, politics, and intellectual issues of Montesquieu's time. It would be as one-sided to judge his thought and politics without reference to the situation as he himself perceived it as it would be to fail to relate them to his class position and interests. If these issues are to be raised about Montesquieu, two questions must be answered: first, what sort of man was he and how was he shaped by his society? Second, what were the principal ideas that led him to formulate his theory as he did?

II
Montesquieu's Life and Milieu

Montesquieu was born in 1689, the year of the Glorious Revolution in England; France was still ruled by Louis XIV. Montesquieu esteemed the English Constitution, which he described in some of his most familiar passages in Book XI of *The Spirit of the Laws* as realizing liberty and embodying the separation of powers. His striking analysis of English society, which he thought excelled all other countries in wealth, in liberty, and in piety, is to be found in Book XIX. For many commentators, then, Montesquieu is the very prototype of a liberal, different from Locke only in details.[13] But to others who have written about Montesquieu, this Anglo-American view of him as a bourgeois liberal is a grave misunderstanding based upon historical anachronism and the failure to specify his class position. For them, Montesquieu was a reactionary landowning magistrate and aristocrat who detested Louis XIV because of his curbing of the nobility and his success in creating a centralized national administration. Seen from such a perspective, there was nothing either progressive or moral about Montesquieu's condemnation of Louis XIV in the *Persian Letters*. Thus when he portrayed Louis XIV as a despot who had violated the ancient constitution of France, when he condemned the Sun King for having impoverished his country by constant and indefensible resort to war as an instrument of national policy, it was only class propaganda.[14]

It is true that Montesquieu was an aristocrat born into a society based upon inequality and hierarchy; it is true that both his distaste for centralized bureaucracy and his arguments attacking absolute monarchy were characteristic of his class. But neither the central principle of his political philosophy nor the organizing categories of his analysis of politics, society, and law can be reduced to a mere class ideology. By tracing the pattern of his life, it will become clearer to what extent Montesquieu was typical of his class, religion, and age, and to what extent his views were transformed by an extraordinarily complex mind, distinctive political vision, and a novel approach to the study of man and society.

Montesquieu's family derived from both the nobility of the sword and that of the robe.[15] The family's genealogy could be traced back 350 years, which in Montesquieu's view made it neither particularly ancient nor new. Yet birth was not everything in Montesquieu's own scheme of things. He was a magistrate, a member of the Academy of Bordeaux, and a local notable in that city. Later in England, he was elected to the Royal Society, the center of physical sciences, and became a Freemason. He was a landowner who liked, as he would say, "to feel his money under his feet." Often he was enmeshed in litigation with his neighbors and peers. It would not be farfetched to describe him as involved in seigneurial relationships with his peasant-tenants, whom he called "my vassals." Of his crops, wine was the most important. It was sold in an international market which flourished in times of peace and which was badly damaged by the wars that occurred so often because of the French royal policy of grandeur and mercantilism. It was England, France's major international rival, that was the principal purchaser of Bordeaux wines. Although much of the city's wealth was based on trade with the West Indies, where sugar production depended upon slavery, Montesquieu was uncompromising in his hostility to slavery in any of its forms.

His childhood curiously combined aristocracy and rusticity. He was born in the chateau de la Brède; his godfather was a beggar chosen to remind the child of his obligation to the poor. He was sent out to nurse with a peasant family for his first three years. His mother died when he was seven; her early death contributed to his detachment and to his distaste for enthusiasm, qualities equally prominent in his writing and in his character. At the age of eleven, Montesquieu was sent away to the Collège de Juilly, a school maintained by the Congregation of the Oratory. This further separation from his family, of a sort more frequent among English than French families, helped accentuate his reserve. At Juilly, Montesquieu acquired a classical education relatively liberal for its day. Malebranche, the great philosopher, was a member of the Congregation. Although not himself present, his influence made itself felt. Montesquieu's Latin studies impressed him with the value of civic virtue and Stoicism.

In 1705, Montesquieu returned to Bordeaux to study law. His paternal uncle, the head of the family, planned to leave his nephew his name, estates, and high judicial office. In the French monarchy, many governmental positions were treated as property that could be sold or bequeathed. This was called venality of office.

Between 1709 and 1713, Montesquieu was in Paris for further legal studies and practice. He came to know some of the most advanced thinkers of his time: Frérét, the Abbé Lama, and Boulainvilliers. Of this group, Boulainvilliers was the most significant for Montesquieu's own thought. For he attacked the absolute monarchy of Louis XIV as violating the ancient constitution of France. The state of Louis XIV did not acknowledge the political rights of the peerage, which, Boulainvilliers claimed, derived from the Franks' conquest of the Gauls. The celebration of feudalism in the closing books of *The Spirit of the Laws* is very much in the vein of Boulainvilliers.

When his uncle died in 1716, Montesquieu inherited his considerable wealth, land, and the legal office of *président à mortier* in the *parlement* of Guyenne at Bordeaux. The *parlements* were ancient judicial organizations that had acquired considerable political significance as well. The office held by Montesquieu was no sinecure. He worked hard at it, but did not much enjoy his life as a judge. Nevertheless, in *The Spirit of the Laws* he supported the position of the *parlementaires* against the monarchy, defended venality of office, and condemned as despotic any attempt to divest the parlements of their political functions.[16]

During Montesquieu's residence in Bordeaux, he participated in the work of its Academy. The provincial academies provided a setting within which the legal nobility, or *noblesse de robe*, developed an intelligentsia with its own doctrines. There they also met learned noblemen of the sword and educated commoners. Montesquieu took to experiments in physiology and natural history; he analyzed echoes and transparency. From this milieu Montesquieu took away a distaste for prejudice, a priori reasoning, and teleological arguments.

During this period of provincial eminence Montesquieu began the *Persian Letters*. The book was published anonymously in Amsterdam in 1721. An immediate and lasting success, it alone would have been enough to ensure its author's reputation. Montesquieu was not always and everywhere serious in this, the wittiest and most delightful of his books. But he wished to do more than to amuse by his irony and irreverence.

After the success of the *Persian Letters*, Montesquieu was accepted by the society of regency Paris and lived the life of an aristocratic rake. His Paris friends secured his election to the French Academy in 1728. He sold his office of *président à mortier* partially because of financial need, and partially because he wanted to live in Paris. As a further result he was at last free to travel.

From 1728 to 1731, Montesquieu was away from France, visiting Austria, Hungary, Italy, Germany, Holland, and England. The two years he spent in England had the greatest effect on his later work. There he made distinguished friends who taught him to view the English constitution through the eyes of the Whig opposition. It was during this stay that he was elected a fellow of the Royal Society and became a Freemason as well.

When Montesquieu returned to France, he was in many regards a different person: more serious and cosmopolitan, more aware of what concerned the leading thinkers and scientists in Europe and England; less narrowly French in culture and political outlook, less the provincial magistrate, less the elegant sceptic. He came to think of himself as a man first and as a Frenchman second: "When I act, I am a citizen; but when I write I am a man and I regard all the peoples of Europe with the same impartiality as I do the peoples of the Island of Madagascar."[17] Free to choose his own mode of life, Montesquieu divided his time among Paris; his family estates in the country near Bordeaux, where he did most of his writing; and the city of Bordeaux, which then had the amenities and good company of a cosmopolitan commercial city. Above all, he became the independent aristocratic scholar dedicated to producing his two last great books, the *Considerations* and *The Spirit of the Laws*.

In Paris he shone among the luminaries of the intellectual salons, now more open to merit than before. Wit, intelligence, and literary fame counted for more than birth. Apparently he did not regret the passing of the old order; he encouraged young *philosophes* and men of letters.

The censorship of the Old Regime did much to strengthen such ties. Malesherbes later held up Montesquieu as an example to Voltaire of how a writer could, by subterfuge and evasion, manage to say substantially whatever he wished. But Montesquieu had to make a considerable effort to have printed books from which Church and State really had little to fear. Even so, *The Spirit of the Laws* was condemned by the Theology Faculty of the Sorbonne and placed on the Index of books prohibited to Roman Catholic readers. Montesquieu had sought to head off such condemnation by enlisting the support of the French ambassador to the Vatican. After a long struggle, the ambassador's efforts failed. But in his final letter, the ambassador sought to console Montesquieu by telling him about a friendly and worldly cardinal who had remarked that he could not understand why so eminent an author should care much about whether or not his books were on the Index.

In 1755 Montesquieu fell victim to an epidemic sweeping Paris. As he lay dying, he asked to be given the last rites of the church. When he chose as confessor a Jesuit who had helped him publish the *Considerations*, the Society of Jesus insisted that he first accept certain conditions. Although Montesquieu denied ever having been in a state of disbelief, he was made to consent to having his final confession made public. It is reported that after receiving the last rites, he said, "I have always respected religion; the ethic of the evangelists is an excellent thing, and the most beautiful gift God could have made to man."[18] Certainly Montesquieu believed in the social and political utility of religion, nor is there any doubt that he held some form of belief compatible with natural religion. But it remains unknown to what degree he believed in the dogmas of his church. He never capitulated to the Jesuits' demands for control of his manuscripts.

III
Montesquieu as Legal Theorist: Comparative and Natural Law

Montesquieu's thought was permanently marked both by his training in French and Roman law and by his reading in public and international law. Inconspicuous in the *Persian Letters* and the *Considerations*, Montesquieu's legal interests emerge as of paramount importance in *The Spirit of the Laws*. To its modern readers, this work presents a good many puzzles, not the least among which are its title and its method. What he wrote about law displayed a new and original theoretical focus. Yet in important respects Montesquieu shared major assumptions of his predecessors in comparative and natural law.

As they did, Montesquieu used the "law of nature" as his standard for judging the actual or positive laws of different nations. Despite the alleged relativism of his thought, he often condemned laws, practices, and institutions as violations of human nature or the law of nature. From a position that ostensibly regards laws as determined by climate and milieu, or as dictated by the internal logic of a particular form of government, Montesquieu often slides into moral and political judgments based upon an absolute standard. Did he see no incompatibility between these two modes of thinking about law? If so, was this due to the fact that practitioners of comparative law such as Hotman and Bodin never gave up natural law? And to what extent did secular natural law theorists such as Grotius use historical precedents and the history of actual practices and institutions as corroborations or proofs?

By pointing up the significance of Montesquieu's background in the law for his legal theory, I hope to clarify, if not his concepts, at least his reasons for combining them as he did. For often he seems to combine both arguments based upon legal precedents and constitutional history on the one side, and another order of arguments deduced from rational, a priori premises on the other. My diagnosis, in brief, is this: Because Montesquieu sought to synthesize the traditions, in so many ways discrepant, of comparative public law and secular natural law, his legal thought was not only enriched but also confused; that when closely examined, the principal theorists of both schools turn out not to make any precise distinction between what is and what ought to be, between what is sanctioned a posteriori by constitutional precedent and what is prescribed a priori as just by natural law. Thus Montesquieu, like Hotman on the one side and Grotius on the other, combined modes of thought that may appear incompatible to us. As Hotman's modern editors have written, he believed that historical precedents demonstrate the truth of abstract propositions.[19]

In the seventeenth century, important changes occurred in the way that the theory of natural law was argued. A new secular version was put forward by Grotius and Pufendorf to replace natural law teachings with theological foundations. Montesquieu wrote: "I give thanks to Messrs. Grotius and Pufendorf for having done so well the work required by one part of my book. They have done so with such genius as I myself could never have attained."[20]

Theorists of natural law assert that law ought to be obeyed, not because rulers or states so command, but because the law itself conforms to some higher principle rooted in nature, morality, deity, or reason. One recent writer has held that whatever the differences separating theorists of the natural law, all its advocates are united by their rejection of the view that no law can be unjust (as has been maintained by the Sophists and by Hobbes). Against this, natural law theorists hold that every positive, or man-made law, is valid to the extent that it meets the standards of natural or ideal law.[21]

Although versions of natural law theories are found in the Stoics and the digest of the Roman law, the *Corpus Iuris Civilis*, Grotius and Pufendorf sought to distinguish the foundations of their own thought from these sources, as well as from the medieval version of St. Thomas Aquinas and his early modern Thomist successors.

In St. Thomas, natural law stresses the dignity and power of man. It applies both to the preservation of life and to inclinations to know the truth about God and to live in society. All actions connected with such inclinations come under the natural law. Secondly, natural law provides the foundation for morality. Here nature and revelation join: Grace does not abolish nature, but perfects it. Finally, natural law is the standard by which all human law and institutions are to be judged. This does not mean that positive law must follow natural law exactly. Much latitude is left to human lawmakers by St. Thomas, who recognizes the significance of circumstances and change. Nor is the content of natural law always the same. It may be modified by either adding to or taking away from it. By itself, natural law is not sufficient to guide men. To establish in detail what has been ordained by natural law, human laws are needed. They also are required in order to restrain evil men from wrongdoing by force and by fear. St. Thomas also held that divine laws are necessary to guide men to their higher duties and destiny. In his view, all laws, whether natural, eternal, or divine, are linked.

It was precisely such connections that were denied by those early modern writers who sought to establish natural law upon foundations that were purely rational and secular. They perceived themselves as breaking decisively with their Thomist predecessors. In this newer view, no theology whatever ought to be included in treatments of natural law. What counted was purely rational construction, compelling assent because of its characteristics: clarity, self-evidence, and internal coherence. This method was deductive like mathematics. Yet the founder of modern natural law, Hugo Grotius (1583–1645), saw no incompatibility between this rationalist, a priori proof of the law of nature, and a second sort of proof based upon a historical, a posteriori method, which supplied evidence from the writing of learned men and from the precedents of history. This twofold method was eclectic; it was to produce difficulties for Montesquieu, as well as for other followers of secular natural law theories.

The next great name after Grotius was Samuel von Pufendorf (1632–94). Both authors wrote in Latin. They were translated into French by Jean Barbeyrac (1644–1744), whose versions, complete with learned notes and his own commentaries, made these works into essential reading for eighteenth-century political philosophers.[22] In the writings of these authors, the nature of man is said to be identical with his faculty of reason; natural law with whatever conforms to right reason. Natural law is thus discovered by reason.

As defined by Grotius, the law of nature is a "dictate of right reason which points out that an act, according as it is or is not in conformity with rational nature, has in it a quality of moral baseness or moral necessity; and that in consequence, such an act is either forbidden or enjoined by the author of nature, God."[23] Yet, Grotius goes on to say, the law of nature would be valid even if there were no God, or if what men did failed to concern God. For God cannot alter natural law. "Just as God cannot cause that two and two should make four, so he cannot cause that which is intrinsically evil be not evil."[24] This theory stresses the analogy between natural law and mathematics; it is rationalistic: "With all truthfulness I aver that, just as the mathematicians treat their figures as abstract from bodies, so in treating law, I have withdrawn my mind from every particular fact."[25] Pufendorf went even further in his rationalism, considering natural law as a necessary and immutable set of laws deduced by reason from the nature of things. This position served as the basis for Book I of *The Spirit of the Laws*.[26]

Such a rationalistic account of natural law introduced considerable problems. What does reason mean? It could be interpreted as intuition, the observation of nature, or noncontradiction (as in mathematics). Grotius, however, did not restrict himself to the a priori method. In his "Prolegomena," his statement that natural law is a set of self-evident truths is followed immediately by proofs based upon history and precedent. In one of his strongest polemical attacks, Rousseau later assailed Grotius for this historical mode of reasoning. No method, Rousseau asserted, could be more favorable to the enemies of liberty than to seek to establish right by fact.[27] It is indeed true that justifications based on precedents were often used by Grotius to prevent drawing revolutionary or even reformist implications from his theory of natural law. Similarly, Rousseau, who for the most part admired Montesquieu, criticized him for his emphasis upon studying the positive law of established governments rather than formulating thefirst principles of law and reason.[28]

Is it true that Montesquieu only concerned himself with the actual laws made by men? Or is it more accurate to say that Montesquieu sought to produce a synthesis of natural law theory with an explanation of how and why laws had come to be what they are? One work on the subject has discovered four discrepant assessments by critics: those who claim that Montesquieu abandoned natural law and lament that he did so; those who agree that Montesquieu's method was an empirical and comparative study of the laws of all peoples and praise him for his innovation in method which led him to abandon the theory of natural law; those progressive or humanitarian critics who hail Montesquieu for the positions he took that were based, they argue, on a belief in natural law; and finally, those who believe that Montesquieu never clearly perceived the options and hence contradicted himself by using one method to explain law, politics, and society, and another method to assert the view of natural law found in *The Spirit of the Laws*.[29]

In my own opinion, Montesquieu held on both to the belief that natural law exists and ought to be used to condemn positive laws that violate it, as well as to a relativism about the different forms that law must and ought to take under different conditions. In Book I of *The Spirit of the Laws*, Montesquieu retained the distinction made by natural law theorists between the general principles of natural law and special applications of it to particular societies and circumstances. This was a commonplace in both St. Thomas and the theorists of secular natural law. Montesquieu repeated that law is human reason and that equity ought to take precedence over man-made laws. As Jean Ehrard has written: "For him [Montesquieu], as for his contemporaries, every philosophy of nature is at once scientific and ethical. Natural right is an integral part of the 'nature of things;' and laws of natural morality have as much objective reality as the mathematical law governing the material world."[30]

Writing in the spirit of the jurist or student of comparative law, as contrasted to the philosophical approach found in Book I, Montesquieu attempted to restrict the degree of possible conflict among different orders of law, including natural and positive laws, by distinguishing them from one another. Human reason, Montesquieu insists, is most sublime when it can understand the differences among these varieties of law and the respective area each is meant to regulate. Subsequent discussions in Book XXVI reveal that, in fact, some legislators do confuse, intentionally or unintentionally, these varieties of law, and for this Montesquieu condemns them. But even after Montesquieu's most comprehensive classification of laws, it is by no means clear what Montesquieu thought to be the relationship between natural law and positive law.[31]

In this connection, his readers must ask themselves whether Montesquieu did not believe that the seraglio, as depicted in the *Persian Letters*; slavery; and religious persecution, as practiced by the Inquisition, were all contrary to nature and the laws of nature. If this is the case, what is the relationship between such reasoning and the sort of explanation he gave for the existence of slavery and despotism in the climates where they were regarded as normal and just?

In the hands of a theorist of natural law such as Grotius, what emerged as most significant about human history was the number of similarities or agreements. These could be used as proofs of the law of nature or of the law of nations. Such comparative study was focused, as Grotius said, on the "best examples," by which he meant ancient Greece and Rome. His texts were full of reference to the classical authors and to the Bible. In the pages of Montesquieu, we encounter a greatly enlarged perspective, one which was intended to take all human experience into account, and not just that of Europe and Christianity. Nor was Montesquieu interested only in similarities as Grotius had been. Comparative study of politics and society involved the perception of differences as well. Clearly, new intellectual influences were at work on Montesquieu. Along with the rationalism found in Book I of *The Spirit of the Laws*, which stressed what humans have in common, Montesquieu also had a vivid sense of their diversity. This produced a different kind of comparative politics as well as a different kind of legal and political theory. The second of these two tendencies is registered in Book I, chapter III. Montesquieu was not a systematic thinker. As has been shown in his treatment of law, comparative and natural, he was more remarkable for the tensions he preserved than for resolving the new problems raised by his method.

IV
The Persian Letters (1721)

This was Montesquieu's first book, written in the form of letters from Europe by two Persians who had never before left their country. Although Montesquieu was not the first to use the device of presenting his own country as it would appear to observers coming from another organized on quite different principles, he displayed a remarkable capacity to treat his own government, society, and religion as phenomena to be investigated objectively. This did not exclude wit, malice, or exaggeration.

The *Persian Letters* is among the first works by a political theorist to apply what has been called the double optic of cultural relativism to his own country, considered as a subject as problematical as any other. As Roger Caillois has written, the *Persian Letters* presupposes a prior revolution in perception and theory: "that of daring to consider as extraordinary and difficult to understand those institutions, those habits, those *moeurs*, to which one has been accustomed since birth, and which are so powerful, so spontaneously respected that in most situations, no alternative to them can be imagined."[32]

Montesquieu did not suggest that his oriental visitors were necessarily correct in their views, or that Persian institutions ought to be eulogized because they were exotic. He had a number of criticisms to make of French political life; it was safest to do so by attributing such views to Persian visitors. The long reign of Louis XIV had produced an aristocratic opposition that regarded the Sun King as a despot who, by introducing absolute practices, had violated the ancient French Constitution, corrupted French society, and introduced institutions previously known only in the orient. More than once in their letters, Montesquieu's Persians comment that government in France curiously resembles that of their own country.

The exaltation of Louis XIV by his apologists in Church and State attempted to base the unlimited power of the king on the absolute power of God. This was as unacceptable to Montesquieu as the philosophical argument made by Hobbes, whom Montesquieu sought to refute in his myth of the Troglodytes. Montesquieu wrote: "All these reflections have made me oppose those learned doctors who depict God as a being who uses his power tyrannically."[33]

Thus Montesquieu deflated absolutist claims to grandeur by Louis XIV. Yet combined with such relativism was an untroubled certainty on his part about the existence and applicability of a universal law of nature valid everywhere, dependent neither upon the laws of any government nor upon any human convention. Montesquieu wrote: ". . . Justice is eternal and does not depend upon the conventions of men."[34] The simultaneous use of relativism and natural law rationalism created a tension Montesquieu never resolved. This problem recurs in Book I of *The Spirit of the Laws*, where Montesquieu attempted to prove that God could never be unjust and that even if there were no God, humans would still be subject to the natural law principle of equity.

Montesquieu was the first major political philosopher who defined his subject matter as truly global, including "the laws, customs, and varied usages of all peoples."[35] In the *Persian Letters*, he registered the new information and speculation made possible by the voyages of exploration, trade, missionary activity, and colonization that Europeans had begun in the fifteenth century. In his *Considerations*, Montesquieu returned to a sustained comparative analysis of two Roman phases of the classical European experience. What is remarkable in *The Spirit of the Laws* is the unprecedented way in which Montesquieu ranged freely through space and time in search of evidence relevant to his argument. In addition to his evident familiarity with classical antiquity, modern Europe, and the novel developments of commerce and government in England, Montesquieu chose, at several crucial points, to rest his argument on sustained analyses of Chinese government and society. To do so was unprecedented in a major book by a European political philosopher.

Both Montesquieu's data and the theoretical use he made of them need to be examined critically. For he was far from emancipated from the prejudices of Christian Europeans of his class and time. Again it is important to detect the internal tensions of his thought. On the one hand, he was among those who contributed most to questioning the hitherto-accepted premises of European culture. Most Europeans viewed other societies through categories that emphasized the superiority of their own religion, technology, and political arrangements. New information did not in itself guarantee general changes in attitudes towards peoples elsewhere. Thus most European attitudes toward non-Western peoples were determined by forces which had more to do with European interests, conflicts, and biases than with the cultures and governments in question. Religious disputes, heresies, and skepticism; acceptance or rejection of unification and centralization, or mercantilism and war as instruments of national policy; the political and social positions of groups and classes—these helped determine what use would be made of the new information that was transforming what was known about the rest of the world.

The sort of ambivalence already noted in comparative law appeared as well in those studies of the non-Western world that were based on the explorations and travels of Europeans. On the one hand, no collection of the customs and institutions of non-European peoples was possible without classification of uniformities; on the other, the principal categories tended to be Europocentric, so that there was a considerable probability that peoples who failed to fit into the European scheme of things might be classified as barbarian, primitive, aboriginal, or like man before the Fall. Both outcomes are to be found in European thinkers: those of the late eighteenth century often preferred to emphasize what was common to all humans everywhere, while in the sixteenth and seventeenth centuries, and again in the nineteenth, dissimilarities were stressed to strengthen claims to the superiority of European religion, commerce, or government.[36]

Montesquieu responded with extraordinary sympathy and flexibility to both tendencies. It was his clear intent to formulate categories that would group similarities among human governments regardless of time and space. In many respects, his work was a triumph of curiosity, research, and objectivity over parochial prejudice. In the *Persian Letters*, he succeeded in achieving a remarkably fresh and detached view of France. Almost every aspect of French life was relativized and made both problematic and amusing. Such a perspective is more than the product of change; it soon comes to serve as a solvent of traditional values and modes of thought, even though Montesquieu was no champion of reform for its own sake.

Such considerations probably did not weigh too heavily upon the first readers of the *Persian Letters*. It is among the very few works of genuine consequence in political philosophy which, combining wit, gaiety, and fable, gain from treating serious matters with irreverence. Unfortunately, only a limited selection of its treasures is possible in this volume. Faced with the necessity of choosing among them, I have decided to leave aside Montesquieu's acute observations of Paris, the rest of France, and those parts of Europe and Asia visited by the Persians. I have had to omit Montesquieu's important early statements about natural law; the futility of seeking the origins of government; the need for religious toleration, the disastrous effects of bigotry, religious and cultural; and his critique of the policy of war and conquest pursued by Louis XIV. Instead I have translated and printed here two sequences of letters: the first is devoted to the myth of the Troglodytes and its unprinted sequel; the second, much longer, consists of the letters that pass between Usbek, the more philosophical of the two Persians visiting Paris, and his seraglio (as Montesquieu calls the harem) of wives and the eunuchs who guard them. Once critics tended to dismiss this part of the *Persian Letters* as mere exoticism and sensual titillation, thus accounting for the enormous popularity of the work (Montesquieu submitted it to a worldly priest who predicted correctly that it would sell like bread). But this sequence, in which a male master treats women as slaves subject to the delegated power of the eunuchs, his ministers, is better understood as a model of a despotic political system.

Yet the *Persian Letters* is not a treatise, but a work of creative imagination by an irreverent young man of genius. It should be read and enjoyed as such. But if the reader has the further concern to connect it to the rest of Montesquieu's work, or to attempt to understand how its contemporary audience was apt to understand the political point of the *Persian Letters*, or the religious, moral, or sexual set of attitudes it presupposes, then Montesquieu ought to be viewed in terms of his own interests and those of his age.

This is not the place to depict those Parisian clubs and salons frequented by Montesquieu during the Regency, which followed the long reign of Louis XIV.[37] The politics of Montesquieu's circle was aristocratic, profoundly anticlerical, skeptical, deist, if not necessarily atheist; it combined the call for liberty, intellectual and political, with attacks on centralized royal power and the denunciation of war as an instrument of national policy. But these views were combined with eulogies of feudalism, when aristocrats played a greater role, and with a deep mistrust of the lower orders of the society.

Even when young, Montesquieu was not a democrat, any more than he was an individualist or a radical. He did not favor wholesale change:

> It is sometimes necessary to change certain basic laws. But the case is rare, and should be undertaken with trembling hands.[38]

> I have often sought that form of government most consonant with reason. It seems to me that the most perfect is that which attains its goals at the least cost, which conforms most to men's inclinations.''[39]

This was neither a sanguine nor a revolutionary outlook; at most it was reformist within the limits of a concept of order that looked to the past for its ideal static pattern. Its theory of despotism had been created by the aristocratic opposition to Louis XIV; its chief theorist was Fénelon, archbishop of Cambrai, and once tutor to the heir to the crown of Louis XIV.[40]

The myth of the Troglodytes comes in answer to the question of how human nature affects politics. A Persian friend inquires of Usbek what is more natural for humans: to satisfy their senses or to practice virtue? Put in this form, the question requires Usbek to choose between the theories of human nature represented by Hobbes and Shaftesbury.[41] Hobbes believed that humans are ruled by their passions, the most politically significant of which is fear. Shaftesbury, on the contrary, thought of humans as having an inherent moral sense of what is right and wrong. Everyone is born with an affection for other humans. Although man is aware of his private interest, he perceives by his native reason that what benefits the public also benefits him. Because of this joint interest, moral virtue is to the advantage of everyone; vice is to the disadvantage of all. Thus Shaftesbury concludes that man discerns and owns a public interest, and is conscious of what affects his fellowship and community.[42] This contrasts vividly with the individualist, egoistic view of human nature and its political implications found in Hobbes, who deduced the need to sacrifice all rights to an absolute sovereign.

By way of developing his own answer, Usbek tells the myth of the Troglo-dytes in four letters. There is a sequel never published by Montesquieu. Like the seraglio sequence in the *Persian Letters*, the myth of the Troglodytes is an appli-cation of creative imagination to politics. With great brevity, Montesquieu sketches the successive states under which the Troglodytes lived: a kingdom, perhaps based on their conquest by a foreign king; a short-lived republic; a state based on the Hobbesian war of all against all; a utopia resembling Fénelon's Bétique; a kingdom based on virtue but excluding wealth; and finally, a king-dom that permits the introduction of new techniques and the accumulation of wealth.

Even in his most rhapsodic sections, Montesquieu manages to bring in a qual-ity of tension, a sense of instability, a dynamic of change, a portent of corrup-tion. All these qualities are rarely found among utopian writers, who often locate their creations in a timeless and unchanging world. Within a few pages, Montesquieu sketches a complex set of political possibilities. Each exacts a cost. None can last forever. Many questions are left unanswered. Often Mon-tesquieu's brevity leads him to indicate rather than to explain why one type of state follows from that which preceded it. Yet Montesquieu's few pages of fable introduce a distinctively modern set of dilemmas, the problems for poli-tics that originate in material and technological advances. Unlike Plato and Fénelon, whose ideal of the good society was intimate and static, Montesquieu does not shrink from considering change and the politics of states larger and more prosperous than the classical cities. As always, Montesquieu is open to the appeals of arguments and authors whose views are not easily reconciled. The consequent tensions reappear in Montesquieu's own thought.[43]

Although Montesquieu's concept of monarchy altered much between the writing of the *Persian Letters* and *The Spirit of the Laws*, his emphasis upon despo-tism remained remarkably constant. While in the *Persian Letters*, Montesquieu's treatment of despotism was imaginative and psychological, in *The Spirit of the Laws* he treated despotism more formally, a crucial concept in the typology of regimes he ranked among his greatest contributions to the comparative study of politics and society. His analysis of the seraglio in the Persian Letters was his single most sustained psychological treatment of a system based upon fear, jealousy, and mutual suspicion.

The concept of despotism had originated with the Greeks, who used the model of the master-slave relationship to describe oriental rule of a sort un-known to the Greek city-states menaced by the Persian Achaemenid Empire (559–330 B.C.). The concept was used to unify the Greeks and mobilize them against the enemy. In Aristotle, despotism was described as a barbaric type of kingship. In it, the power of the monarch over his subjects, although indistin-guishable from that exercised by a master over slaves, was nevertheless con-sidered by the ruled to be sanctified by custom, and hence to be legitimate. Such a form of rule was said to be characteristic of non-Hellenic, or barbarian peoples (whom the Greeks regarded as slaves by nature). Despotism was profoundly repugnant to the Greeks, because they thought of themselves as possessing reason and hence the capacity and the tradition of ruling themselves.[44]

In devoting so large a part of the Persian Letters to depicting the inner life of the seraglio, Montesquieu created an image of despotism altogether novel in its detail, its compelling account of the human passions that sustain it, and above all, its representation as a system of power. Before the *Persian Letters*, oriental despotism had been used as code words only by the aristocratic and Protestant groups opposed to Louis XIV. In a letter Fénelon wrote that under that ruler "despotism is the cause of all our troubles."[45] Boulainvilliers claimed that, under Louis XIV, despotism and egalitarianism had debased the ancient nobility whose ancestors were Frankish conquerors of the Gallo-Romans.[46]

Because of Montesquieu's widely accepted new typology, later stated in *The Spirit of the Laws*, the concept of despotism became enormously significant in political discourse in the second half of the eighteenth century. In France, "despotism" supplanted the concept of tyranny as the term most often used to designate a system of total domination, as distinguished from the exceptional abuse of power by an individual ruler. In the mid-century debate about the origin and form of the French Constitution, Voltaire, who championed the version that justified absolute royal sovereignty, felt compelled to attack Montesquieu's use of the concept of despotism.

In the seraglio letters, there are three parties to a relationship that is despotic: Usbek, the master of the seraglio, who is absent in Paris; his eunuchs, to whom he has delegated power; and his wives. This is a system of power that involves a set of paradoxes and contradictions. Its ostensible purpose is to maintain the conditions regarded by its master, at least, as requisite for maintaining purity, obedience, and modesty proper to marriage as practiced by the Persians. Of course, there arises immediately the question of whether the seraglio is compatible with human nature and the law of nature. Relativism cuts two ways, and if customs and institutions are to be regarded as merely the products of a society's physical environment and historical experience, then what is regarded as natural by Westerners and Christians is as arbitrary as any oriental practice, such as the seraglio.

Usbek believes the seraglio is connected to virtue and duty; he sees its maintenance as closely connected to that of authority and dependence. Usbek wishes to be loved by his wives as their husband rather than feared as their master. Yet he, like them and the eunuchs, is part of a system which by its logic links love to fear, the distinguishing characteristic of despotic rule. Despotism cannot be enlightened, because it works only through fear, and this cannot be moderated or checked, although Usbek attempts to do so. It is his eunuchs who reveal to him the implacable logic of despotic rule. But Montesquieu does not exaggerate the omnipotence or permanence of this system. Even within it, some sort of consent is necessary, as Roxana points out in her final letter. Not only is absolute rule more subject to corruption than any other regime, but when sedition occurs, it produces more violent effects than disorder in other systems. None of the three sets of participants in the despotic order of the seraglio can escape its contradictions.

The political system of the seraglio is based upon internal contradictions that make its maintenance difficult and its authority unstable. In the *Persian Letters* Usbek is himself both the voice of Western critiques of the seraglio and, in practice, the master who consents to the use of brute force when told that only in this way can order be restored. Yet the master is consumed by jealousy and fear that his wives will be enjoyed by someone other than himself. His wish to be loved is incompatible with the structure of the seraglio. As for the eunuchs, they owe their position to their lost manhood and must seek compensation in the exercise of power. As the first eunuch writes: "I remember always that I was born to command them, and when in fact I do so, I feel as though I have once again become a man."[47]

When Usbek grants the eunuch unlimited power, its use produces the breakdown, rather than the reestablishment of order. The wives declare that when subjected to such treatment they no longer love Usbek. Roxanna takes a lover and commits suicide when he is discovered. It is made clear that the wives' submission depended ultimately, not upon fear of absolute power, but upon love. As Roxanna writes in her final letter: "I may have lived in slavery, but I have always been free: I have reformed your laws by those of nature, and my spirit has never lost its independence."[48]

Yet although love is essential to rule, as is consent to obedience, nevertheless love and consent are not sufficient conditions. For a legitimate order ultimately depends upon an institutionalized form of authority. Montesquieu preferred the type of authority limited by law, by internal and external checks on the ruler, and by a free competition of interests. For such qualities he praised England in the *Persian Letters*, points he made even more clearly in his *Considerations*.

V

Considerations on the Causes of the Romans' Greatness and Decline (1734)

This work is today perhaps the least known of Montesquieu's major works. It remains distinguished notably for its style, clarity, and remarkable analysis of historical causation and the nature of politics. Montesquieu was attracted to

Roman history, in part because it offered the most complete record of a political society available to him, and also because Rome's fundamental transformation after becoming an empire seemed to point to a moral applicable to the aggressive foreign policy of Louis XIV. The *Considerations* contributed greatly to the development of what the eighteenth century was to call "philosophical history."[49] Gibbon wrote that his own work on Roman history had been inspired by the *Considerations*. More than a century later it was Tocqueville's first model for what was to become the *l'Ancien Régime et la Révolution*.

To Rome Montesquieu applied an analysis that already anticipated *The Spirit of the Laws*: the claim that although chance plays some part in human events, these may always be rationally explained; the emphasis upon the orientation of political actors through religion, ideas, maxims, and public opinion (in the *Considerations*, Montesquieu did not emphasize climate or milieu); a definition of politics in a free society as requiring some disunion and group conflict; and the concept of the "general spirit" of a society.

Perhaps the single most telling passage in the *Considerations* occurs in Montesquieu's theory of causation:

> It is not fortune that rules the world. . . . On this point, consult the Romans, who enjoyed a series of consecutive successes when their government followed one policy; an unbroken set of reverses when it adopted another. There are general causes, whether moral or physical, which act upon every monarchy, which advance, maintain, or ruin it. All accidents are subject to these causes. If the chance loss of a battle, that is, a particular cause, ruins a state, there is a general cause that created the situations whereby this state could perish by the loss of a single battle.[50]

This statement, which received much attention in France after the defeat of 1940, referred in its original context to the place held by war and conquest in Roman policy. Montesquieu, summing up his analysis, concluded—by a process of a sort that a later age would call dialectical—that Rome was first made and then ruined:

> Here, in a word, is the history of the Romans: by following their original maxims, they conquered all other peoples. But after such success, their republic could no longer be maintained. It became necessary to change the form of government. Their new maxims, contrary to those with which they had begun, were applied to the new form of government. This caused the Romans to fall from their former greatness.[51]

Montesquieu here combined judgments of fact and value in a way dear to him. On the one hand, he was generalizing about the effects of scale upon a government's structure and functions; on the other, he was concluding that the Romans had fought too much and conquered too much. Violence, first used as a weapon against other nations, was in turn employed at home. Roman decadence was inherent in the means used to attain greatness. In the *Considerations*, Montesquieu recast themes prominent among writers opposed to the foreign policy of Louis XIV and the mercantilism he and his ministers favored.

The *Considerations* also provides a set of detailed illustrations of Montesquieu's meaning when he asserted that virtue is the principle of republics. By this he meant that citizens must be attached to their state by principles that lead to genuine subordination of personal interest to country; that republics, so far from being disorganized, must demand and receive iron discipline; and that all legislation must support the frugality and patriotism requisite to the government's principle.

The *Considerations* contains a striking first formulation of Montesquieu's treatment of politics in a free society, where the texture of interpersonal and intergroup relations is much looser than in a despotism. In a free state, divergences and even conflicts among groups are essential, for such a society is based upon the conciliation of recognized groups, each with its own interest. The virtues of consensus and unanimity are overrated by partisans of order and absolutism:

> The historians never tire of repeating that internal divisions ruined Rome. What they fail to see is that these divisions were necessary, that they had always existed, and should have continued to exist.
> . . . As a general rule, it may be assumed that whenever everyone is tranquil in a state that calls itself a republic, that state is no longer free. What constitutes union in a political body is difficult to determine. True union is a harmony in which all the parts, however opposed they may appear, concur in attaining the general good of the society, just as dissonances in music are necessary so that they may be resolved in an ultimate harmony. Union may exist in a state where apparently only trouble is to be found. . . .
>
> But underlying the unanimity of Asiatic despotism, that is, every government where power is not checked, there is always a more serious type of division. The tiller of the land, the soldier, the merchant, the magistrate, the noble are related only in the sense that some of them oppress the others without meeting any resistance. If this be union, it can be so not in the sense that citizens are joined to one another, but rather that sense in which corpses are united when buried in a mass grave.[52]

What was philosophical history as it was understood by those seeking to follow Montesquieu's method? History was to be understood neither by reference to theological final causes such as Providence, nor by reference to chance, even to the limited extent allowed for by Machiavelli, whose *Discourses* otherwise served as a model. A second emphasis of philosophical history, if a negative one, consisted in the rejection of fact, detail, or erudition for its own sake. Montesquieu's style in this book reflects its author's preoccupations: its sparse, stripped-down maxims are historical generalizations at a high level of abstraction. A third characteristic of philosophical history was its turning away from teaching by examples taken from great heroes, as had been done by Plutarch, so much admired and imitated in the Renaissance. On the whole, Montesquieu played down military heroes. He detested the world that had been created by the policy of the balance of power in seventeenth- and eighteenth-century Europe.

Montesquieu's movement away from splendid heroes and martial victories pushed him in the direction of sociological and economic analyses. Not the state exclusively, but the society—its nature, its internal logic, deriving from its structure and type—became to an equal extent the object of his investigation. The explanation of history is to be sought not in political, but in social and economic history. The way in which property is distributed and inheritance provided for, the means of creating wealth and creating new techniques in agriculture and industry, the attention given to commerce, the understanding of the effects produced by different sets of institutions and legal systems—these ought to stand at the center of the historian's concerns. History should, in the phrase of Giannone, become *historia civile*, that of civil society. In *The Spirit of the Laws*, Montesquieu was to argue that commerical societies are inclined to peace rather than to war, to maximizing the liberty of individuals, rather than the interest of one nation at the expense of all others.[53]

The last article of philosophical history was that historians, rather than confining their work to those societies that were Christian or that had played a part in the historians' own development, should break out of such bounds and write truly universal history. All great civilizations deserved consideration as part of the human past. It must be noted that Montesquieu differed from some other philosophical historians in that he did not hold to any form of the theory of progress. Unlike those who believed that history should principally record the advances that had been made and analyze the reasons for them, as well as the obstacles to further progress, Montesquieu in his *Considerations* was more interested in decline and corruption and in their roots in the structure of politics and society.[54] Similarly, he was as much interested in societies that contain contradictions as he was in those that are well integrated. Finally, although Montesquieu was among the first to stress those general characteristics that distinguish one society from another, he nevertheless did not minimize the possibilities of mitigating or transforming such characteristics by the use of political power and wise legislation.

V I
The Spirit of the Laws (1748)

The Spirit of the Laws is a work which began but did not end within the traditions of comparative and natural law. This complex, overarching book encompasses political and legal philosophy, as well as comparative politics and political sociology. Montesquieu's declared intention was to determine the principles by which human or positive laws ought to be judged. His data were drawn from that unrivaled body of evidence available in the recorded laws of all nations, not just those of modern Europe and classical antiquity. This massive documentation he ordered by the categories of a new method.

Montesquieu addressed himself to the issues raised by political philosophers, and must be classified among them. Yet his book was on law, and many of the key passages focused on legal questions. He had been a practicing judge before he became a specialist in comparative, natural, and feudal law. It was Montesquieu's legal training that led him to his life's work and to the materials he was to organize in his own way. From his study of the law, he derived his conviction that any good government must be subject to legal restraints, and that there can be no liberty without law. As a member of the legal aristocracy, he placed great emphasis upon precedent and tradition.[55]

However, Montesquieu was not interested in the actual practice of French law. *The Spirit of the Laws* is not a summary of existing law, but is a method of studying jurisprudence: "For my purpose is to treat not laws, but their spirit."[56] Thus Montesquieu searched both for the causes of positive laws and for a theory of law in general that would provide a standard for assessing particular laws. This part of his enterprise was philosophical.

The professional French jurists of Montesquieu's time were outraged by his definition of law as "the necessary relations that derive from the nature of things."[57] Nor did they find acceptable his resort to natural law arguments when he wished to criticize fundamental abuses.

Montesquieu was no less independent in his relationship to the school of secular natural law. From their combination of deductive rationalism with appeal to historical precedent, both Grotius and Pufendorf had drawn conclusions justifying absolutism, had sanctioned the rights of conquerors, and had accepted slavery as legitimate. These aspects of their thought were no more tolerable to Montesquieu than they would be to Rousseau. Whenever the views of natural law theorists conflicted with his own, Montesquieu explicitly rejected their legal theory, put some parts of it to uses unknown to their original formulators, or added arguments foreign to them.

An example of Montesquieu's independence occurs when he dismisses treatments of the so-called right of conquest by Grotius and Pufendorf, the basis of their justification of slavery:

> The authors of our public law . . . have fallen into very great errors. . . . Because of the arbitrary power they have assumed to belong to conquerors, these have been assigned a right to kill, a right unknown to me. From this right, they have drawn consequences as terrible as the principles themselves. . . . It is clear that once the conquest is completed, the conqueror no longer has a right to kill, since he no longer is in a situation that involves his preservation, the only sort of defense nature permits.[58]

However, like Grotius, Pufendorf, and Barbeyrac, Montesquieu found in deductive rationalism a sympathetic method that could be used scientifically. His espousal of such views is especially marked in Book I of *The Spirit of the Laws*. Again he saw no inherent incompatibility between rational demonstration and empirical, even historical, verification. The notion of a lawful universe created by God was as congenial to him as to them. Yet other parts of Montesquieu's work were more sociological and historical. To the notion that a law ought to conform to the rational principle of justice, he added another sense of "ought": laws ought to be consistent with the nature and principle of the government, with the climate, and all the other elements that make up the general spirit of a nation.[59] What counted most in such discussions were Montesquieu's distinctive typology of governments and his theory of causation.

Ostensibly descriptive and explanatory, both had another function as well. They contributed tacitly to Montesquieu's political argument. This is not to say that Montesquieu's thought was purely ideological, but rather that he was not exclusively a social scientist. He was a political philosopher aware of how many practical consequences may flow from adopting certain methods and assumptions. He knew that Hobbes had made law and justice dependent upon human convention and individual will. In Montesquieu's view, such a doctrine facilitated absolute rule. The divine right of kings, on the other hand, as argued by Bossuet and James I, depended upon the theory of sovereignty. The king on earth is like God in heaven—he cannot be limited by any law because his will is law.

Another political emphasis can be seen in Montesquieu's objection to Spinoza, whom he viewed as a determinist who left no room for human agency.

When Montesquieu formulated his own theory in "An Essay on the Causes that May Affect Men's Minds and Characters," he took care to avoid statements that would have endorsed as necessary any existing order or law.[60] Instead Montesquieu concluded that moral may overcome physical causes. Within limits, men, by legislation and other purposive action, can ameliorate their environment and attain goals apparently incompatible with their milieu. Thus even in hot climates, slavery is not required in order to till the land.

Montesquieu's use of comparison is most often intended to prove that viable alternatives exist to deplorable laws and practices. It is for this reason that Montesquieu does not reduce politics to a derivative function of social or economic process. Many evils can be removed or ameliorated, although some cannot. As always, Montesquieu equivocated. His activism had limits. He could see that hasty and direct attempts to eradicate abuses may create greater evils. One part of his mind delighted in discovering meaningful functions for ostensibly useless customs and institutions. And he too often viewed as necessary those infringements of human liberties that took place outside of Europe. Nevertheless he spoke out against slavery as no previous political philosopher had done, including John Locke.

Montesquieu wrote as a citizen of the world anxious for practical effect, rather than as a detached analyst outside the practices and laws under examination. Although not a revolutionary, nor even a democrat, he espoused humanitarian reform and criticized the cruelty of punishments then meted out by the criminal law. Beccaria, the great spokesman for abolition of cruel punishments and reform of penal law, described how Montesquieu had merited "the secret thanks of the unknown and peace-loving disciples of reason."[61] War, religious intolerance, intellectual repression, and violations of political liberty were other targets of Montesquieu's vigorous criticism. On all these subjects, he was at one with the *philosophes* and the early Enlightenment.

Yet there was another and profoundly different side to his thought, and it was this that disturbed Voltaire and Helvétius. Montesquieu defended the selling of office, exalted the political power of the *parlements* as essential to constitutional monarchy, declared the nobility's privileges essential to liberty, and scorned the political capacity of the people. In his theory of the French Constitution, he took the remote feudal past as the standard by which to measure the institutions of his own time. Thus once again Montesquieu's thought turns out to be characterized by complex tensions that cannot be reduced to any one single "ism," such as "liberalism," or analyzed away as the alleged ideology of his class.

How political was Montesquieu's thought? Much depends upon what meaning is attached to the term, "political." Some critics have claimed that by accepting uncritically the Greek notion of the knowledgeable and disinterested legislator, Montesquieu naively attributed too much efficacy to politics, to deliberate efforts to achieve the public ends by constitutional engineering.[62]

Other critics have asserted that Montesquieu was among the first political philosophers to give up the identification of the political with the common good.
Thus he is alleged to have substituted society for the polity.[63] Instead of direct
political action, he is said to have accepted surrogate, quasi-automatic mechanisms, constitutional, social, or economic, as producing acceptable outcomes in
modern states. Individual, group, and regional interests were to replace the
active and omnipotent sovereign state served by a bureaucracy and centralized
administration. In short, on this view, Montesquieu regarded the political as
nothing more than that institutionalized conflict among groups and estates that
characterizes free regimes. His emphasis upon moderate constitutions with
such devices as the separation of powers has led to the charge that he was a
liberal who thought politics ought to be restricted to preventing the accumulation and exercise of power, a purely negative objective.[64]

Certainly there is some basis for such assertions about the antipolitical qualities of Montesquieu's thought. But there are quite contrary indications as well.
Both tendencies in *The Spirit of the Laws* need to be identified and assessed.

No part of his thought reveals more about Montesquieu's orientation than his
attacks upon those theorists who had justified the absolutisms of early modern
Europe. Of these, Hobbes was the single most important. From the time that he
wrote the myth of the Troglodytes in the *Persian Letters* and his early treatise on
man's duties, Montesquieu sought to refute Hobbes. Montesquieu wrote: "He
tells me that in and of itself justice is nothing; it is only what the laws of a
government ordain or forbid."[65] Against this Montesquieu had written in the
Persian Letters, ". . . Justice is eternal and does not depend upon conventions of
men. If it did so, then this would be a dreadful truth we should have to hide from
ourselves."[66] In his early treatise on moral duties and political obligation, the
Traité général des devoirs, Montesquieu derived justice from the existence and
sociability of reasonable beings, not from human laws or the individual wills of
these beings.[67]

There was an extraordinary consistency in Montesquieu's life-long opposition to Hobbes and Spinoza. Some critics have called Montesquieu's sincerity
into question. In their view, he attacked Hobbes and Spinoza only to conceal his
agreement with them.[68] Yet in Book I of *The Spirit of the Laws* Montesquieu
reproduced verbatim passages from his early unpublished work of 1725. This
demonstrates that he was not writing simply to take in the censors. When he
defended himself against clerical attacks after the publication of *The Spirit of the
Laws*, he wrote of Book I:

> . . . the end in view is to attack Hobbes. His system is terrible be-
> cause it makes all human virtues and vices depend upon laws men
> have made for themselves. Furthermore he wishes to prove that all
> men are born into a state of war, and that the first law of nature is

the war of all against all. This system, like that of Spinoza, over-turns all religion and all morality.[69]

The preface of *The Spirit of the Laws* puts forward Montesquieu's claims for his work. Most controversial was Montesquieu's contention that he found no fault with the existing order. Every nation will find in his book, he wrote, the justifications for its principles; he would be delighted if he could provide all men everywhere with new reasons for loving their governments, laws, and duties.

Much of what follows in *The Spirit of the Laws* is, however, critical of prevailing institutions, laws, and practices in France and elsewhere. Furthermore, in his preface, Montesquieu goes on to praise enlightenment and to condemn prejudice. In the body of his work, Montesquieu appeals to justice, humanity, reason, religious toleration, and political liberty. Does this mean that Montesquieu was a *philosophe*, a concealed adherent of the Enlightenment and the *l'Encyclopédie*, that he belonged to the party of humanity and that his ideal was the heavenly city of the eighteenth-century philosophers?[70]

In this same preface, Montesquieu wrote some lines that are so clearly conservative that it is not difficult to understand why Burke admired their author. Montesquieu's constitutionalism based on tradition, his emphasis on the general spirit of a nation as determining what its laws ought to be, his opposition to large-scale change based on general ideas—all these central positions were conservative. Montesquieu believed that not progress but corruption was the law of history. On balance, however, it appears that instead of choosing one clear-cut option, he maintained a tension that could lead either to rationalist and reforming, or to historical and conservative positions.

An equally controversial part of his preface dealt with the design and method of *The Spirit of the Laws*. Montesquieu claimed that his work of twenty years was unified by a design that the reader could discover by careful study. He stated that he had established principles, under which all particular cases fall. All history follows from these principles, and so every law is connected to another, or derives from a more general law. Ever since critics have been proposing analytical schemes (all of which differ) that claim to reveal Montesquieu's design. This is to assume that because he claimed unity for his thought, he in fact achieved it. Nothing is more dubious. Perhaps after the projected new critical edition of *The Spirit of the Laws* has established just when Montesquieu wrote which portions of his book, it may be possible to go further toward resolving definitively the question of its unity. That day is not yet here.

No less perplexing is the question of the meaning and significance of the philosophical theory of law Montesquieu provided in Book I. Almost all commentators today take a dim view of the opening book. Many of his contemporaries shared this estimate. It is a paradox about Montesquieu that his reputation has been able to survive what even his admirers concede to have been a disappointing beginning. Book I was meant to provide the philosophical foundation on which Montesquieu was to place the enormous weight of his life's work. Had Montesquieu consistently relied on his initial definitions of law, his work would have been less of an achievement. In a sense, his inconsistency saved him.[71]

There are two ways of describing Montesquieu's intentions in Book I that may clarify it. First of all, he understood himself to be summarizing a consensus of philosophical thinkers in the tradition of secular natural law, rather than offering an altogether novel theory of his own. If so, he may have regarded Book I as less of an advance than his new typology of governments, his theory of causation, his restatement of limited constitutional government, and his assessment of how the effects of the climate affect politics. Secondly, although he relied for the most part upon the metaphysical and methodological commonplaces of the natural law school, Montesquieu wished to adapt them to his own political position.

Montesquieu was far more critical of absolute monarchy. Book I must be seen as an attempt to destroy the philosophical foundations of absolutism in all the forms known to Montesquieu by at once maintaining the arguments of the natural law school, but rejecting the defense of the absolute state by Grotius and Pufendorf. Despite its abstract character, Montesquieu's theory of law is political. It lays the basis for the theory that liberty is possible only under the limitation of law, and institutions that support it.

Because of human nature, Montesquieu holds, passions may lead human beings to disregard reason. They need to be reminded of their duties to their creator, and even more of their moral and political obligations. These cannot be forgotten because humans are made to live in society, and hence need laws. Montesquieu again follows the secular natural law school in basing law upon the inherent sociability of human nature, as well as human passions, which can and should be restrained by reason. Unlike some natural law theorists, he makes no use whatever of the notion of social contract.

Montesquieu wished to refute Hobbes on a number of points: to show that man is by nature sociable rather than seeking to dominate his fellows; that the state of nature is not a state of war. To do this, Montesquieu returns to the comparison and contrast between men and animals he had begun in chapter I. An implicit part of his argument is the distinction between humans as created by God, the first stage, in which the laws of nature are those shared with the animals, and humans as living in civil society, the second stage, when they need positive laws.

Without conceding that there was ever a presocial condition, or that any sort of compact was made to bring humans into civil society, Montesquieu explores what they were like when created. The key to understanding the laws of nature is to be found in animals, who have no desire to attack one another. Hence peace is the first law of nature (*loi naturelle*).[72] This is one point on which he wished to refute Hobbes, who argued that the state of nature is a state of war.

When Montesquieu gives his version of the laws of nature, he refers also to the weakness and timidity of humans as first created. Thus each felt inferior to every other; the idea of equality would be unlikely in these circumstances. The desire to subjugate others could not have been the first to occur to humans. The idea of sovereignty and domination is so complex that it must have come much later.[73] Most of this chapter relies very heavily on Pufendorf, whose principal targets were Hobbes and Spinoza.

To these general principles of being obliged to do good to others and to avoid doing them harm, Montesquieu applies the term "natural." They are thus the substance of the law of nature. But then he confuses the issue by extending the term "natural" to the sort of adaptation that must be undergone by general principles when applied to particular circumstances.

When Montesquieu turns to positive or human laws, he uses this second sense of "natural." A government is natural, he asserts, when it conforms to the genius of the people for whom it was established. So great are the differences among the general spirits of nations that the laws of one are almost never suited to another. Thus laws ought to be relative to the nature and principle of a government, to its physical conditions, to its mode of life, to its political constitution, religion, wealth, numbers, commerce, *moeurs* and *manières*. All these taken together make up the spirit that ought to animate a nation's laws. Sometimes there are internal contradictions or anomalies, and these ought to be eliminated. To investigate all these considerations is the program of *The Spirit of the Laws*.

The relationship of Book I to the rest of *The Spirit of the Laws* is difficult to determine. Montesquieu, on numerous subsequent occasions, refers to the "natural," that is, the prescriptive aspects of domestic and international law. On the other hand, most of his attention focuses on laws as "natural" in the second and discrepant sense of being congruent with the general spirit of a nation, or else with the "nature" and principle of its government. Therefore, when Montesquieu uses the term "ought," he sometimes does so in the moral sense of obligation. More often he uses "ought" in the sense of conforming to the nature or principle of a government, or to the general spirit.

Books II through VIII make up perhaps the single most integrated section in *The Spirit of the Laws*. There Montesquieu sets out his own distinctive classifications of governments. He then analyzes the nature and principle of each, and derives the consequences that ought to follow from their laws, *moeurs*, and education. Finally, he deals with the sort of fatal corruption that must occur when the principle of a government is flouted or abandoned. This section Montesquieu regarded as among his most significant intellectual contributions.

Montesquieu was making a number of vital political arguments by his classifications of governments, by reconceptualizing monarchy and despotism. Despotism is perhaps his greatest innovation in the classifications of government. As defined by Montesquieu, there is little to be said in favor of despotism, except that it is the most efficient way of ruling extended empires where the population has no tradition of self-government and where the climate favors acceptance of arbitrary rule. Hence, if any characteristic of despotism occurs in another form of government, it must be viewed as pathological. If delegation of authority to a powerful chief minister and bureaucracy is a characteristic of despotism, then it must not be allowed in a monarchy.

Montequieu asserted that in oriental governments the despot could do what he wished without any limiting laws or traditions and that the despot owned the lands and property of all his subjects. In short, when Montesquieu argued that European monarchies were threatened with despotism, he posited the consequent disappearance of liberty, of the rule of law, of economic prosperity, and of the institution of private property.

What do these conclusions indicate about the role of evidence in Montesquieu's method? Clearly, induction from facts is not what he understood himself to be doing. Rather, either facts provide clues to the internal structure of governments and societies, or else facts illustrate principles or laws. It is important to understand that for Montesquieu facts are significant to the extent that their connections and interdependence are understood as comprising wholes. These wholes or types, then, are to be understood in terms of clear and interconnected concepts, such as the nature and principle of a government. Reason, then, is not to be limited to philosophical questions; it can be applied to the analysis of legal, political, and social structures. What reason can reveal are the causes of the laws and institutions of a society being what they are; reason also provides us with the standards by which we can judge whether these laws and institutions meet the standards of justice, liberty, and humanity.

Montesquieu was a great practitioner of comparative political analysis. Nothing is more important for the understanding of his method than the uses he made of comparison, the typology he devised to facilitate it, the quality of his data, and the standards he applied to his evidence. In his "Essay on the Causes" Montesquieu singled out comparison as the single most valuable capacity of the human mind. Comparison is to him indispensable for the analysis of human collectivities. At the very least, Montesquieu argued that we can understand political and social phenomena only when we can stipulate some arrangement alternative to that in question. Second, he insisted that only by dividing human societies into types can comparative method be put on a rigorous basis. At his most ambitious, he claimed to have discovered certain general laws applicable to all governments. By them every individual datum can be explained; every law can be linked to another or derived from another and more general law.

Montesquieu's interests were almost equally divided between establishing similarities among classes of polities or societies widely separated in time and space, on the one side, and on the other, arriving at the understanding of what distinguishes one from the other. He has been praised for his achievements in both types of comparative analysis. Montesquieu was fascinated by differences in political and social systems, in their complexity, their organic and unplanned historical development. On occasion he discovered the hidden wisdom of custom and could refer to the generally beneficent, if unintended, consequences of faith.

Nowhere is his ambivalence as an analyst better displayed than in his discussion of feudal laws and institutions, which Marc Bloch called the first treatment of feudalism as a social and political system. This vast piece of comparative historical sociology appended to *The Spirit of the Laws* began with an extended organic metaphor, in which Montesquieu likened the system formed by feudal laws and practices to a huge oak tree.[74] As one approaches, its trunk but not its roots are visible. In order to see them, it is necessary to dig deep beneath the surface. Thus the organic approach to feudalism inherent in this metaphor is combined with the aspiration to achieve a scientific analysis. In Montesquieu's view, all human laws and institutions are susceptible to comparative investigation of a sort that will produce general laws.

Montesquieu believed himself to be breaking new ground, a judgment shared by many who came after him. Ernst Cassirer wrote: "Montesquieu in fact grasped a new and fruitful principle and founded a new method in social science. The method of ideal-types, which he introduces and first applies effectively, has never been abandoned; on the contrary, it reached its full development only in the sociology of the nineteenth and twentieth centuries."[75]

Throughout his analysis Montesquieu used such ideal types. As Montesquieu phrased it:

> I have had new ideas; I have had to find new terms, or else to give new meaning to old ones. . . . It should be noted that there is a great difference between saying that a certain quality . . . or virtue is not the spring that moves a government, and saying that it is nowhere to be found in that government. If I say that this wheel, this cog are not the spring that makes this watch go, does it follow that they are not in this watch? . . . In a word, honor exists in a republic, although political virtue is its mainspring; political virtue, in a monarchy, although honor is its principle.[76]

In Books II–VIII, Montesquieu classified governments in terms of three types, each of which is characterized by its nature and principle. By the "nature" of a government he meant the structure, the framework within which the person or group holding power must function; by "principle," that passion which must animate those involved in a form of government if it is to operate at its strongest and best. When a government is functioning properly, a legislator who violates the principle of government will provoke revolution. On the other hand, when a government is debilitated by the weakening of its essential principle, it can be saved only by a good legislator capable of strengthening it. The persona of the legislator is used by Montesquieu in the classical sense of an exceptional person called in by a society to give it basic laws. But the retention of this fiction produced an ambiguity when joined to what is novel in Montesquieu's thought, the limits placed upon legislation by the physical and moral causes that combine to form the general spirit of a society. Sometimes he suggested that the legislator adapt laws to the general spirit of the society, sometimes that he use laws and even religion to combat that spirit.

When classified by their nature, governments fall into three categories. A republic is that form in which the people as a whole (democracy), or certain families (aristocracy), hold sovereign power. A monarchy is that in which a prince rules according to established laws that create channels through which the royal power flows. (Montesquieu's examples of such channels include an aristocracy administering local justice, parlements with political functions, a clergy with recognized rights, and cities with historical privileges.) Despotism is the rule of a single person, directed only by his own will and caprice.

The principles of these governments differ: virtue is the principle of republics; honor, of monarchies; and fear, of despotism. Montesquieu subdivided republics into democracies and aristocracies. His image of the first was taken from classical Greece and Rome. When he assigned virtue to them as their distinctive principle, he meant those political qualities requisite to their maintenance: in the case of democracies, love of country (*patrie*), belief in equality, and the frugality and asceticism that lead men to sacrifice their personal pleasures to the general interest.

Montesquieu's model for aristocracy was drawn from early modern Italian republics such as Venice. This is why he classified aristocracies, along with democracies, as republics. Although such aristocratic republics required virtue on the part of its governing class, the virtue required of them was moderation of aspiration and conduct. For their characteristic weaknesses sprang both from implacable internal rivalry among aristocrats and from the envy they aroused when they insisted upon maintaining too great differences between their class and the people.

Montesquieu thought that monarchy, as found in France and other European states of his time, was the modern regime best suited to ruling free societies intermediate in scale and commercial in their economy. The principle of monarchy he defined as honor, based on *esprit de corps*, the sense of belonging to an exclusive and superior social group, which demands and receives preference on the basis of birth. When such privileges are granted voluntarily by the monarch, the nobility of a monarchy is recognized as a semi-autonomous, intermediate group (between the king and people). The nobility, although its claims are selfish and exclusive, helps maintain liberty by resisting any attempt by the crown to exceed its constutional prerogatives. Montesquieu summed up his conviction that such a nobility is essential to a monarchy (as opposed to despotism) in the phrase: "Without a monarch, no nobility; without a nobility, no monarchy. For then there is only a despot."[77]

Montesquieu made the concept of despotism into a regime type that became so universally used in a pejorative sense during the second half of the eighteenth century that it helped undermine the legitimacy of the French monarchy. Because of Montesquieu, in France "despotism" replaced "tyranny" as the term for a corrupted monarchy. The French Revolution was described by those who made it as the overthrow of despotism.[78] The term, first used by nobles and members of *parlements* like Montesquieu himself, later became irresistible to Rousseau, Robespierre, and Saint-Just, whose commitments were anything but monarchical and aristocratic.

In the reconceptualization of regime types presented in *The Spirit of the Laws*, Montesquieu took into account virtually every development of the concept of despotism from its formulation in Greece to its early modern identification with slavery and its most recent form as a system of government. Like the other two types of government, despotism had to be analyzed in terms of its nature or structure and its principle or operative passion. Yet Montesquieu did not expect to find any of his types empirically embodied in all its aspects. Montesquieu makes this point clearly about despotism.

> It would be an error to believe that there has ever existed any-where in the world a human authority that is despotic in all its aspects. . . . Even the greatest power is limited in some way. If the grand seigneur . . . were to attempt to impose some new tax, the resulting outcry would be such as to make him observe the limits to which he had not known he was subject. Although the king of Persia may be able to force a son to kill his father . . . the same king cannot force his subjects to drink wine. Every nation is dominated by a general spirit, on which its very power is founded. Anything undertaken in defiance of that spirit is a blow against that power, and as such must necessarily come to a stop.[79]

Although a number of the strands previously associated with the concept of despotism recur in Montesquieu's formulation, it shares the significant innovations made in his way of theorizing about politics. Thus despotism was for him, not simply a structure of state power and offices, but a system with a characteristic political structure and social organization propelled by fear, a passion peculiar to it. Montesquieu refused to reduce social organization to political form, or political form to social organization. In his view, both the political institutions and the social organization of despotic societies are simple, while those of a monarchy, as he defines it, are complex. This he argues by analyzing the ties that unite societies living under free and despotic governments respectively. Montesquieu also contrasts the characteristics of free societies, with those of despotisms, which suppress conflict in the name of order, refuse to recognize the status of intermediate groups and classes, and insist upon immediate and unquestioned obedience to commands. In a free society, the texture of relations among persons and groups is much looser than in a despotism. Disagreements and even conflict are essential to the one; fatal to the other.[80]

In Book III, Montesquieu contrasted the distinctive modes of obedience requisite to despotic governments on the one side, and free governments on the other. The positive side of Montesquieu's political thought cannot be understood without reference to the characteristics of despotism. Many critics who have found Montesquieu's definition of freedom as security from fear to be unsatisfactory have not grasped his contrast with despotism, which he sees as actuated by that passion. Similarly, the essential features of politics in a free government are the limitation of power, the recognition and accommodation of groups conceded to have some autonomy, the regular discussion between them and the sovereign of alternatives to proposals judged to be adverse to their interests by the parties affected by legislation, and the preference for obedience based on consent.

In Book IV, Montesquieu dealt with the education or social training essential to each type of government. These must ensure that all citizens be inspired by the same passion, the principle requisite to its maintenance. Most of the book is devoted to moral education in republics. In a republic, the principle that must be inculcated is the love of *patrie* and its laws, the persisting preference for the public over the private good. Because every citizen participates in the government, he must be possessed of the passion that will preserve it. To the type of education required by republics and monarchies, Montesquieu contrasts that of despotic government.

The passive obedience required under despotism presupposes education of a peculiar kind: the subject must be ignorant, timid, broken in spirit, requiring little regulation by law. Social relations must also follow a pattern: in a despotism, every family is, as a matter of policy, isolated from every other. Only religion and custom can moderate despotism, and these are less effective and regular in their operation than the basic laws which limit governments that willingly observe them. Even in the sphere of economic life, despotism exerts noxious effects. The general uncertainty created by the caprice of the despot and his viziers impoverishes the mass of men; commerce is unrewarding; labor's results, incalculable; and hence potentially profitable activities are left undone.[81]

By contrast the nature of monarchy requires laws that recognize constituted powers set between the king and the people. Although the king is sovereign, monarchy by its nature entails requires that there be fundamental laws restraining his will and caprice. Power should flow through the channels of groups or estates freely consented to by the king. First among them is the nobility, without which a monarchy turns into a despotism. There must also be a constituted body that includes the clergy. This is as valuable in a monarchy as it is pernicious in a republic. Other bodies mentioned by Montesquieu as essential to a monarchy are those including lords with feudal prerogatives, such as acting as judges, and cities with privileges for their citizens. Finally, there must be courts with the power to register or not to register laws of the king. These courts must be in the hands of a quasi-independent judiciary.

Since honor is the principle of monarchy, the laws ought to support the nobility governed by its code of honor. The nobility must be hereditary. All legal provisions that preserve the existence of noble families are necessary to a monarchy. Taxes must be collected in a way that does not affect adversely the population's willingness to work. Since monarchies can execute policy faster than republics, there is some danger that laws will be carried out too quickly. The *parlements*, which hold the power to register laws, should question potential abuses. Delay is, therefore, a protection of liberty.

In Book VIII, Montesquieu deals with corruption, or what happens to a government when it deviates from the principle, or passion, that is its spring. To abandon its principle is to corrupt the state by changing its basic nature. Once that occurs, the most excellent laws begin to work against the state. But if the principle of a state is in force, then even defective laws produce excellent results. So great is the power of the principle that it overrides all obstacles.

Montesquieu is here following the logic inherent in a method that refuses to draw conclusions applicable to all types of states. Rather he deduces his generalizations from the specific structure and ruling passion of each type. Thus his analysis is applied to how and why corruption differs in each of the governments. The argument is deductive, the evidence serving to illustrate the general points being made.

Since their principle is virtue, republics become corrupt when virtue is lost. Corruption differs in democracies and aristocracies, the two forms of republic. Democracies are corrupted in two ways: either the spirit of equality is lost, or it becomes exaggerated. When inequality becomes the dominant principle, democracy turns into aristocracy; when extreme equality is dominant, democracy turns into the despotism of a single ruler. Montesquieu is more interested in the second mode. Whereas for Plato, democracy is by its nature extreme, for Montesquieu, there is a normal, moderate mode of democracy. This "consists, not in creating a situation in which everyone commands, or in which no one is commanded, but rather in our obeying or commanding only our equals."[82] Thus Montesquieu defines true equality, not as having no master, but as having only equals as masters. In a well-ordered, moderate democracy, men are equal only as citizens. They do not resent the legitimate authority of their magistrates or judges.

Monarchies become corrupted with the disappearance of honor as a principle. Then constituted bodies (*corps*) are deprived of their prerogatives; the towns, of their privileges; the nobles, of the honors and functions due them. In a sentence aimed at Louis XIV, Montesquieu describes how a monarchy may be corrupted into the despotism of a single person by a king who centers everything on himself, summons the state to his capital, the capital to his court, and the court to himself.

Montesquieu considers China as a potential counterexample not assimilable to his classification, that is, as ruled by a principle combining fear, honor, and virtue. China is a crucial case both here in Book VIII, which concludes Montesquieu's examination of the types of government, and in Book XIX, which concludes his treatment of causation. It is, perhaps, the first time in the history of Western political thought that so much attention is given to a non-European state. Thus Montesquieu did in fact seek to take the whole world into account. On the other hand, in both books China is declared to be an oriental despotism on the basis of evidence selected to buttress Montesquieu's case. This demonstrates how Europocentric he remained in his view of the world. Political liberty is an European achievement; despotism, the usual condition of non-Europeans.

No part of *The Spirit of the Laws* is better known and more often misrepresented than Montesquieu's treatment of the relationship between liberty and the structure of a nation's constitution (Book XI, chapter 6). For many scholars and students, Montesquieu's political theory is still identified with his alleged statement that constitutional mechanisms, such as the separation of powers, alone determine whether or not a government is free. Such a legalistic interpretation of Montesquieu is indefensible. It is not based on a close reading or proper understanding even of the texts from this single chapter cited by those who so interpret him. Furthermore, such a narrowly constitutional reading ignores the principal thrust and novelty of Montesquieu as a theorist.

In Book XI, Montesquieu understood himself to be investigating those characteristics of a nation's constitution that create and maintain liberty. This was but one part of his treatment of liberty, its institutional characteristics, social supports, and psychological bases, considered in relation to the government as a whole. Although he thought that England offered the best single case of constitutional liberty, Montesquieu believed that the English constitution had evolved without plan or conscious construction. By making explicit its principles, Montesquieu opened the way to deliberate construction of constitutions. Probably he himself came closest to this notion when he made use of the classical concept of the "legislator," a person called in to construct a scheme of government for a state. Either he was an expert from another state, or if from the same state, he was excluded from any subsequent part in the institutions he had devised. When the American and French Revolutions occurred, Montesquieu's theories received the close attention of those engaged in debating the details of the new constitutions. Montesquieu made the single most important statement of eighteenth-century constitutional theory prior to these actual cases of revolution and reconstruction, which he thus influenced without having anticipated.

What were the constitutional principles set forth by Montesquieu? How novel were they? To what extent did his originality consist in arranging and combining strands of thought previously separated? To what extent did the component parts of his theory fit into a single coherent theory?

No progress can be made toward understanding Montesquieu's thinking about constitutional principles without distinguishing four theories often confused with one another: the mixed constitution, the balanced constitution, separation of powers, and checks and balances. All four theories are varieties of constitutionalism. But they are constructed in terms of differing elements, functions, and goals of government and society. Since they have been formulated at various times and on discrepant bases, these four theories to some extent overlap, and to some extent are contradictory.[83] Montesquieu's originality consists in his distinctive assembly and combination of these theories, rather than in inventing any one of them. All had already figured in English constitutional discussions.[84]

The oldest is the theory of the mixed constitution. It classifies the pure forms of government, establishes distinctions between their ideal and vitiated forms, and concludes that the ideal constitution is a judicious mixture of monarchy, aristocracy, and democracy. The theory of the balanced constitution, on the other hand, was stated in terms either of a balance of power among different parts of the government or of the society. A typical statement was made by Blackstone in his *Commentaries* (1765–69), who found the balance to exist in the relationship among the people, nobility, and king.

In Book XI, Montesquieu gave three definitions of governmental powers. Of these, two are abstract, focusing on the functions presumably performed by every government. In the first, with which he began chapter VI, Montesquieu divided political power into legislative and executive functions; he then subdivided the executive function into executive power, by which he meant the conduct of foreign affairs (which executes the law of nations), and the judicial power (which executes domestic laws).

The second statement of governmental functions occurs shortly after the first, and is used thereafter by Montesquieu: "these three powers: that of making laws, that of executing public decisions, and that of judging crimes or disputes arising among individuals."[85] It was a great and lasting innovation for Montesquieu to isolate, and place on the same level as the other two, this last function, which he always called the power of judging (*la puissance de juger*) rather than the judicial power (*le pouvoir judiciaire*). But although he intended that the power of judging not be dependent upon the other two, he did not give the judicial power that equality with the legislative and executive achieved in

American doctrine. Yet Montesquieu did establish the trinity of governmental functions, as divided into legislative, executive, and judicial.

The third statement he made of governmental functions is in his summary of the British Constitution:

> Here, then, is the fundamental constitution of the government being discussed. Since the legislative body is made up of two parts, each is made dependent upon the other by their mutual power to reject legislation. Both will be connected by the executive power, which itself will be connected to the legislative.[86]

> These three powers ought to produce repose, or inaction. But since the nature of things requires movement, all three powers are obliged to act, and to act together.[87]

Montesquieu here referred to the executive and the two chambers of Parliament. Such a breakdown derives from the theory of the mixed constitution and refers to the representation of the aristocracy in the House of Lords and of the people in the House of Commons. Each is allowed a part in making law in order to protect its legitimate interests against the other. Such a notion plays no part in the theory of the separation of powers. And, it should be noted, insofar as this is a theory of the balanced constitution, it fails to assign any role to that branch concerned with the power of judging.[88] Rather, Montesquieu declared that considered from the point of view of the balanced constitution, the judicial branch has no part to play:

> "As for the three powers mentioned above, the judicial, in a sense, has no force. This leaves but two. They need a power so constituted that it can temper both of them, and this can be done by that part of the legislative body which is composed of nobles. . . ."[89]

According to Montesquieu, any constitution that achieves political liberty must be based upon at least two principles: the separation of powers and the balance of powers. Although distinct, they are related and support each other. Those who hold power always seek more. Hence any constitutional separation of powers needs to be maintained by checks upon one branch by another. For this reason the executive branch must be given a veto power to check the legislative whenever it seeks to monopolize power. Similarly, if the executive seeks to gather all power into its own hands, it should be subject to check by the legislative. Montesquieu held that all executive officers, except the chief executive himself, may be called into account for their actions by the legislature.

Where does this leave Montesquieu's doctrine of the separation of powers?

Two interpretations have dominated the field. The first is continental and European, and tends to appear in the work of jurists rather than political philosophers. It represents Montesquieu as asserting that for constitutional liberty to exist, there must be a complete separation of agencies, functions, and persons. The other interpretation is that of Madison, who held that the separation of powers entails only that all power should not be concentrated in the same set of hands. Such separation is best secured by a partial separation and blending of powers, that is, separation of powers modified by a partial application of the theory of checks and balances. Some other commentators have argued that Montesquieu was concerned only with the nonconfusion of powers rather than their rigid separation.

What they mean by this is that, in their view, Montesquieu wished only to provide a constitutional basis for each branch, but did not wish to separate either functions or persons. He may have been clearer about what he sought to avoid than in his view of the principles immanent in his model, the English Constitution.

Many commentators have distorted Montesquieu by neglecting his negative model of despotism and concentrating exclusively on that view of England presented in Book XI, chapter 6. Such conventional interpretations also miss significant points in political sociology added by the later chapter 27 of Book XIX. Its title is "How a Nation's Laws May Contribute to Its *Moeurs, Manières,* and Character."[90] Montesquieu's analysis stresses the effect of the political upon the social: the English Constitution has affected considerably that nation's *moeurs* and *manières*. In this chapter, Montesquieu added further elements that have not been sufficiently noticed by those who accuse him of either not knowing or misrepresenting the operation of the English Constitution in his time. Montesquieu here placed great stress upon the distinctive role of parties in English political life, and upon freedom of thought and expression, as its prerequisites. Under the English Constitution, there were two visible powers, the executive and legislative (the judicial attracted less attention from the public because juries were drawn from the people itself). Thus there is no judicial institution comparable in its prestige and symbolism to that of the executive or legislative branches. And because the individuals who make up the society are free and dominated by their passions, they tend to prefer either the executive or the legislative branch. Despite the advantages enjoyed by the executive branch, which can use its patronage to buy support, the public rallies against it when it appears to be overwhelmingly the victor.

Citizens in a free state, according to Montesquieu, invariably support the weaker side in a political struggle. The existence of parties makes it unlikely that either the executive or legislative branch can achieve permanent domination over the other. The constitution thus encourages frequent changes in the support of party by citizens and in the monarch's choice of prime minister.

Although Montesquieu relates the *moeurs* and *manières* of the English to their constitution, his point about parties is a new argument. It fits into his description of England as a society with characteristics that reinforce the disposition of the legal and political parts of the government in such a way that undesirable concentration of power is avoided. This derives from what may be called Montesquieu's political sociology: the general attitudes of citizens produce political consequences. Thus the unanticipated and unplanned consequences of liberty reinforce the political structure. He welcomes political parties because he believes that conflict within limits is not only inevitable but necessary to a free government. He further suggests that free men tend to swing from one party to another whenever it seems that one party may achieve a permanent dominance. This implies that freedom depends upon countervailing forces.

Montesquieu also asserted here that political liberty presupposes freedom of thought and expression: "If a state is to enjoy and preserve liberty, everyone must be able to say what he thinks. In a free state, therefore, a citizen may speak and write anything not expressly forbidden by the laws."[91]

England, as here described, is not a republic in Montesquieu's stipulated sense, i. e. , that its principle or spring is love of equality and the *patrie*. Nevertheless, individual interests are not dominant, nor do the English calculate benefits. Their attachment to liberty is based on passion, rather than reason: "[N]o other nation loves its liberty more. To defend it, the nation stands ready to sacrifice its wealth, its comforts, its interests. . . ."[91]

Books XI and XII both deal with the laws that comprise political liberty. Book XI considers political liberty in relation to the constitution under which the citizen lives; Book XII, the protections afforded to the citizen against accusations under the criminal law that might menace his person, his property, and his honor.

Montesquieu, after remarking on the confusion that surrounds theoretical discussions of liberty in general, proceeds to eliminate those definitions he judges irrelevant to political liberty. Independence, or the right to do what one wishes, cannot be political liberty. "If a citizen could do what the law prohibits, he would no longer possess liberty because all others would have the same power."[93] Nor should political liberty be confused with the liberty defined by philosophers considering the exercise of free will. In Book XI, the issue is the constitution under which a citizen lives. He is free when that constitution is "so framed that no one is compelled to do what is not made obligatory by law, nor forced to abstain from what the law permits."[94] This formulation is clearer than the notoriously ill-phrased one that preceded it: "In a state, that is, a society where laws exist, liberty can consist only in being able to do what one ought to will, and in not being constrained to do what one ought not to will."[95]

In Book XII, Montesquieu takes up the liberty of the citizen in relation to his person, property, and honor. There he equates liberty with security (tacitly contrasting this with the fear endemic to despotic systems). Such security depends more upon the nature of the criminal law than anything else. The citizen's liberty depends upon his having adequate procedural protections when he is accused. For it is then that his security is most directly menaced.

This was particularly true in Montesquieu's time, when severe punishments were meted out in cases of sacrilege, heresy, witchcraft, and homosexuality. Montesquieu argued that these offenses, then punished by death at the stake, did not merit such penalties by the state. The only correct principle of punishment is proportionality. Acts that damage individuals slightly should be punished slightly. Offenses against the church should be punished by exclusion from it, not by criminal penalties. Offenses against the Deity should be left to divine vengance. Only when someone has intentionally deprived another of his security ought punishment be severe. Montesquieu condemned vague definitions of high treason as opening the way to arbitrary abuse of state power. Montesquieu carefully distinguished opinion from action. Indiscreet speeches and irreverent writing ought not to be treated as high treason, which applies only to overt actions.[96] However, in the presence of genuine danger, the protection of individuals may be subordinated to the preservation of the state.[97]

Montesquieu condemned the cruel punishments of his day, the use of torture as a means of obtaining evidence, and the use of executive decrees to imprison without trial. He denied the efficacy of extreme penalties. Finally, he argued that free governments practice leniency; severity of punishment is more fitting for despotic governments, whose principle is fear, than for a monarchy or republic whose springs are honor and virtue respectively. In nondespotic states, the purpose is to prevent, not to punish, crimes. There the legislator seeks to inspire good *moeurs*. For in moderate governments, the love of *patrie*, shame, and the fear of blame are internal restraints more effective than the external cruel sanctions of despotisms.[98]

What is the relationship between political liberty and the three types of government? Montesquieu holds that neither democracy nor aristocracy are by their nature free politically. They may or may not be so.[99] Everything depends upon whether, within a given government, political power is moderated or checked. And this is the case only when the political structure is so ordered that one part of the government has the power to check another. Only in monarchy is liberty always present. For when it is not (according to the stipulative definition given by Montesquieu), the state is no longer a monarchy but a despotism.

In Books X and XV, Montesquieu set out to refute the justifications of slavery, conquest, and colonialism found in legal theorists of absolutism. Slavery, the absolute right held by a master over the life and property of a slave, Montesquieu argued, violates natural law. Nor is it justifiable even on utilitarian grounds. Its effects are deleterious to master and slave alike. No matter what the climate, all necessary work can be performed by freemen. Slavery is in the long run fatal to both monarchies and republics.[100]

Montesquieu did not accept any of the justifications for total domination given in the Roman Law or by later jurists such as Bodin, Grotius, Pufendorf, or Hobbes. He denied that the claim to enslave men could be justified, as they had argued, by asserting that conquerors were being merciful when they spared those they had defeated in return for enslaving them. The reasons given by jurists were absurd. Even in war, only necessity can create the right to kill. A victor has no right to murder a captive in cold blood. Nor does a man have a right to sell himself into slavery. Such a sale presupposes a price. But to give up one's status as a freeman is an act of such extravagance that it cannot be supposed to be the act of a rational being. And how can the enslavement of children as yet unborn be justified by any act or promise on the part of their parents or ancestors?

Slavery violates both the natural and the civil law. A criminal may be justly punished because the law he has violated has been made in his favor, and he had benefited from it. But the same cannot be true of the slave, to whom law can never serve any purpose. This violates the fundamental principle underlying all human societies.[101]

As for other arguments offered in defense of slavery, Montesquieu riddled them with scorn. Often they derived from nothing more than the contempt felt by one nation for another with different customs; often, from the absurd pretension that a nation could be reduced to slavery in order to simplify the task of converting it to the true faith. Such reasoning had encouraged those who had ravaged the Americas to believe that they merited absolute power. How pleasant to act as a bandit and to be considered a good Christian. Slavery derived from the desire of a few for unlimited voluptuousness and luxury; slavery appealed to the basest of human passions. Whose desires would not be kindled by the prospect of becoming the absolute master of another's life, virtue, and property? As for Negro slavery, it derived, not only from such passions thinly disguised by sophisms, but also from the most contemptible of human prejudices. To unmask those who defended the African slave trade, Montesquieu reverted to the irony of the *Persian Letters*.[102] This section, together with that deriding the Inquisition, is incompatible both with the image of Montesquieu as a self-serving *parlementaire* concerned to defend the privileges of his class and with that of him as a quasi-bourgeois citizen of Bordeaux, the center of the French slave trade.

Book XIX states Montesquieu's general theory of causation. What constitutes an adequate explanation of why a people has certain laws, political organization, and social structure, and not others? Montesquieu's most comprehensive answer was his theory that every society has its distinctive *esprit général*, which is determined not only by physical causes such as climate and terrain, but even more by what he called moral forces: religion, laws, maxims, precedents, *moeurs, manières*, economy and trade, and its style of thought. What results from such moral and physical forces is a distinctive pattern, ordering every important aspect of a society.[103]

This general spirit, as formulated by Montesquieu, possesses none of the metaphysical attributes later found in the German notion of the *Volksgeist*. For him, the general character of a society can be explained empirically by the upbringing or education it imparts to its members. This is done in three ways: through the family, through schools, and through the social practices of the society. These settings may all teach the same thing; they may contradict one another. The modern world is critically affected in this regard by the contradiction between what is taught by religion, on the one hand, and by the society's practices on the other—a state of affairs unknown to classical antiquity.

Thus Montesquieu's theory calls attention to the integration or contradiction among the several aspects of a society. Its general character derives from a number of causes, physical and moral, whose respective effects may be assessed after careful investigation. To the extent that any one cause is established as predominating, the rest recede in importance. It is not assumed that integration is always the characteristic state of a society; Montesquieu allows for contradictions.

The notion that every society possesses some general principle that distinguishes it from other societies plays a significant part in Montesquieu's theory. He warned rulers against making laws that ran contrary to the spirit of their peoples, and provided examples of the disastrous results of such errors.

Montesquieu believed that political society requires a certain amount of repression of men's wills and imagination. However, this repression may be accomplished in a variety of ways, either directly, by a centralized and omnipotent state or ruler, or indirectly, by such means as religion or principled self-repression on the part of citizens brought up to put the common good above personal interest. Thus Montesquieu treated laws and constitutions as but one way of affecting human conduct. It is the method used by governments. The civil society uses other means: religion, *moeurs*, and *manières*.[104] Montesquieu did not underrate what can be done by laws that have behind them the coercive power of the state. But here he wished to call attention to forces outside government that could both limit state action and perform a function equivalent to laws by using essentially social means to restrain human passion, will, and imagination. Montesquieu, however, was not committed to the thesis that society is everything and government, nothing. Rather he wished to specify the numerous and complex ways in which the political and social interact. He did not attempt to reduce government to a derivative function of society, or vice versa.

Among the essentially social forces that may affect government, religion is particularly important. Montesquieu's treatment of religion developed from his early rationalist theory of elites manipulating the credulous, which he found in Machiavelli, to a more sophisticated theory. When using the first mode of analysis, Montesquieu treated religion as something that could be used by rulers, much as they used laws. Thus both religion and law could be employed to defeat the worst effects of climate.[105] And Montesquieu agreed with Machiavelli that it is easier to enforce laws in a religious country than elsewhere. But this theory began to be transformed when Montesquieu argued that if religion is an effective force in a state, there is, to that extent, less need for control by the state and its sort of power. Religion, Montesquieu argued, can even save a state, which, left to its own police power, would be overturned.[106] In Rome, at one point, the survival of the state depended upon religion and *moeurs*.

Montesquieu emphasized the political and social effects of religion, seen always as operating within a given type of state. The most sacred and true dogmas may produce the worst consequences, if these dogmas should turn out to be incongruent with the general spirit of a society, or the principle of a state. In a despotic state, religion is the only restraint upon the ruler. In a republic, it is dangerous to allow the clergy to gain strength, while, in a monarchy, a strong clergy helps maintain liberty. Religion also can determine men's orientations toward politics, economic activity, population, and liberty. In a sentence which later caught Max Weber's attention, Montesquieu called attention to the fact that the English had been the people who had best known how to combine religion, commerce, and liberty.

Two other moral causes affecting the general spirit and closely resembling religion in their operation are *moeurs* and *manières*. Both may be used as surrogates for laws of the state: "When a people has *bonnes moeurs*, its laws need not be complex."[107] *Moeurs* and *manières* are usages unmentioned in law because they could not be so established, or were not intended to be. Laws govern men's actions *qua* members of a political unit. As for *moeurs* and *manières*, the first apply internalized restraints upon conduct not specifically prohibited by law, and the second, external restraints upon such conduct, but the sanctions applied are social rather than legal.[108]

This part of Montesquieu's theory emphasized social determinants of behavior, rather than legal sanctions. Yet, and this was consistent with his pluralist view of causation, he did not attempt to establish a hierarchy of causes with priority assigned to nongovernmental as against governmental action. Montesquieu represented the general spirit as potentially determined by any one or by a combination of the seven causes he identified. Tocqueville adopted Montesquieu's style of analysis when he argued that, although the success of the United States had been due more to its constitution than to its climate and terrain, the *moeurs* of the Americans had been most important of all.[109]

What were the political implications of Montesquieu's theory of the general spirit? On the whole, this represents the more conservative and historicist aspects of Montesquieu's thought, in contrast to the critical and reforming qualities that emerged from his adaptation of secular natural law. In part, his theory of causation constituted an argument against uniformity and centralization, and a plea for pluralism and sharing of power. Implicitly he was recommending moderation and patience in politics, both to the ruler—whether king, people, or aristocracy—and to the ruled. Patience is the central virtue implicit in his definition of politics as an instrument that is like a smooth old file doing its work by wearing away resistance slowly.[110] The concluding books of *The Spirit of the Laws* illustrate these points, as do the opening books on the three governments and Book XI on the separation of powers.

In Book XXIX, where Montesquieu discussed legislators and laws, he began with a striking sentence: "What I say, and it seems to me that I have written this book for no other reason than this, is that moderation ought to be the spirit of the legislator. Political good is like moral good in always being located between two extremes."[111] Montesquieu combined this appeal to moderation with an appeal to the past, or to his image of the past as seen from the perspective of his profession and order.

Books XXVII, XXX, and XXXI give Montesquieu's view of French history; they also provide his version of the precedents that ought to govern the French Constitution. Montesquieu skillfully reconciled the claims and interests of the older military nobility (*noblesse de l'epée*) with those of the legal nobility of the *Parlements* (*noblesse de robe*). The constitutional position Montesquieu argued was that the entire French *noblesse* held title by historical right to quasi-autonomous political powers, those of the intermediary orders. These had been usurped by the monarchy and its agents. This claim, the *thèse nobilaire*, rested upon the contention that the first kings of France had originally been limited by the institutions brought in by the Frankish conquerors of Gaul. As against this version of history, royalist defenders of the *thèse royale*, such as the Abbé Dubos, contended that the Frankish kings had been officers of the Roman Empire. Justinian had ceded Gaul to them. Hence, they and their descendants held power legitimately; it was the feudal lords who had usurped royal prerogatives. Thus seen, feudal institutions represented a lapse from the legitimate order. Montesquieu did not share the views of the Abbé Dubos.

This historical dispute masked but slightly a political conflict. As Montesquieu himself wrote, two major explanations of the original constitution of the French monarchy were extant: "The Count de Boulainvilliers and the Abbé Dubos have both constructed their systems: the first appears to be a conspiracy against the third estate; the second, a conspiracy against the *noblesse*."[112] Montesquieu claimed to strike a balance between the two, but in fact he came much closer to the position of Boulainvilliers. Although the work of Montesquieu as a theorist ought not to be assessed simply in terms of his class position, it would be a mistake to ignore the question of its influence upon his political values, his theory of politics, and his scheme of analysis, taken as a whole.

For the politics of his own time, Montesquieu's single most important doctrine in *The Spirit of the Laws* was the theory that intermediary bodies, such as the nobility, the *parlements*, the local courts of seigneurial justice, and the church, were all indispensable to political liberty. These and other constituted bodies, provinces, towns, guilds, professional associations, all had their rights, legal powers, and privileges, none of which could be removed since they all derived from the original institutions of the realm. And their present function was to balance one another and to serve as a barrier to despotism. Needless to say, such constituted bodies were not to be treated as equal. Such an arrangement would violate the essential principle of monarchy, which rests upon honor derived from inequality. The great, those most distinguished by birth, wealth, or honor, should have a share in legislation equal to their advantages. This, Montesquieu specified, was the power to check the people, just as the people should have the power to check them.[113]

It has been justly remarked that Montesquieu's analysis of the British Constitution demonstrates that he did not believe in rule by one class.[114] In addition to there being a body of nobles, there should also be a body representing the people, that is, those who are not noble. Classes were to be distinct. But the nobility was a vital element in the balance. A hierarchical form of society, a noble class jealous of its privileges, these were ingredients essential to the preservation of liberty. In Montesquieu's time and later in the eighteenth century, the nobility, regrouped and at once more confident and more powerful, was not content with its share of power. It went on to demand more, as well as resisting initiatives of the king and his agents. Hence Montesquieu's political doctrine was not conservative, although it based its claims of legitimacy on historical arguments about arrangements made in the remote past.

This backward-looking political theory that sought to produce change is at the bottom of what appears to be a contradiction in Montesquieu's political values. On the one hand, there is his opposition to large-scale change planned on the basis of abstract ideas; on the other, there are proposals for removing abuses and providing services that did not then exist. The reasons for a state having endured are complex and largely unknown. If the entire system is changed, then unanticipated difficulties may arise. Piecemeal change is best; precedents should guide policy.[115]

In Montesquieu's view, long-established institutions tend to reform a people's *moeurs*, while new institutions tend to corrupt them.[116] A prudent administration seldom proceeds to its ends by direct means. It changes by law only what has been established by law; it attempts to change the *moeurs*, not by legislation, but through introducing new *moeurs* by the personal example of the rulers. The uniformity sought by a centralized administration leads to despotism. Why seek to have the same weights and measures everywhere, the same regulations applicable to trade, the same laws everywhere in the state, and the same religion? Is it always less of an evil to change than to suffer what is? Wisdom consists in knowing in what cases uniformity is necessary, and in what cases, diversity.[117] Montesquieu did not oppose all that was new, nor did he defend all that existed. In addition to attacking slavery, severe punishments, and religious persecution, he argued that the state owes all its inhabitants an assured subsistence, nourishment, clothing, and a mode of life that promotes good health. It is also the state's duty to provide for orphans, the sick, and the old; it should feed the people in the event of famine.[118] Montesquieu's own values emerge clearly from his discussion of slavery. He took the position that slavery was incompatible with the general spirit of both republics and monarchy. Yet he added that if slaves were emancipated, their liberty should be civil, not political. Even in popular governments, power should never be allowed to fall into the hands of the lowest classes (*le bas peuple*).[119] Montesquieu, however, stressed the worth of education and denounced prejudice. With greater knowledge, human beings become less cruel; Montesquieu supported at least this aspect of the Enlightenment.[120] He was neither a reactionary nor, strictly speaking, a conservative.

The French monarchy would have been different in significant respects had all of Montesquieu's recommendations been accepted. He would have remodeled the administrative, legal, and penal systems of France. Montesquieu would have had the monarchy freely embrace the industry, toleration, and political liberty practiced in the commercial society he saw emerging across the Channel.[121] He saw no glory in war and little point in conquest in Europe or establishing colonies elsewhere in the world. Did these positions make him a liberal?

As always with Montesquieu, any answer must be carefully qualified. He defended the privileges of his class even when they were clearly abuses. There is some truth in the view that his theory of monarchy and his theory of despotism were both designed to cement an alliance between the crown and the nobility. It may even be that the real point of his theory of the separation of powers was less concerned with liberty than with distributing powers in such a way that aristocratic privilege could be equally well protected against attacks from above or below.[122]

Montesquieu combined several perspectives in such a way as to preserve their tensions. The attractiveness of civic life in a republic, as he depicted it, later became an ideal for many of those who drew up the constitutions and the political programs of the American and French Revolutions. His model of politics as a bargaining process among groups, and as depending upon countervailing powers, was adapted by Madison, who also drew upon Montesquieu's psychological and sociological rationales for the separation of powers. American federalism was to lean heavily upon Montesquieu's solution to the problem of how small republics can survive.

Few other political theorists can match the subtlety, moderation, and continuing suggestiveness of Montesquieu's mind. For these qualities readers today should be grateful.

French Terms Used in the Translation

Décadence

This term figures in the title of Montesquieu's book, *Considérations sur les causes de la grandeur des Romains et de leur décadence*. Montesquieu did not believe in the theory of progress; his philosophy of history has been described as "pessimism in moderation." (Henry Vyverberg, *Historical Pessimism in the French Enlightenment* [Cambridge, Mass., 1958]) It stressed flux and the eventual corruption from within of all states. At the end of the most famous chapter of *The Spirit of the Laws*, that celebrating the government of England (Book XI, chapter 6), Montesquieu wrote: "Since everything human must end, the state discussed here will lose its liberty and perish. Rome, Sparta, Carthage—all have perished. This state will perish when its legislative power becomes more corrupt than its executive." Book VIII of *The Spirit of the Laws* is a full-scale treatment of how the principles of each of the three types of government may be corrupted. (In his *Considérations*, Montesquieu had argued that the political decadence of Rome was inherent in the very maxims and laws that had produced its successful expansion. Thus corruption of principle and decadence are due, not only to the instability of the human condition, but to inherent defects in the nature and principles of all three types of government. Yet there is much that the legislator may do to mitigate and delay the effects of these causes of decadence.

Esprit

This word had as many diverse meanings for Montesquieu as did "spirit" for a contemporary Englishman such as Samuel Johnson. Some of them will be discussed in the explanations of *Homme d'Esprit* and *Esprit général* below. The meanings most important for the title of *De l'Esprit des loix* are:

1. The essential, underlying, or fundamental meaning of a text, constitution, or set of laws. Often used in the sense of "spirit" as opposed to "letter."

2. The distinguishing characteristic of a collectivity, or type. "The *esprit* that animated the Greek republics was that of contentment, both with the extent of their territories, and with their laws." (Book VIII, chapter 16)

3. Montesquieu himself criticized the French for confusing in the word *esprit* four concepts distinguished by the English of his time: wit, humour, sense, and understanding.

Esprit Général

Those common and distinguishing characteristics of a society which result from a number of diverse causes, physical or moral. Montesquieu's most significant statement of this organizing concept occurs in Book XIX, chapter 4: "Men are ruled by many causes: climate, religion, laws, maxims of government, examples drawn from the past, *moeurs, manières*. Out of them is formed the general spirit of a nation."

Homme d'Esprit

1. Intelligent man, sensible man.
2. Wit.

Lois

1. Laws. Part of a distinction between *lois, moeurs,* and *manières*. Laws are positive and operate by sanctions; they regulate public life, the actions of men considered as citizens. Book XIX is particularly concerned with this set of distinctions. *Lois* are part, but not all, of the *Esprit général*.
2. Those institutions established by the specific provisions of a lawgiver, that is, by a person or persons called in to institute the general framework of a constitution, without subsequently participating in it. *Moeurs* and *manières* are not, thus, consciously created, but are usages evolved by the nation as a whole over time.
3. A term of jurisprudence covering a wide variety of rules. Montesquieu's set of distinctions, which opens Book XXVI, became the standard text for the rest of the eighteenth century. (F. Brunot, *Histoire de la langue française,* vol. VI, 1, 457) There is a treatment of *lois,* at once more philosophical and more confusing, in Book I of *The Spirit of the Laws.*

Manières

1. Customs. *Manières* resemble *moeurs,* but differ from them. (See entry for *moeurs.*) By *manières* Montesquieu meant that type of conduct not regulated by law. Unlike *moeurs,* which use internal restraints, the violation of *manières* calls forth sanctions, but these are social and not legal. Montesquieu's impact upon general usage may be measured by the difference between the definition given by *The Dictionary of the French Academy* (1748) and that written by Saint-Lambert in the *Encyclopédie*. In the *Dictionary, manières* is defined as a mode of behavior (*façon d'agir*); in the *Encyclopédie* as standing in the same relation to *moeurs* as does worship to religion.
2. Thus *manières* often means "behavior" or "conduct" in Montesquieu.

Moeurs

1. *Moeurs*, a technical term for Montesquieu, and hence best understood in the sense he himself used it, as related to, but distinguished from *manières*. Both *moeurs* and *manières* are to be understood in opposition to *lois*. In the eighteenth century, *moeurs* was usually translated into English as "manners," or "morals"; *manières* as "customs," or "behavior."

The key exposition of *moeurs* and *manières* occurs in Book XIX, chapter 16 of *The Spirit of the Laws*:

> *Moeurs* and *manières* are usages unmentioned by law, either because they could not be so established, or else because they were not meant to be.

> There is this distinction between laws and *moeurs*: laws are directed primarily at men's actions *qua* citizens; *moeurs*, at their actions *qua* men. There is this distinction between *moeurs* and *manières*: *moeurs* are more concerned with conduct considered from the inside; *manières*, with conduct considered from the outside.

2. *Moeurs*, therefore, refer to nonlegal internalized restraints established by custom. Diderot in his article in the *Encyclopédie* followed Montesquieu's usage almost literally; the French Academy's *Dictionary* (1748) uses the less technical sense of a nation's mode of life (*manière de vivre*), including its laws.

Nation

All the people or inhabitants of the same *pays*. The French Academy's *Dictionary* (1740) notes that this still means *patrie*, place of birth," and that sometimes it means "the whole of the state in which one was born; sometimes, the province, country, or city. It is worth noting that at this time the English meant by "nation" something closer to the sense in which it is now used. Johnson's *Dictionary* gives: "A people distinguished from another people, generally by their language, origin, or government." Among the sources cited by Johnson was Temple, who wrote: "A *nation* properly signifies a great number of families, derived from the same blood, born in the same country, and living under the same government."

Patrie

When Montesquieu began to write, *patrie* still meant "the place where one was born, one's native country or soil." The French Academy's *Dictionary* (1740) defines it as the place (*pays*) or the state (*état*) where one was born. Sometimes, it says, *la patrie* refers to provinces; sometimes to cities. "Paris is his *pays*." It is not inaccurate to say that in Montesquieu's time, *la patrie, la nation*, and *le pays* were synonyms. (See entry for *la nation*.) In general usage, there was no trace of the emotional charge that was to emerge in the words of the "Marseillaise" (written in 1792; made the French national hymn in 1795).

Yet there was another specialized tradition of usage for *la patrie*. Upon this tradition Montesquieu built and to it he also contributed. In 1688 La Bruyère wrote in his *Caractères* (X, 4): "Under a despotism, there is no *patrie*. Other things replace it: interest, glory, the service of the ruler." Montesquieu, by making love of *patrie* and love of equality into the principle or spring of republics (Montesquieu's Preface, *The Spirit of the Laws*) greatly strengthened the implication of La Bruyère that there can be a *patrie* only where citizens possess rights.

Pays

1. Country, land, region.
2. Native land, native soil.

SELECTED BIBLIOGRAPHY

Louis Althusser, *Politics and History* (New York, 1971).

Raymond Aron, *Main Currents in Sociological Thought* (2 vols; New York, 1968), I.

Alain Grosrichard, *Structure du Serail* (Paris, 1974).

Nannerl Keohane, *Philosophy and the State in France* (Princeton, 1980).

David Lowenthal, "Montesquieu," in Strauss and Cropsey, eds., *History of Political Thought* (3rd ed.; Chicago, 1988).

Charles-Louis de Secondat, Baron de Montesquieu, "An Essay on the Causes That May Affect Men's Minds and Characters," trans. with an introduction by Melvin Richter, *Political Theory* 4 (1976), 132–62.

Franz Neumann, "Introduction," *The Spirit of the Laws* (New York, 1949).

Thomas L. Pangle, *Montesquieu's Philosophy of Liberalism* (Chicago, 1973).

J. G. A. Pocock, *The Machiavellian Moment* (Princeton, 1975).

Melvin Richter, "Montesquieu, the Politics of Language, and the Language of Politics," *History of Political Thought* X (1989), 71–88.

——, *The Political Theory of Montesquieu* (Cambridge and New York: Cambridge University Press, 1977).

Robert Shackleton, *Montesquieu. A Critical Biography* (Oxford, 1961).

Judith Shklar, *Montesquieu* (Oxford, 1987)

PERSIAN LETTERS

Myth of the Troglodytes

Letter X

Mirza to his Friend Usbek at Erzerum

Only you could make up for the absence of Rica; only Rica could console me for your departure. We miss you, Usbek, you were the soul of our group. It required much violence to break the obligations created by heart and mind.

Here we continue to argue much; and at the center of our discussion is the question of ethics. The issue yesterday was whether men achieve happiness through the pleasures and satisfactions of the senses, or by the practice of virtue. I have often heard you say that men are born to be virtuous, that justice is a quality as proper to them as existence. Please explain to me what you mean.

I have talked with some mullahs, but their citation of passages from the Koran made me despair.[1] For I speak to them not as a true believer, but as a man, as a citizen, as a father of a family.[2] Adieu.

From Ispahan, the last of the moon of Saphar, 1711

Letter XI

Usbek to Mirza at Ispahan

You disparage your own reason and seek out mine. You demean yourself when you consult me in the belief that I am capable of instructing you. My dear Mirza, only one thing is more flattering than your high opinion of me and that is your friendship.

To do what you have asked of me does not, in my view, require highly abstract reasoning. There are certain truths that cannot be learned by rational persuasion alone, but in addition need to be felt. Such are the truths of ethics. Perhaps a bit of history will touch you more than subtle philosophical argument.

In Arabia there once was a small people called the Troglodytes, descendants of the ancient Troglodytes, who, if the historians are to be believed,[3] resembled beasts more than men. Their descendants were in no way deformed, they were neither hairy like bears, nor did they hiss [like serpents]; they had two eyes. But they were at once so wicked and cruel that they lacked any principle of equity or of justice.

They were ruled by a king of foreign origin who treated them severely in order to correct their wicked nature. But conspiring against him, they put him to death, and exterminated the entire royal family.

Having succeeded in their coup, they assembled to choose a government. After many a disagreement, they created magistrates. Immediately after having been chosen, these were found unendurable and were massacred in turn.

Once liberated from their new yoke, this people consulted only the savage disposition natural to them. All of them agreed that they would no longer obey anybody, that everyone would confine himself to looking out for his own interests without taking into account those of others.

This unanimous decision pleased everyone. They said: "Why should I become involved and kill myself working for people about whom I could not care less. I shall think of myself alone. I shall live happily without concern for others. I shall provide for all my needs. If successful, I shall not care if all the other Troglodytes are miserable."

It was the season to plant the fields. Every individual said: "I shall cultivate my land only to the extent that I need grain; anything more would be useless to me; I shall not take such trouble for nothing."

Not all the soil in this little kingdom was of the same quality. Some of the terrain was arid and mountainous; some, located on lower ground, was watered by several streams. That year there was a great drought. The land on high ground had no water; while that below could be irrigated and was very fertile. Thus the mountain people all died of hunger because the others were so hard-hearted that they refused to share their harvest.

The next year was very rainy. The high lands were extraordinarily fertile; those below were submerged. Half of the people once again cried famine. These miserable people found themselves confronted by others as unyielding as they themselves had been.

One of the principal inhabitants had a very beautiful wife. His neighbor fell in love with her and carried her off. A great quarrel broke out. After many insults and many blows, they agreed to submit the matter for decision to a Troglodyte, who had had a good reputation at the time of the republic. They went to him and attempted to state their respective cases. "What difference does it make to me," said this man, "whether this woman belongs to one or another of you? I have my field to cultivate. Perhaps I have a better way of using my time than to settle your differences and to work on your business while neglecting my own. Please leave me in peace and don't bother me with your disputes." With that, he left them to attend to his land. The abductor, who was the stronger, swore that he would die before giving up this woman. Her husband was wounded by the injustice done him by his neighbor and the harshness of the judge. Returning home in despair, he came across a young and beautiful woman on her way back from the fountain. He no longer had a wife, and this woman pleased him. His satisfaction became even greater upon learning that she was the wife of the man whom he had wished to act as a judge, the man so insensitive to his misfortune. He carried her off to his home.

There was another man who owned a fertile field, which he cultivated with great care. Two of his neighbors united, expelled him from his house and took over his field. They agreed to join in defending themselves against anyone who might seek to take it from them and indeed managed to stay there for several months. But then one of them, tired of sharing what he might have for himself, killed the other and became sole master of the field. His tenure did not last long. Two other Troglodytes came and attacked him. Since he was too weak to defend himself, he was massacred.

Another Troglodyte, who was very close to being naked, saw some wool for sale, and asked its price. The merchant replied, "Naturally I ought not to expect more for my wool than what would enable me to buy two measures of grain. But I am going to sell it for four times that amount. Then I can get eight measures." Needing the wool, the first had to pay that price. "That pleases me," said the merchant. "Now I can buy grain." "What did you say?" replied the buyer. "You need grain? I have some for sale. But the price may surprise you. As you know, grain costs a great deal, and famine prevails almost everywhere. Give me back my money, and I shall give you one measure of wheat. I shall not dispose of it on any other terms, even if you were to die of hunger."

Meanwhile a cruel disease was ravaging the country. A skilled physician from a neighboring country arrived and prescribed remedies so effective that he cured everyone in his care. Once the disease was over, he went to all those he had treated and asked for his fee. Everywhere he was met by the refusal to pay. He returned to his country, exhausted by the rigors of his long voyage. But soon after he heard that the same disease had reappeared and once again was afflicting that ungrateful land. This time its inhabitants did not wait for him to come to them, but came to him. "Go away," he told them. "You are unjust men. Your souls are filled with a poison more lethal than the disease you wished cured. You do not deserve a place on earth because you have no humanity; the rules of equity are unknown to you. Were I to oppose the justice of the angry gods punishing you, I should myself offend them."

From Erzerum, the 3rd of the moon of Gemmadi II, 1711

Letter XII
Usbek to the Same at Ispahan

You have seen, my dear Mirza, how the Troglodytes perished because of their wickedness, how they were the victims of their own injustice. Out of all their families, only two escaped the misfortunes that befell their nation. Those surviving families included two extraordinary men: they possessed humanity; they knew justice; they loved virtue. They were as much united by their upright hearts as by the corruption of the others. When they saw how widespread was the desolation, they could feel only pity. This furnished the purpose of a new union. With a mutual solicitude, they worked for the common interest; between them, there were no differences other than those that stemmed from a sweet and tender friendship. In the most remote part of the country, separated from compatriots unworthy of them, they led a happy and tranquil life. The earth, cultivated by such virtuous hands, seemed to produce almost spontaneously.[4]

They loved their wives, and were tenderly cherished by them. All their attention was devoted to raising their children in the ways of virtue. To their children, they always pointed out the misfortunes of their compatriots; and continually held up their sad example. Above all, their children were made to feel that the interest of individuals always consists of the common interest; that he who wills the separation of these interests wills their loss; that virtue neither costs us dear nor is painful to practice; that justice to others is a blessing to ourselves.

Soon they had the consolation of virtuous fathers – that is, to have children like themselves. The young people growing up under their eyes increased because of happy marriages; their numbers continued to grow; their union remained what it had always been; and virtue, far from being weakened by such numbers, was strengthened by the greater number of examples.

Who could describe the happiness of the Troglodytes? So just a people must have been cherished by the gods. As soon as the Troglodytes opened their eyes and recognized the gods, they learned to fear them. Thus religion came to make gentler those *moeurs* that Nature had left too unrefined.

They instituted festivals in honor of the gods. Young girls decked in flowers joined the young boys in celebration by dances to the harmonies of rural music. Then followed banquets characterized by both joy and frugality. Here simple Nature spoke, and taught how to give and receive their hearts. Here virginal chastity made that surprised confession which was soon to be ratified by paternal consent. Here tender mothers were delighted to predict from afar tender and faithful unions.

The Troglodytes would go to the Temple to request favors of the gods. But they prayed neither for riches nor for burdensome abundance; to do so would have been unworthy of the happy Troglodytes. Rather they came to the foot of the altars only to seek health for their fathers, marriage for their brothers, the tender love of their wives, the love and obedience of their children. Girls came for no other purpose than to make the tender sacrifice of their hearts; they sought no blessing other than to be able to make a Troglodyte happy.

In the evening, after the flocks had returned from the meadows and the weary oxen had brought back their plows, the Troglodytes would assemble and after a frugal meal, sing of the injustices and misfortunes of the first Troglodytes, of the rebirth of virtue in a new people and its consequent felicity. They celebrated the greatness of the gods, who always bestowed their favors upon those men who prayed for them, and punished by their inevitable wrath those who did not fear them. Then they would describe the delights of life in the country and the happiness of an existence graced by innocence. Soon they yielded to a sleep undisturbed by care or pain.

Nature supplied their desires as well as their needs. In this fortunate country, cupidity was unknown. When they exchanged presents, the giver always thought himself to be the most fortunate. The Troglodyte people regarded itself as a single family. Their flocks were almost always intermingled; the only trouble the Troglodytes spared themselves was to separate them.[5]

From Erzerum, the 6th of the moon of Gemmadi II, 1711

Letter XIII
Usbek to the Same

I could not tell you enough about the virtue of the Troglodytes. Once upon a time one of them said, "My father must plow his field tomorrow. I shall get up two hours before he does, and when he goes to his field, he will find it already plowed."

Another said to himself, "It seems to me that my sister has taken a liking for a young Troglodyte, who is related to us. I must speak to my father and persuade him to arrange the marriage."

Another was told that robbers had carried off his flock. "I am very angry about that," he said. "There was a pure white heifer that I had wished to offer to the gods."

One of them was heard to tell another, "I must go to the Temple to thank the gods. My brother, so much loved by my father and dear to me, has recovered his health."

Or else, "A field that borders on my father's is so exposed to the heat of the sun that those who cultivate it must suffer every day that they do so. I must go there and plant two trees so that those poor people may from time to time rest in their shade."

One day when a number of Troglodytes had come together, an old man spoke of a young person whom he suspected of having committed a crime and whom he had reproached for it. "We cannot believe that he has committed this crime," said the young Troglodytes, "but if he has, may he be the last of his family to die."

Another Troglodyte was informed that strangers had pillaged his house and carried away everything there. "If they had not been unjust men," he replied, "I would have wished that the gods might grant them a longer enjoyment of those goods than was given to me."

So much prosperity did not go unenvied. Their neighbors joined together and on the basis of some empty pretext sought to seize the Troglodytes' flocks. As soon as they heard of this resolve, the Troglodytes sent ambassadors to them, who spoke as follows:

"What have the Troglodytes done to you? Have they carried off your wives, or stolen your cattle? No, we are just and we fear the gods. What, then, do you ask of us? Do you wish wool for your clothes? Do you wish milk for your flocks, or the fruits of our soil? Put down your arms, come to us, and we shall give you all that. But we swear by all that is most sacred, if you enter our land as enemies, we shall regard you as an unjust people, and treat you as wild beasts."

Those words were rejected with scorn. These savage peoples came armed into the lands of the Troglodytes, which they thought to be defended only by their innocence.

But the Troglodytes were well prepared to defend themselves; they had placed their wives and children in the midst of their defenses. They were more astonished by their neighbors' injustice than by their numbers. A new ardor burned in their hearts. One man wished to die for his father; another, for his wife and children; a third, for his brothers; a fourth, for his friends; and everyone for the Troglodyte people. Anyone killed in battle was at once replaced by another, who was spurred not only by the common cause, but also by the death of an individual he had to revenge.

Such was the combat between injustice and virtue. Those cowardly peoples who sought only booty were not ashamed to flee. They yielded to the virtue of the Troglodytes without even being touched by it.

From Erzerum, the 9th of the moon of Gemmadi II, 1711

Letter XIV

To the Same

Since their people was increasing in number every day, the Troglodytes thought it appropriate to choose a king. They agreed that the crown should be offered to whomever was most just. They all cast their eyes upon an old man who was venerated both for his age and long-continued virtue. He had not wished to attend this meeting, and had retired to his home, his heart filled with sadness.

Deputies were sent to inform him that he had been chosen. "God forbid," he said, "that I commit this wrong against the Troglodytes, that anyone should think that I am the most just among them. You offer me the crown, and if you absolutely insist, I must accept it. But realize that I shall die of grief to have seen Troglodytes born free, but now become subjects." After these words, he burst into tears. "O miserable day," he said. "Why did I have to live so long?" Then he cried out in a severe voice: "I see well what is happening, O Troglodytes: Your virtue is beginning to weigh upon you. In your present situation without a chief, you must be virtuous despite yourself. Otherwise you could not carry on: you would relapse into the misfortunes of the first Troglodytes who were your ancestors. But this yoke appears too difficult to you; you would prefer to be in submission to a prince and to be governed by his laws, for they would be less rigorous than your *moeurs*. You know that from then on you could satisfy your ambition, acquire riches, and languish amidst the pleasures of a coward. Provided only that you avoid major crimes, you would no longer need virtue." He stopped a moment, and his tears began to flow even more than before. "Well then, what would you have me do? How could I give orders to a Troglodyte? Do you hope that because I have issued an order he will do a virtuous deed? But he would have done the same thing without me, urged on by nothing more than the inclination of his nature. O Troglodytes, I am coming to the end of my days. My blood is becoming colder in my veins. Before long I shall be seeing again your revered ancestors. Why do you ask me to afflict them? Why must I be obliged to tell them that I have left you under another yoke than that of virtue?"[6]

From Erzerum, the 10th of the moon of Gemmadi II, 1711

Sequel to the Myth of the Troglodytes[7]

It was a grand spectacle to see all the Troglodytes joyous while the prince was dissolved in tears. When he appeared the next day before the Troglodytes, his face showed neither sadness nor joy. He appeared to be preoccupied with the task of government. But the secret disquiet that was devouring him soon put an end to his life. Thus died the greatest king who ever ruled over men.

For forty days, he was mourned; everyone believed that he had lost his own father. Everyone said: "What has happened to the hope of the Troglodytes? We lose you, dear Prince. You believed that you were unworthy of commanding us. Heaven has revealed that we were not worthy of obeying you. But we swear by your sacred spirit that since you did not wish to govern us by your laws, we shall conduct ourselves by the example you provided us."

It became necessary to elect another prince. One remarkable aspect of the situation was that no member of the dead monarch's family claimed his throne. The wisest and most just member of this family was chosen to be king.

Toward the end of his reign, some believed it necessary for the Troglodytes to establish commerce and the arts. The nation was assembled, and that course was decided.

The king spoke in the following way: "You wished me to assume the throne and believed me virtuous enough to govern you. Heaven is my witness that the happiness of the Troglodytes has been the only object of my concerns. I have the honor of knowing that my reign has not been sullied by the cowardice of even a single Troglodyte. Would you now prefer riches to your virtue?"

"My Lord," replied one of them, "we are fortunate; we work upon excellent soil. Shall I dare to say it? You alone will decide whether or not wealth will be pernicious to your people. If they see that you prefer wealth to virtue, they will soon accustom themselves to do the same; and in that your taste will govern theirs. If you promote someone in your service, or choose him simply because he is rich, you may be certain that this will be a mortal blow that you have delivered to virtue. You will have created imperceptibly as many dishonest men as have observed this cruel distinction made by you. You know, my lord, what is the basis of your people's virtue: it is education. Once this education is changed, even the man who is not daring enough to become a criminal will soon blush at being virtuous.

"We have two things to do: to make avarice and prodigality equally disgraceful. Everyone must be responsible to the state for the administration of his property. Any coward who lowers himself to the point of denying himself an honest subsistence ought to be judged no less severely than the man who dissipates the inheritance of his children. Every citizen must dispense his own wealth as fairly as he would that belonging to another."

"Troglodytes," said the king, "wealth will be admitted into your country. But I tell you that if you are not virtuous, you will rank among the most miserable peoples in the world. In your present state, I need only be more just than you. This is what marks my royal authority, and I could never find anything more majestic. If you seek to distinguish yourselves only by your wealth, which is intrinsically worthless, then I shall have to distinguish myself by the same means in order not to remain in the poverty that you will scorn. Then it will become necessary for me to load you down with taxes, and for you to devote a considerable part of your subsistence to support me in the pomp and magnificence that will serve to make me respectable. At present I find all my wealth within myself. But if the situation were to alter, then you would have to spend everything you have in order to enrich me. Then you will not at all enjoy the wealth of which you make so much; it will all pass into my treasury. O Troglodytes: There is a lovely tie that can bind us together. If you are virtuous, then I shall be; if I am virtuous, then you will be."

Seraglio Sequence

Letter II
Usbek to the Chief Black Eunuch
at His Seraglio at Ispahan

You are the faithful guardian of the most beautiful women in Persia. To you I have confided those who are dearest to me in all the world; in your hands, you hold the keys to those fateful doors that open only to me. As long as it is you who guard this place so dear to my heart, it is at ease and is perfectly secure. You stand guard in the silence of the night, as in the tumult of the day. When virtue falters, you correct it by the infinite pains you take. Should the women you guard ever be inclined to stray from their duty, you would make them lose hope of ever succeeding. You are the scourge of vice and the pillar of fidelity.

You command them; you obey them. You fulfill blindly their every wish; you make them carry out in the same way everything prescribed by the laws of the seraglio. You attain glory in performing for them the most degrading services; you submit with respect and fear to their legitimate orders; you serve them like the slave of their slaves. But by a reversal of power, you take on the prerogative to command like myself as master whenever you fear that the laws of decency and modesty are not being fully observed.

Never forget the oblivion from which I rescued you. Once you were the meanest of my slaves; I put you where you now are, and confided to you the delights of my heart. Maintain the most complete humility toward those who share my love; at the same time, make them feel how completely they are subordinated to you. Make every innocent pleasure available to them; beguile them when they feel uneasy; amuse them with music, dancing, and delicious drinks; persuade them to come together often. If they wish to go to the country, take them there. But strike down any man who attempts to speak to them. Encourage cleanliness, the image of the soul's clarity. From time to time, speak to them of me. How much I should like to see them once again in that charming place they so adorn. Farewell.

Tauris, the 18th of the moon of Saphar, 1711

Letter IX

The First Eunuch to Ibbi at Erzerum

As you accompany your master on his voyage, and cross provinces and kingdoms, cares do not much affect you. At every moment, you see something new, and this in turn diverts you and makes time pass imperceptibly.

That is not at all my situation. Imprisoned in the most dreadful of places, I am always surrounded by the same objects, and devoured by the same preoccupations. Weighed down by fifty years of effort and anxiety, I groan when I realize that during all of my long life, I have not enjoyed one serene day, not one tranquil moment.

At the time my first master conceived of his cruel plot to confide his women to me, he used a combination of promises and threats to force me into the act that separated me forever from my true self. Tired of the debasing services I was forced to perform, I reasoned that I was sacrificing my passions for the sake of ease and wealth. What an unhappy decision that was! Preoccupied by what I would gain as compensation, I failed to realize the extent of my sacrifice. I expected to gain immunity from the attacks of love once I lost the capacity to satisfy it. Alas, the effects of the passions were extinguished, not the causes. Far from being relieved of them, I found myself surrounded by stimulants that have never ceased to provoke me. When I entered the seraglio, everything there made me regret what I had lost; I was continually excited; the thousand charms bestowed by nature on my charges only made me miserable. My situation was made even less tolerable by the sight of my happy master. During that time of troubles, I never led a woman to his bed, never undressed her, without another attack of rage in my heart and despair in my soul.

In this way I passed my miserable youth. I had no confidant. I was consumed by the melancholy and anger that weighed upon me. I had to assume the greatest air of severity toward precisely those women that most tempted me. Otherwise I should have been lost. Had they discovered my true feelings, what advantage would they have not taken?

I remember that one day, while putting a woman into her bath, I was so overcome that reason left me, and I dared to touch a forbidden place. My first thought was that I should not survive that day. However, I was fortunate, and escaped the thousand deaths that awaited me. But the beauty to whom I had revealed my weakness, exacted a high price for her silence. My authority over her came to an end, and after that, she forced me to overlook any number of things, which, if discovered, would have cost me my life.

At last the fires of youth were extinguished. Now that I am old, I find myself at peace in that regard. I look at women with indifference, and I pay back all the scorn and torments they once made me suffer. I remember always that I was born to command them, and when in fact I do so, I feel as though I have once again become a man. Ever since I have been able to view women coldly, I have hated them. My reason now serves to expose all their weaknesses. Although I guard them for another, I feel a secret joy when I make them obey. When I deprive them of everything, I feel as though it were I who had exercised the prerogative. This always provides vicarious satisfaction. The seraglio has become my little empire, and there, my ambition, the only passion left me, is in part satisfied. It gratifies me to see that everything depends upon me, that I am at all times indispensable. I accept willingly the hatred of all the women I guard, for this strengthens my position. Thus they are not dealing with someone who fails to appreciate what they are doing for him. I put an end to their pleasures, however innocent. I make myself into a barrier that cannot be removed; I put a stop to whatever plans they may make; I arm myself with refusals; I bristle with scruples; I never stop talking of duty, virtue, decency, and modesty. I drive them to despair by my constant reminders of the weakness of their sex, and the authority due their master. Then I complain of the severity I am forced to use. I pretend that I have no motives other than their own interest and my great affection for them.

This is not to say that I have been spared an infinite number of disagreeable experiences. Every day these revengeful women seek retaliation for what I do to them, since they suffer great setbacks at my hands. Between us there is an ebb and flow of command and submission. They seek constantly to have the most humiliating tasks assigned to me; they affect boundless contempt for me. Without any regard for my age, they awaken me ten times a night for the merest trifle. I am overwhelmed by orders, commands, tasks, caprices. They seem to take turns in keeping me occupied and to become increasingly bizarre in their wishes. Often they amuse themselves by making me redouble my vigilance; they pretend to confide in me. Sometimes one comes to tell me that a young man has appeared outside the walls; sometimes that a noise has been heard, or that a letter is to be passed. All this causes me much apprehension, and this amuses them. They are delighted to see me torturing myself in this way. On other occasions, they cause me to guard them day and night. They know very well how to feign illnesses, fits of fainting and of terror; no pretext is lacking to manipulate me into doing what they wish. At such times, I must obey blindly and comply without qualification, for a refusal to do so from someone like me would be unprecedented, and they would have the right to ask that I be punished. And, my dear Ibbi, I should rather die than have that happen.

Nor is that all. Never for a moment am I certain of my master's favor, so many are the enemies who possess his heart and wish my ruin. When they are with him, I am not heard; at those times, nothing is denied them and I am always wrong. The women I lead to my master's bed are incensed against me. Is it likely that they will act in my behalf, or that my side will emerge the stronger? I have everything to fear from their tears and sighs, from their embraces and even the pleasures they give. Here is the place of their triumphs; their charms terrify me; their services of the moment efface everything I have done in the past; no satisfaction can be expected by me from a master who no longer is himself.

How many times have I been in favor when I went to sleep, only to find myself in disgrace when I awoke? The day I was so ignominiously whipped around the seraglio – what was it that I had done? I left a woman in the arms of my master. As soon as she saw his passions were inflamed, she launched torrents of tears. She complained, and so orchestrated her demands, that they increased in proportion to the love she aroused. How could I defend myself at such a critical moment? I was lost when least I expected it; I was the victim of an amorous negotiation, of a treaty signed by sighs. This, my dear Ibbi, is the cruel situation in which I have always lived.

How fortunate you are! You need concern yourself only with the person of Usbek himself. You can easily please him and maintain yourself in his favor until the end of your days.

From the seraglio of Ispahan, the last day of
the moon of Saphar, 1711

Letter XXII

Jaron to the Chief Eunuch

The further Usbek travels from his seraglio, the more his mind is filled with thoughts of the women dedicated to him. He sighs, his eyes fill with tears; his grief turns bitter, his suspicions increase. He wishes to increase the number of those guarding his women. He is sending me back, along with all the other negroes who accompany him. He fears no longer for his own security, but rather for those who are a thousand times dearer to him than himself.

I am coming, therefore, to live under your laws, and to share your concerns. Great God! How much must be done to make a single person happy!

Nature seems to have put women into a condition of dependence, from which it then released them. This created disorder between the two sexes, because their rights were now reciprocal. You and I are now involved in a scheme for a new sort of harmony: we serve to create hatred between women and ourselves; love between men and women.

My face will become severe, I shall assume a somber expression. Joy will no longer be seen on my lips. On the outside, I shall appear tranquil; but within, I shall be uneasy. Long before old age, I shall be wrinkled by care.

It would have been pleasant to have followed my master into the Occident. But my will belongs to him. Since he wishes that I guard his wives, I shall do so faithfully. I know how I ought to conduct myself with that sex, which, if not allowed to be vain, then tends to become proud. It is easier to destroy women than to humiliate them.

I prostrate myself before you.

From Smyrna, the 12th of the moon of Zilcade, 1711

Letter XXVI

Usbek to Roxana at the Seraglio at Ispahan

How fortunate you are, Roxana, to be in the gentle land of Persia, rather than in these corrupt countries, where neither decency nor virtue are known! How fortunate you are! You live in my seraglio, as in the abode of innocence, inaccessible to the assaults of men. You live happily in a situation where, fortunately, it is impossible for you to falter in your virtue. Never has anyone sullied you with lascivious glances. . . .

. . . women here have lost all discretion. They present themselves without veils to men, as though seeking to be conquered; they invite men's stares; they talk to men in mosques, during walks, and even receive the opposite sex in their own homes; the custom of attendance by eunuchs is unknown to them. Instead of that noble simplicity and charming modesty that reigns where you are, there is a brutish impudence, to which it is impossible to become accustomed.

. . .

But what am I to think of European women? Their skill in making up their faces, the ornaments with which they adorn themselves, the care they take with their bodies, their preoccupation with pleasing the opposite sex – these are so many stains upon their virtue, and outrages to their husbands.

Do not think, Roxana, that I believe these women carry their impropriety as far as their conduct might suggest, that their excesses extend to what is most horrible of all, of actually violating their marriage vows. Very few women are so abandoned as that. In their hearts, they carry a certain mark of virtue engraved there at birth, and which their upbringing weakens but does not destroy. They may be lax in those external duties imposed by modesty, but when it comes to taking the final step, nature revolts. Thus when we imprison you so strictly, and have you guarded by so many slaves, when we restrain your desires when they go too far, it is not that we fear the ultimate infidelity, but because we know that it is impossible that purity be excessive, and that it may be corrupted by the slightest stain.

. . .

From Paris, the 7th of the moon of Rhegeb, 1712

Letter XXXIV

Usbek to Ibben at Smyrna

Although Persian women are more beautiful than French women, the French are prettier. It is as difficult not to love the first, as it is not to be pleased by the second; the first are more tender and modest, the second, gayer and livelier.

What makes women so beautiful in Persia is their ordered life: they neither gamble, nor keep late hours; they drink almost no wine, and almost never expose themselves to the air. It must be admitted that the seraglio is better fitted for health than for pleasure. Life there is uniform and unexciting; it is based on subordination and duty. Even its pleasures are grave; its joys, severe. These are seldom enjoyed, except as connected with authority and dependence.

Even Persian men lack the gaiety of the French. In Persia, there is nowhere to be seen that freedom of spirit, and that look of satisfaction which I find here in all ranks and conditions of men.

This is even worse in Turkey, where whole families may be found, no member of which, from father to son, has laughed since the establishment of the monarchy.

This Asiatic gravity is due to the absence of social intercourse; they see each other only when ceremony prescribes that they do so. Friendship, that gentle engagement of the heart, which makes life so pleasant here, is there almost unknown. They retire into their homes, where always the same company awaits them. Thus each family is isolated.

One day, while discussing this with an inhabitant of this country, he said to me: "What repels me most about your *moeurs* is that you are obliged to live with slaves, whose hearts and minds can never transcend their base condition. From your infancy, which they dominate, these craven creatures weaken those sentiments of virtue that derive from nature. Really, you must put your prejudices aside. What can be expected of an upbringing at the hands of a wretch, whose honor depends upon guarding the wives of another man, and prides himself upon the vilest of human occupations? Even fidelity, the one virtue possessed by such a person, is contemptible because it stems from envy, jealousy, and despair. Burning with vengeance against both sexes, and rejected by both, he consents to being tyrannized by the stronger on the condition that he be allowed to torment the weaker. Since everything that distinguishes his position presupposes imperfection, ugliness, and deformity, he is esteemed only because he is unworthy. Riveted forever to the door he guards, he is harder than the bolts and bars securing it. Yet he prides himself upon having held for fifty years this unworthy post, where as the representative of his master's jealousy, he has made full use of his own sordid qualities.

From Paris, the 14th of the moon of Zilhage, 1713

Letter LXII

Zélis to Usbek at Paris

Since your daughter is now seven, I thought it was time for her to be brought into the interior of the seraglio, rather than waiting until she was ten before confiding her to the care of the black eunuchs. It is never too early to take away the liberties of childhood from a young person, and give her a pious upbringing within those holy walls where modesty dwells.

For I am not of the opinion of those mothers who confine their daughters only when they are about to receive their husband. To do so is to condemn them to the seraglio, rather than to consecrate them to it; is to force them to submit to a mode of life, which they should have been taught to love. Must everything be made to await the force of reason, and nothing be left to the gentle effects of habit?

It is futile to speak to us of the subordinate position in which nature has put us. It is not enough to make us feel this submission; we must be made to practice it, so that it may sustain us at that critical time when the passions begin to make themselves felt and encourage independence.

Were it only duty that attached us to you, we might sometimes forget it. Were it only inclination that served as the bond, a stronger inclination might overcome the first. But when the laws give us over to one man, they remove us so far from all others, that we might as well be a hundred thousand leagues away.

Nature, so industrious when favoring men, did not limit itself to giving them desires; it also wished that we too should have them, in order to become active instruments of their felicity. Within us, nature has kindled the fire of passion, so that men might live in tranquillity. If they lose it, we are meant to return them to this condition in which they are exempt from strong feelings in a way that we ourselves never can be.

Nevertheless, Usbek, you ought not imagine that your situation is more fortunate than my own. I have sampled here a thousand pleasures unknown to you; my imagination has worked incessantly to make me realize their worth. I have lived, and you have but languished.

I remain freer than you in the very prison in which you confine me. If you redouble your efforts to guard me, I only enjoy your uneasiness. Your suspicions, jealousy, and irritation are but marks of your dependence.

Continue, dear Usbek, to have me guarded night and day; do not believe that even ordinary precautions are enough. Add to my happiness, while assuring your own. Know that I dread nothing but your indifference.

From the seraglio at Ispahan, the 2nd of
the moon of Rebiab I, 1714

Letter LXIV
The Chief of the Black Eunuchs to Usbek at Paris

I am, magnificent lord, in a plight I scarcely know how to describe. The seraglio is in appalling disorder and confusion: among your women, a state of war exists; your eunuchs are divided among themselves; nothing but complaints, grumbling, and reproaches can be heard. My remonstrances are scorned, everything seems permissible in this time of license, and my title now means nothing in this seraglio.

Every one of your wives considers herself superior to all the rest by birth, beauty, wealth, wit, and your love for her, and, on the basis of one or another of these qualities, demands preference on all other points as well. At every moment, I lose that long-suffering patience, which nevertheless has unfortunately had the effect of making all of them discontent. My prudence, even my good nature (a virtue rare and almost unknown in the post I occupy) have become useless.

May I reveal to you, magnificent lord, the cause of all these disorders? It is altogether due to your heart and the tender regard you have for them. If you did not stay my hand; if, instead of remonstrances, you allowed me to use punishments; if, instead of allowing yourself to hear their complaints and tears, you sent them to weep before me, who am never softened by this sight – I should soon fit them with the yoke they ought to bear; and wear down their imperious and independent humor.

At the age of fifteen, I was abducted from the depths of my native Africa. I was first sold to a master who had more than twenty wives or concubines. Having judged from my grave and taciturn air that I was fitted for the seraglio, he ordered that I be made ready. I was forced to undergo an operation that was painful at the beginning, but then turned out to be fortunate for me, since it gave me access to the ear and confidence of my masters. I entered the seraglio, a new world for me. The chief eunuch, the most severe man I have ever seen, exercised absolute rule. Divisions and quarrels were unknown there; a profound silence reigned everywhere. All the women were put to bed and awakened at the same times throughout the year. They entered the bath in turn; they left it at the slightest sign from us. As for the rest of the time, they were almost always confined to their rooms. He had one rule, which was to make them observe the strictest cleanliness. On this point he took inexpressible pains, the slightest refusal to obey was punished mercilessly. "I am a slave," he said, "but I belong to a man who is your master and mine, and the power I hold over you was given to me by him. It is he who chastises you, not I, who only aid him." Those women never entered my master's room without being summoned. This favor they received with joy, but did not complain if denied it. In short, I, who was the lowliest of the black eunuchs in that peaceful seraglio, was a thousand times more respected there than in your own, where I command everyone.

As soon as the chief eunuch recognized my talent, he began to take notice of me. He recommended me to my master as capable of working in accordance with his own views, and of succeeding him in his post. That I was very young did not disturb him; he believed that my vigilance would compensate for my inexperience. Shall I tell you? I became so trusted by him, that he no longer made the slightest difficulty about entrusting me with the keys to those terrible places he had so long guarded. It was under this great master that I learned the difficult art of command, and was trained according to the maxims of inexorable government. Under him I studied the feminine heart. I learned how to profit from the weakness of women and never to be surprised by their haughtiness. Often he liked to watch me carry them to the point where their last defenses against instant obedience were broken down. Then he allowed them to return to their previous condition gradually, and desired that I appear to give way for a time to them. But to appreciate him, he had to be seen at those moments when he found them on the verge of despair, suspended between entreaty and reproach. Withstanding their tears without being touched in the least by them, he prided himself upon such triumphs. "This is how women must be governed," he would say contentedly. "Their number present no difficulty to me; no change would be needed to rule all the women of our great monarch. How can a man hope to enslave their hearts, if his faithful eunuchs have not previously broken their spirits?"

He was not only firm, but astute as well. He read their thoughts and their dissimulations; their studied gestures, the faces they prepared, did not protect them in the least from him. He knew of even those acts they took most pains to conceal, and of their most secret words. He made use of some of them to inform him about others; he rewarded willingly even the slighest confidence. Since they came to their husband only after having been summoned, the eunuch could choose anyone he wished, and call his master's attention to whomever he wished to favor. This distinction was their reward for having revealed a secret. His master had been convinced that good order required that the eunuch make the choice, so that his authority might thus be increased. That was how he governed, magnificent lord, in that seraglio that was, I believe, the best ordered in Persia.

Free my hands, allow me to do what obedience requires. In a week, order will replace confusion. This is what your glory demands, and your safety requires.

From the seraglio at Ispahan, the 9th of
the moon of Rebiab 1, 1714

Letter LXV

Usbek to His Wives at the Seraglio at Ispahan

I hear that the seraglio is in disorder, that it is full of quarrels and internal divisions. When I departed, did I not bid you to live in peace and on good terms? You promised me to do so. Was this done only to deceive me?

It is you who will be deceived, if I decide to take the advice of the grand eunuch and use my authority to make you live in the way I urged you.

But I can resort to such violent means only after having exhausted all others. Thus do on your own account what you would not do on mine.

The first eunuch has good reason to complain. He says that you do not respect him. How can you reconcile such conduct with the modesty prescribed by your condition? During my absence, is not the care of your virtue confided to him? It is he who is the guardian of this sacred treasure. But the scorn with which you treat him shows how much of a burden to you are those charged with making you live according to the laws of honor.

And so I am requesting you to change your conduct. Behave in such a way as to enable me to reject again those proposals that would affect adversely your liberty and repose.

For I should like to make you forget that I am your master, and think of me only as your husband.

From Paris, the 5th of the moon of Chahban, 1714

Letter CXLVII

The Chief Eunuch to Usbek at Paris

Things have arrived at a state that can no longer be tolerated; your wives have the illusion that your departure has left them immune to any punishment whatever. Horrible things are happening here. I myself tremble at the prospect of telling you this painful story.

Several days ago, Zélis, while going to the mosque, let her veil drop and appeared with her face virtually exposed before the entire populace.

I have found Zachi in bed with one of her slaves, something completely prohibited by the laws of the seraglio.

By sheer chance, I have intercepted a letter that I am sending you. I have never been able to discover to whom it was sent.

Yesterday evening, a young man was found in the seraglio garden; he escaped by scaling the walls.

If you add to that everything else that has not come to my attention, surely you have been betrayed. I await your orders. Until the happy moment when I receive them, I shall be in a desperate situation. But if you do not permit me to treat all these women as my discretion dictates, I cannot answer for any of them. Every day the news I shall have to give you will be as sad as this.

From the seraglio at Ispahan, the 1st of
the moon of Rhegeb, 1717

Letter CXLVIII
Usbek to the Chief Eunuch at the Seraglio at Ispahan

Receive by this letter unlimited power over the entire seraglio; command with as much authority as I myself possess. Let fear and terror be your accompaniment. As you hasten from one apartment to the next, inflict punishment and correction. Put everyone into a state of dismay; make them dissolve in tears before you. Interrogate everyone in the seraglio; begin with the slaves. Do not spare the objects of my love; subject them all to your formidable inquiry. Expose the most hidden secrets. Purify this sordid place and return it to the virtue it once possessed. From this moment, I make you responsible for even the slightest fault. I suspect Zélis of being the one to whom was addressed that letter you intercepted. Investigate that with the eyes of a lynx.

From . . . , the 11th of the moon of Zilhage, 1718

Letter CXLIX
Narsit to Usbek at Paris

The chief eunuch has just died, magnificent lord. Since I am the oldest of your slaves, I have assumed his place until you make known your choice of his successor.

Two days after his death, one of your letters, addressed to him, was brought to me; I have taken good care not to open it. Respectfully I wrapped and locked it away until you reveal your holy will to me.

Yesterday a slave came in the middle of the night to tell me that he had found a young man in the seraglio. I arose, investigated the matter, and concluded that it was a vision.

I kiss your feet, sublime lord, and I beg of you to have confidence in my zeal, experience, and age.

From the seraglio at Ispahan, the 5th of
the moon of Gemmadi I, 1718

Letter CL
Usbek to Narsit at the Seraglio at Ispahan

Wretch that you are! You have in your hands letters that contain orders to be carried out immediately and with violence. At a time when the slightest delay makes me despair, you remain calm for no reason whatever.

Terrible things are taking place; perhaps a half of my slaves deserve to die. I am sending you the letter on that subject, which the chief eunuch wrote me before his death. Had you opened the package addressed to him, you would have found orders to shed blood. And so read these orders. Unless you carry them out, you yourself will die.

From . . . , the 25th of the moon of Chalval, 1718

Letter CLI

Solim to Usbek at Paris

If I remained silent any longer, I should be as guilty as all the criminals you have in your seraglio.

I was the confidant of the chief eunuch, the most faithful of your slaves. When he saw that his end was near, he summoned me and said these words: "I am dying with but one regret: that my last view of the world has revealed the criminal guilt of my master's wives. May Heaven protect him from all the evils I foresee. After I am dead, may my ghost return to warn these perfidious women by my threats to return to their duty, and thus intimidate them once again. Here are the keys to these fearful places; take them to the oldest of the black eunuchs. But if after my death, he fails to be vigilant, make certain to warn your master of this." After saying these words, he died in my arms.

I know what, some time before his death, he wrote you about your wives' conduct. In the seraglio there is a letter that, had it been opened, would have spread terror. The letter you wrote after that was intercepted three leagues from here. I do not know what is going on; everything is turning out for the worst.

Meanwhile your wives have shown no discretion whatever. Since the death of the chief eunuch, it seems as though they can do anything they wish. Only Roxana has remained within the bounds of duty and retains her modesty. Every day sees the further decline of *moeurs*. The faces of your wives no longer have their former expression of vigorous and austere virtue. In such a place as this any new joy is, in my view, an infallible proof of some new satisfaction. Even in the smallest things, I perceive hitherto unknown liberties being taken. Even among your slaves there prevails a certain laxity toward their duties and the maintenance of rules – that surprises me. No longer do they display that ardent zeal to serve you which once seemed to animate the entire seraglio.

For a week your wives have been in the country at one of the most isolated of your houses. It is said that the slave in charge of it has been bribed, and that the day before their arrival, he hid two men in a stone compartment in the wall of the main room. It was from there that they emerged after we had retired at night. The old eunuch now in charge of us is an imbecile who can be made to believe anything.

I am possessed by the anger to revenge all these betrayals. If Heaven willed that you be better served, and you were to consider me capable of command, I promise you that even if your wives were not virtuous, they at least would be faithful.

From the seraglio at Ispahan, the 6 th of
the moon of Rebiab I, 1719

Letter CLII

Narsit to Usbék at Paris

Roxana and Zélis wished to go to the country; I did not believe that I ought to refuse them. Fortunate Usbek! Your wives are faithful; your slaves, vigilant: the places I command are those that virtue seems to have chosen as her sanctuary. Rest assured that nothing will happen here that could offend your eyes.

An unfortunate occurrence has caused me much pain. Some Armenian merchants, newly arrived at Ispahan, had carried one of your letters for me. I sent a slave to get it. On his return, he was robbed and the letter lost. Therefore write to me soon, for I suppose that with this change of command, you will have important orders for me.

From the seraglio at Fatima, the 6 th of
the moon of Rebiab I, 1719

Letter CLIII

Usbek to Solim at the Seraglio at Ispahan

I put my sword into your hand. I entrust to you what now is most precious to me in all the world – my vengeance. Take up your new office; but bring to it neither tenderness nor pity. I am writing to my wives that they are to obey you blindly. Distracted by their many crimes, they will not be able to withstand your eyes. I must rely upon you to assure my happiness and peace of mind. Return my seraglio to me as it was when I left it; but begin by making it atone for what it has done. Exterminate the guilty; make those tremble who consider becoming so. What can you not expect from your master for such signal services? It depends only upon yourself for you to surmount your condition and to gain as reward everything you have ever desired.

From Paris, the 4th of the moon of Chahban, 1719

Letter CLIV

Usbek to His Wives at the Seraglio at Ispahan

May this letter fall upon you like thunder in the midst of lightning and storm. Solim is your chief eunuch, not to guard you, but to punish you. The entire seraglio will abase itself before him. He is to judge your actions in the past, and, in future, he will make you live under a yoke so severe that even if you do not regret having lost your virtue, you will regret having lost your liberty.

From Paris, the 4th of the moon of Chahban, 1719

Letter CLV

Usbek to Nessir at Ispahan

Happy is the man who, knowing the value of a gentle and quiet life, puts his heart at ease among his family and knows no country other than that in which he was born.

I am living in a barbarous place, exposed to everything that annoys me, removed from everything that interests me. A somber sadness seizes me; I am falling into a dejection beyond belief – it seems to me that I am destroying myself, and that I shall rediscover myself only after grim jealousy has been kindled in my soul where it gives birth to fear, suspicions, hatred, and regret.

. . .

What a poor thing I am. I want to see my country again, perhaps only to become even more wretched. Yet what am I to do there? I am going to expose my head to my enemies. Nor is that all. I shall enter my seraglio where I must demand an accounting for that disastrous period of my absence. And if I find some who are guilty, what shall I do? If even the notion is overwhelming from this distance, what will it be like when my presence creates the inescapable reality? What will it be like if I am forced to see and hear what I cannot imagine without becoming furious? And, finally, what will be the outcome, if the punishments I myself pronounce become eternal scars inflicted by my confusion and despair?

I shall return to imprison myself within those walls more terrifying to me than to the women guarded there. With me I shall bring back all my suspicions, none of which will ever be allayed, no matter how eager my wives' embraces. In my own bed, in their arms, I shall feel nothing more than disquiet. At a time when reflection is inappropriate, I shall be driven to it by my jealousy. Scum unworthy of human nature, debased slaves, whose hearts are forever closed to all feelings of love – you would cease lamenting your condition, if you knew the misery of mine.

From Paris, the 4th of the moon of Chahban, 1719

Letter CLVI
Roxana to Usbek at Paris

Horror, darkness, and terror reign in the seraglio; it is shrouded in terrifying gloom. Within a tiger vents his rage upon us: he has had two white eunuchs tortured, who only continue to avow their innocence; he has sold a number of our slaves, and forced us to exchange among ourselves those who remained. Zachi and Zélis, in their own rooms during the darkness of night, have been subjected to infamous treatment; no fear has kept that sacrilegious person from laying his vile hands on them. He keeps each of us locked up in her apartment, and, although we are thus isolated, he insists that we be veiled. No longer are we permitted to talk to each other; writing would be considered a crime; we are free only to weep.

An army of new eunuchs has entered the seraglio to besiege us day and night; our sleep is constantly interrupted by their investigations based on suspicions, whether real or feigned. All that consoles me is the thought that all this cannot last long, and that these sufferings will end when does my life. That will not be long, cruel Usbek. I shall not grant you enough time to put an end to these outrages.

From the seraglio at Ispahan, the 2nd of
the moon of Maharram, 1720

Letter CLVIII
Zélis to Usbek at Paris

A thousand leagues from me, you judge me guilty; a thousand leagues away, you punish me.

When a barbarous eunuch laid his vile hands on me, he did so at your command. It is the tyrant who outrages me, not his instrument.

Whenever your caprice dictates, you may redouble your abuse of me. My heart is at peace, since it cannot love you any longer.

Your soul has been debased, and you have become cruel. You can be certain that this will bring you no happiness.

Farewell.

From the seraglio at Ispahan, the 2nd of
the moon of Maharram, 1720

Letter CLIX
Solim to Usbek at Paris

I pity myself, magnificent lord, and I pity you: never before has so faithful a servant fallen into such despair as mine. Here are your misfortunes and mine. I tremble as I write.

I swear by all the prophets in heaven that ever since you confided your wives to my care, I have watched over them night and day, that never for a moment have I suspended my anxieties. I began my ministry with punishments, which I have discontinued, without giving up the austerity natural to me.

But what am I saying to you? Why do I boast here of a fidelity that has been so useless to you? Forget all my past services; consider me a traitor; and punish me for all the crimes I have been unable to prevent.

Roxana, proud Roxana! O Heaven! From now on is there anyone we can trust? You suspected Zélis while feeling perfectly secure about Roxana. But her fierce virtue was a cruel deception veiling her treachery. I have surprised her in the arms of a young man, who attacked me when he saw that he had been discovered. Twice he stabbed me with his dagger. The eunuchs, brought running by the commotion, surrounded him. He defended himself for a long time, wounded several of them; and even tried to reenter Roxana's bedroom, so that he could die before her eyes, or so he said. But finally he succumbed to numbers, and fell at our feet.

I do not know, sublime lord, whether I can wait until your severe orders arrive. You have entrusted your vengeance to me; I ought not delay it.

From the seraglio at Ispahan, the 8th of
the moon of Rebiab I, 1720

Letter CLX
Solim to Usbek at Paris

I have made my decision. All your misfortunes are coming to an end; I am going to mete out punishment.

Already I feel a secret joy. My soul and your own shall be calm again. We shall exterminate all crime; even innocence will pale.

All you women seem to have been created only to ignore all your senses and to be unworthy even of your desires. Eternal victims of shame and modesty, how I should like to bring you in great multitudes into this unhappy seraglio and astound you by all the blood I am about to shed.

From the seraglio at Ispahan, the 8th of
the moon of Rebiab I, 1720

Letter CLXI
Roxana to Usbek at Paris

Yes, I have deceived you. I have corrupted your eunuchs, toyed with your jealousy, and known how to make a place of delights and pleasures out of your abominable seraglio.

I am about to die; poison will soon circulate through my veins. What keeps me here now that the one man who made me want to live is no more? I die, but my soul will be well accompanied. I have just sent off before me those sacrilegious guardians who have shed the most beautiful blood in the world.

How could you have believed me so credulous as to imagine that I had come into the world only to adore your every caprice? that while permitting yourself everything, you had the right to frustrate all my desires. No! I may have lived in slavery, but I have always been free: I have reformed your laws by those of nature, and my spirit has never lost its independence.

You ought to thank me for the sacrifice I have made to you. I have abased myself to the point of appearing faithful; I have, like a coward, confined to my heart what I should have told all the world. Finally, I have profaned virtue by allowing that name to be applied to my submission to your whims.

You were astonished not to find in me the transports of love. Had you known me well, you would have discovered all the violence of hate.

But for a long time you enjoyed the pleasure of believing that a heart like mine had been subjugated by you. We were both happy: you believed me to be deceived; and I deceived you.

No doubt this language will appear novel to you. Is it yet possible after having filled you with sorrows, for me to compel you to admire my courage? But all is over. The poison is consuming me. My strength is ebbing. The pen falls from my hands. I feel even my hatred weakened; I die.

From the seraglio at Ispahan, the 8th of the moon of Rebiab I, 1720

End of the *Persian Letters*

A Note on Chronology in the *Persian Letters*

Montesquieu's chronology in the *Persian Letters* has been studied by scholars (most notably Robert Shackleton, "The Moslem Calendar in *Lettres persanes*," *French Studies* VIII [1954] pp. 17–27). Their conclusion is that Montesquieu sought to find exotic-sounding equivalents in the Moslem calendar, which is lunar, for the Western calendar, which is solar. Montesquieu's resolution of the problem was to begin the year with March and to call it by the corresponding Moslem name (although the Moslem month in fact started in the middle of March). The principal sources of Montesquieu's knowledge were Chardin's *Voyages en Perse et autres lieux de l'Orient*, and Tavernier's *Les Six Voyages en Turquie, en Perse et aux Indes*. Montesquieu took his Persian spelling from Chardin, except for two changes. He wrote Rebiab for Rebiah, and Chalval for Cheval. The following three columns give Montesquieu's terms for the months, the usual Moslem spelling, and the Western calendar. All years given in the *Persian Letters* are in the solar years of the Christian era. Thus dates are composite: oriental months; Christian years.

Montesquieu	*Moslem*	*Western*
Maharram	Muharram	March
Saphar	Safar	April
Rebiab I	Rabia I	May
Rebiab II	Rabia II	June
Gemmadi I	Jumada I	July
Gemmadi II	Jumada II	August
Rhegeb	Rajab	September
Chahban	Shaban	October
Rahmazan	Ramadan	November
Chalval	Shawwal	December
Zilcade	Dhu-l-Kada	January
Zilhage	Dhu-l-Hijja	February

CONSIDERATIONS ON THE CAUSES OF THE ROMANS' GREATNESS AND DECLINE

CHAPTER III
How the Romans Could Expand[1]

Since the peoples of Europe now possess approximately the same techniques, the same arms, the same discipline and style of warfare, the prodigious success of the Romans appears incredible. Furthermore, today there is such a disproportion in the power of states, that a small one cannot, by its own efforts alone, overcome the subordinate position assigned it by Providence.

All this calls for reflection. Otherwise, we might witness events without understanding them, and, imperfectly aware of the differences between the two situations, believe, when turning to ancient history, that men then were other than we ourselves now are.[2]

In modern Europe, experience has continued to demonstrate that a prince ruling a million subjects cannot, without destroying himself, maintain a force of more than ten thousand men. Thus only great nations can have armies.

Things were otherwise in the ancient republics. For that proportion of soldiers to the rest of the population, which today stands at one to a hundred, then could easily be maintained at the level of one to eight.

The founders of these ancient republics had divided up their lands equally among their citizens. Only this could have created a powerful people, that is to say, a well-ordered society. At the same time, this brought into being a strong army, for each of its members had an equal and very great interest in defending his homeland (*patrie*).

When these land laws ceased to be rigidly observed, the situation became what it is today: the greediness of certain individuals, and the prodigality of others produced a concentration of landed estates in the hands of a few. Then to meet the mutual needs of the rich and poor, the arts came into being. This had the effect of leaving almost no citizens or soldiers, for the lands that formerly supported them now had to sustain those slaves and artisans who were the instruments for the luxuries of the new owners. Otherwise the state, which had to be maintained, even though no longer based on its original principles, could not have continued to exist. Before this corruption took place, most of the state's primary resources were divided among the soldiers, that is, those who tilled the soil.[3] But after corruption set in, such revenues came into the hands of the rich, who then passed them out to slaves and artisans. It was their taxes that provided in part, support for the soldiers.

Such slaves and artisans were not at all fitted for war. They were cowardly, already corrupted by the luxury of the cities, or by the nature of their occupations. In addition, since they had no land of their own, and could profit equally well from practicing their occupations anywhere, they had little to lose or to conserve.

Rome and Athens had approximately the same population, according to a census taken at Rome sometime after the expulsion of its kings,[4] and another made by Demetrius of Phalerum at Athens.[5] Rome had 440,000 inhabitants; Athens, 431,000. But Rome was at the height of the power created by the establishment of its original laws; while the laws of Athens had been altogether corrupted. At Rome a quarter of its inhabitants were citizens who had passed the age of puberty; at Athens, the figure fell to less than one-twentieth. Thus the power of Rome was five times greater than that of Athens, which is the relationship of one-fourth to one-twentieth.

The Spartan kings, Agis and Cleomenes, discovered that instead of the nine thousand citizens who had inhabited their city at the time of Lycurgus,[6] the number had fallen to seven hundred. Of these, scarcely one hundred possessed land;[7] the rest lacked all courage. These kings reestablished the original land laws.[8] Sparta then recovered its former power and became once again formidable to all the Greeks.

It was the equal division of lands that first made Rome capable of emerging from its humble condition. This truth made itself felt after Rome became corrupted.

Rome was but a tiny republic when the Latins refused to provide those troops they had pledged. Immediately ten legions were raised from the city itself.[9] Of this, Livy remarked, "Rome, which now threatens to overflow the bounds of the world, could scarcely match this feat, were an enemy to appear before its walls. This constitutes irrefutable proof that we are no greater than we were.

Indeed, all we have done is to augment the luxury and wealth that obsess us."

"Tell me," said Tiberius Gracchus to the nobles,[10] "who is worth more, a citizen, or a perpetual slave; a soldier, or a man useless in war? In order to have a few more acres of land than other citizens, are you willing to renounce your hopes of conquering the rest of the world? Do you wish to take the risk of seeing enemies seize those lands you deny to us?"

CHAPTER VI
The Means Used by the Romans to Subjugate All Other Peoples[1]

Even amid such great success, at a time when men usually become careless, the senate continued to act with the same profundity as before. While Roman armies routed all their opponents, the senate devoted itself to making permanent the victories won on the battlefield.

The senate constituted itself a tribunal that passed judgment on all other peoples. Once a war was ended, it was the senate that decided what penalties and what rewards ought to be meted out. It deprived conquered peoples of some part of their territory, which it then gave to the Romans' allies. In this way, it achieved two things: it attached to Rome those kings from whom it had little to fear, and much to hope; and it weakened those others, from whom it had nothing to hope, and everything to fear.

The Romans used their allies to make war upon their enemies. Then they destroyed their agents of destruction. Philip was defeated by the Aetolians, who then were immediately themselves wiped out because they had joined Antiochus. He was vanquished with the aid of the Rhodians. After these had received extraordinary rewards, they in turn were humbled for all time because of their alleged demand that peace be made with Perseus.

When the Romans had several enemies to deal with, they offered a truce to the weakest, which counted itself fortunate to have put off its ruin.

While engaged in a great war, the senate pretended not to notice any injuries and waited in silence for the time of punishment. If a people sent to it those guilty of offense, the senate would refuse to punish them. It preferred to hold the entire opposing nation responsible, and thus to defer a more opportune revenge.

Since they inflicted incredible evils upon their enemies, no leagues were formed against the Romans. Those furthest removed from the Romans had no wish to come any closer to them.

For this reason they were seldom attacked. But the Romans never ceased to make war against those they chose to attack at the time and in the way most convenient to themselves. Of all the peoples attacked by the Romans, there were few indeed that would not have endured every insult that stopped short of war itself.

Their custom was always to address other nations as though Rome were their master. When they did so to nations that had not as yet felt their power, the Roman ambassadors were certain to be mistreated, thus providing an excellent pretext for making a new war.[2]

Since they never acted in good faith when they made peace, their true intention being to invade all other peoples, Roman treaties came to nothing more than temporary suspensions of war. The Romans set conditions that always led to the ruin of the state that accepted them. They insisted that garrisons abandon their fortifications, or limited the number of troops holding strong points, or demanded that horses or elephants be handed over to them. If their opponents were a sea power, the Romans would force them to burn their ships, or, on occasion, to move further inland.

After having destroyed a ruler's armies, the Romans would proceed to ruin his finances by imposing excessive taxes or forcing him to pay a tribute. Under the pretext that the defeated should pay the costs of a war, the Romans devised a new sort of tyranny. For the conquered ruler was forced to oppress his subjects, and thus lost their love.

When they granted peace to a ruler, they took a brother or a child as hostage, thus enabling them to torment his kingdom whenever they took the fancy to do so. If the Romans held the nearest heir, they intimidated the incumbent; if their hostage was removed by several degrees from the succession, they used him to stir up revolts among his people.

Whenever a sovereign's authority was challenged by a ruler or people, these were immediately given the title, ally of the Roman people, thus making them sacred and inviolable.[3] In this way, no king, however great, could be sure for a moment of his subjects or even his family.

Although to be an ally of the Romans meant assuming a servile relation to them, nevertheless this status was much sought after.[4] For in that case, a state could be certain that it would be troubled only by the Romans, and it was not unreasonable to hope that their demands would be less than from all other sources combined. Thus it was that peoples and kings showed themselves ready to render every type of service to the Romans; no degradation was excluded that might lead to obtaining this end.

Their allies differed in kind. Some were united to the Romans by privileges, and participation in their greatness, as in the case of the Latins and the Hernici; others, like their colonies, by the very fact of having been established by the Romans; there could be attachments based upon good service, as Masinissa, Eumenes, and Attalus, all of whom owed their realms or their expansion to the Romans; states could become allies by treaties freely negotiated; they could become subjects through long continuance of alliances, as had the kings of Egypt, Bithynia, and Cappadocia, and most Greek cities; and finally, many more, by treaties forced upon them as the condition of peace, like Philip and Antiochus. For the Romans never granted peace to an enemy without imposing an alliance upon it, that is, they never conquered peoples who could not contribute to the defeat of still other states.

Whenever they left cities free, the Romans created two factions:[5] the first, defending local laws and liberty; the second, taking the position that the only law was what the Romans willed. Since the second faction was always stronger, it was clear that what was called liberty existed only in name.

Sometimes they used succession as their pretext for making themselves masters of the country. Thus they entered Asia, Bithynia, and Libya on the basis of the wills left by Attalus, Nicomedes,[6] and Apion, while Egypt passed to them by that of the king of Cyrene.

To keep great rulers permanently weak, the Romans set the condition that no state that was their ally could have the same relationship to other states that were also in league with the Romans.[7] Since they never refused an alliance with any neighbor of a powerful ruler, this condition, when incorporated into a peace treaty, deprived him of all allies.

In addition, after conquering such a ruler of importance, they stipulated in the treaty, that he could not make war to resolve his differences with allies of the Romans (that is, in most cases, with all his neighbors), but must, instead, submit to arbitration. In this way, he was stripped of all military power for the future.

Finally, so as to reserve all such power to themselves, they deprived even their allies of it. In the case of the slightest quarrel, the Romans sent ambassadors who forced the parties involved to make peace. This policy may be observed in the way that they put an end to the war between Attalus and Prusias.

Whenever a prince made a conquest that left his forces exhausted, a Roman ambassador would appear to tear his prize out of his hands. Among a thousand such examples was the case in which the Romans, by a word, expelled Antiochus from Egypt.

The Romans, knowing the capacity of the European peoples to make war, established as a law that no Asian ruler could enter Europe and subdue any people whatever.[8] The principal motive of their war upon Mithridates was that he, in defiance of this principle, had forced a small number of European barbarians to surrender to him.[9]

When they saw two peoples at war, the Romans, despite the fact that they had neither alliances nor disputes with either of them, never failed to appear on the scene, and, like our knights-errant, to take the side of the weaker. As Dionysius of Halicarnassus remarked, it was an ancient custom of the Romans always to aid those who asked for it.[10]

None of these Roman customs were derived from separate actions taken at random, but rather from principles that remained constant. This can be easily seen from the fact that the maxims they used against the great powers were precisely the same as those they had originally practiced against the small cities that surrounded them.

The Romans made use of Eumenes and Masinissa to subjugate Philip and Antiochus, just as they had employed the Latins and Hernici in the case of the Volsci and Tuscans; they made the Carthaginians and the kings of Asia give up their fleets, just as they had done with the ships of Antium; they put an end to the political and civil ties that existed among the four parts of Macedon, just as they had broken in the past the union of the small Latin towns.[11]

But above all, their constant maxim was to divide. The republic of Achaea had been formed by an association of free cities; the Roman senate declared that henceforth each city would be governed by its own laws, without reference to any common authority.

The republic of the Boeotians was likewise a league of many cities. Yet in the war against Persia, some sided with the king of that country, while others supported the Romans. This faction the Romans agreed to favor, but only on the condition that the common alliance be dissolved.

Had these maxims been followed by a great ruler of our own time, he, when he saw one of his neighbors dethroned, would have used all the power at his disposal to support him, but to limit him to that island that remained faithful to him. By thus dividing the only power that could oppose his designs, he would have derived immense advantages even from the misfortune of his ally.[12]

When there were internal disagreements in a state, the Romans would pass judgment. In this way, they were certain of finding opposed to themselves only that party they had condemned. If the crown was disputed by two princes of the same blood, the Romans sometimes would declare both of them to be king:[13] if one of them were a minor,[14] the Romans would decide in his favor, and, as protectors of the universe, would assume his tutelage. For they had carried things to such a point that peoples and kings were their subjects without knowing precisely by what title, the Romans having established that merely having heard of them was enough to owe them obedience.

Never did they make war far from their borders unless they had secured as an ally a neighbor of the enemy. In this way, their army was reinforced. Since this was never large in numbers, they always kept another army in that province closest to the enemy, and a third in Rome ready at all times to march.[15] Thus they exposed but a very small part of their forces, while their enemy put all of his into the balance.[16]

On occasion they took advantage of their language's subtlety. They destroyed Carthage, saying that they had promised to preserve the state, but not the city.[17] It is well known that the Aetolians entrusted themselves to the Romans' good faith and were deceived. The Romans pretended that "to entrust oneself to an enemy's good faith"[18] meant acquiescence to the loss of all sorts of things: persons, land, cities, temples, and even sepulchers.

They were even capable of making an arbitrary interpretation of a treaty. When they wished to humble the Rhodians, the Romans stated that when in the past, they gave them Lycia, they did so not unconditionally, but only so long as the Rhodians remained friends and allies.

When one of their generals sued for peace in order to save his army from destruction, the senate, which refused to ratify this act, profited from the cessation of hostilities, and continued the war. Thus, when Jugurtha surrounded a Roman army, which he then let go under the terms of a treaty based on the Romans' word, the senate sent against him the very troops he had released. After the Numantians had forced the capitulation of twenty thousand Romans, who were about to die of hunger, this surrender, which had saved so many citizens, was repudiated at Rome. It was pretended that the good faith of the state was not involved, and the consul who had signed the peace agreement was returned to his former captors.[19]

Sometimes they made peace with the ruler on reasonable terms. Then, when he had carried out his part of the agreement, they added terms of a kind that forced him to reopen war. And so, after making Jugurtha[20] hand over his elephants, horses, treasures, and those Romans who had deserted to him, they then demanded that he give himself up. Since such a fate is the worst imaginable for a ruler, it can never be a condition of peace.

Finally, they set themselves up in judgment upon the faults and individual offenses of kings. They heard all the complaints of those involved in quarrels with Philip; they sent agents to see to their security; they held proceedings to accuse Perseus of several murders, as well as to take sides against him in his disagreements with citizens of cities allied to the Romans.

Since they judged a general's glory by the amount of gold and silver he displayed in his triumph, he left nothing to a vanquished enemy. Rome continued to enrich itself, and every war left it better fitted to undertake the next.

Those peoples, friendly or allied to Rome, were all ruined by the enormous gifts made to retain its favor, or to add to it. Even a half of the money they spent for this purpose would have sufficed to conquer the Romans.[21]

Masters of the universe, they claimed all its treasures. For all this, they were less rapacious as conquerors than in their capacity as legislators. After learning of the enormous wealth of Ptolemy, king of Cyprus, they enacted a law, proposed by a tribune, by which they declared themselves his heirs, although he was still alive, and proceeded to the confiscation of his goods, although he was their ally.[22]

Soon the cupidity of individuals succeeded in making off with whatever had escaped public greediness. Magistrates and governors sold the injustice they dealt out to foreign kings. Two competitors would ruin themselves in the contest to purchase protection that was worthless so long as their rival still retained some resources. The Romans lacked even that justice of thieves, who carry a certain integrity into their practice of crime. Finally, they created a situation in which rights, legitimate or usurped, went unrecognized unless payment was forthcoming. To obtain recognition of their claims, rulers plundered temples, confiscated the goods of their richest citizens, committed a thousand crimes in order to bestow upon the Romans all the money in the world.

But nothing served Rome better than the respect it instilled everywhere. Before it kings fell silent, and were reduced to a sort of stupefaction. What was at stake was not simply the extent of their power. The Romans attacked their very persons. To risk a war was to expose oneself to captivity, death, the ignominy of a Roman triumph. As a result, those kings who lived in pomp and luxury did not dare to confront the Roman people. Their courage gone, they hoped only that their patience and servility might delay somewhat the misfortunes with which they were threatened.[23]

Now I must ask you to consider how the Romans managed their affairs. After the defeat of Antiochus, they were masters of Africa, Asia, and Greece. Yet they held almost no cities. This made it appear as though they conquered only so as to be able to give away the fruits of their victory. Nevertheless, when they made war upon a ruler, they crushed him, as it were, by applying the weight of the whole universe.

It was not as yet the time to take direct possession of those countries that had been conquered. Had the Romans kept those cities they had taken from Philip, they would have opened the eyes of all the other Greeks. If, after the Second Punic War, or that against Antiochus, they had taken possession of territory in Africa or Asia, they could not have kept these conquests, which lacked a solid base.[24]

Before the other nations could be commanded to obey as subjects, it was necessary to wait until they became accustomed to doing so in their capacity as independent allies. And in this way, they gradually became absorbed in the Roman Republic.

Among the principal foundations of their power was the treaty they made with the Latins after the victory of Lake Regillus.[25] Examine it: not a word would arouse suspicion of empire.

This was a gradual method of conquest. After a people was defeated, the Romans were content to weaken it. Conditions were imposed that undermined it imperceptibly. If a revolt occurred, then an even greater degree of Roman control was imposed. Thus a people became subject to the Romans without even knowing when this had taken place.

Thus Rome was, properly speaking, neither a monarchy nor a republic, but the head of that body formed by all the peoples in the world.

Had the Spanish, after the conquests of Mexico and Peru, followed this plan, they would not have found it necessary to destroy everything in order to conserve everything.

It is the usual folly of conquerors to attempt to impose their own laws and customs upon all other peoples. This achieves nothing, for obedience can be obtained under all governments, whatever their form.

But Rome, imposing no general laws, created no dangerous relationships among its peoples. These were united only by their common obedience, and without being compatriots, they were all Roman.

It may be objected that empires founded upon a legal system of fiefs have been neither long lasting nor powerful.[26] But nothing could be more opposed to the method of the Romans than that of the barbarians. To sum up the difference in a word, the first was the product of force, the other of weakness; in the first, it was subjection that was extreme, in the second, independence. In countries conquered by the Germanic nations, power was in the hands of the vassals, while the prince had only legal right. In the case of the Romans, it was quite the opposite.

CHAPTER VIII
The Internal Divisions that Always Existed at Rome[1]

During the time that Rome was conquering the universe, a hidden war was going on within its walls. This resembled volcanic fire, which bursts out as soon as something is added to its usual activity.

After the expulsion of the kings, the government of Rome became aristocratic: the patrician families alone obtained all the magistracies, all the dignities,[2] and consequently, all military and civil honors.[3]

The patricians, who wished to prevent the return of the kings, sought to encourage an attitude already at work among the people.[4] But they succeeded better than they had wished. By imparting to the people a hatred for the kings, they also brought into existence an immoderate desire for liberty. Since royal authority had passed in its entirety into the hands of the consuls, the people became aware that they did not at all possess that liberty, which they had been told was so worthy of love. They sought, then, to humble the consulate, to have plebian magistrates, and to share the curule magistracies with the nobles.[5] The patricians were forced to cede everything that was demanded of them, for birth and honors could not lead to great advantages in a city where poverty was public virtue, and where wealth, that silent means of attaining power, was despised. Power had to revert to the greater number, and aristocracy turned gradually into a state dominated by the people.

Those who owe obedience to a king are less tormented by envy and jealousy than those who live in a hereditary aristocracy. The monarch is so far removed from his subjects, that he is almost unperceived by them; his strength so far exceeds their own, that they cannot imagine any comparison that might offend them. Nobles, on the other hand, rule in plain view, and are not so far removed from others as to remove the possibility of constant odious comparisons. Thus it has always been the case and it remains so still, that the people detest patrician senators. From this point of view, the most fortunate republics are those in which birth plays no part in the awarding of office. For the people resent less that authority they have in their own power to confer on whomever they choose, and which they may recall at their pleasure.

Discontented with the patricians, the people withdrew to Mons Sacer. There deputies were sent to appease them. Since each member of the people promised to come to the aid of every other in the event that the patricians did not keep their pledges,[6] it was judged wisest to create a magistracy with the power of preventing injustice to plebeians.[7] Otherwise, continued popular action would have created a constant danger of sedition and encroached upon the prerogatives of the magistrates. But by a malady eternal among men, the plebeians, after having obtained tribunes in order to defend themselves, used these magistrates to attack the patricians. Little by little, these were deprived of their prerogatives, thus producing an interminable set of quarrels. The people was supported, or more exactly, animated by the tribunes; the patricians were defended by the senate, made up almost exclusively of men from that class. These cared more for the ancient maxims of government and also feared that the people might elevate one of its tribunes to a dominating position as tyrant.

The resources of the people were its own power, its superiority in voting, its capacity to refuse military service, its threat to withdraw from the polity, the bias of the laws it had made, and finally, its judgments against those who had resisted it too strongly. The senate defended itself by its wisdom, its justice, and the love of country it inspired; by the benefits it produced and by its wise distribution of the republic's treasures; by the respect felt by the people for the glory achieved by the principal families and for the virtue of the great personages;[8] by religion itself, by the ancient institutions, and the suspension of the days set aside for assembly, this under the pretext of unfavorable auspices; by their clients; by setting one tribune against another; by the creation of a dictator,[9] by the preoccupation with new wars, or with those misfortunes that joined the interest of all classes, and finally, by a paternalistic willingness to cede to the people one part of their demands so that it might abandon the rest. Nor did the senate ever abandon the maxim that the preservation of the republic was to be preferred to the prerogatives of any order or any magistracy whatever.

As time went on, the plebeians so humbled the patricians that this distinction[10] among families became meaningless, and men of both orders were elevated on the same basis to the highest honors. Then there occurred new disputes between the common people, stirred up by its tribunes, and the principal families of both the patricians and plebeians, who were classed together under the name of the "nobles." These had the support of the senate, itself made up of this group. Because the ancient *moeurs* no longer existed, because individuals had acquired immense riches, and it was impossible that such wealth would not carry power with it, the nobles resisted more effectively than had the patricians. This accounts for the death of the Gracchi, and of many of those who collaborated with them in their plan.[11]

I must discuss the censors, a magistracy that contributed greatly to the maintenance of the Roman Republic. The censors made up the voting list of the people. What was more, since the power of the republic derived from discipline, the austerity of its *moeurs*, and the constant observance of certain customs, the censors corrected those abuses not anticipated by the law, or not subject to the jurisdiction of ordinary magistrates.[12] For there are bad examples worse than crime; more states have perished because their *moeurs* have been violated than because their laws have been broken.[13] At Rome, the censors prevented everything that could introduce dangerous innovations, change the hearts and minds of the citizens, and in this way endanger, by family or public disorder, what I may perhaps be allowed to call the continuity of tradition. The censors could expel from the senate whomever they chose; they could deprive an equestrian of the horse provided him by the people; they could transfer a citizen from one tribe to another, or even place him in the status of those who paid for the city's costs without sharing its citizens' privileges.[14]

M. Livius punished the people itself by placing it in disgrace. Of the thirty-five tribes, he put thirty-four into the category of those without citizens' privileges.[15] "For," he said, "after condemning me previously, you then made me consul and censor. It follows, then, that either you were at fault in punishing me, or, if I were guilty, you erred in elevating me to consul and afterwards to censor."

M. Duronius, a tribune of the people, was expelled from the senate by the censors for having broken the law that set limits on the sum to be spent on banquets.[16]

The censorship was a truly wise institution. The censors were not given the power to deprive anyone of a popularly elected office, for that would have infringed the power of the public.[17] But they could reduce citizens' order and rank, and deprive them, so to speak, of any nobility possessed as private individuals.

It was Servius Tullius who divided the Roman people into centuries in the way so well explained by Livy[18] and Dionysius of Halicarnassus.[19] Tullius divided 193 centuries into 6 classes, and put the lowest class of the people (*le bas peuple*) into the last century, which made up the sixth class. Thus the lowest class of the people was excluded from the suffrage in fact, although not in law. As it turned out later, it was decided that, except for certain exceptional cases, suffrage was to be determined by membership in tribes. There were 35 tribes, each of which had a voice, 4 in the city, and 31 in the countryside. The principal citizens, all of whom cultivated land, as a matter of course were entered as members of the tribes in the countryside. The city tribes included all members of the lowest class of the people,[20] which being thus restricted, had little influence. This was regarded as the salvation of the republic. When Fabius returned to the four tribes of the city those members of the lower classes Appius Claudius had distributed among all the others, he received the title, Very Great.[21] The censors examined the condition of the republic every five years, and redistributed the people into tribes so as to prevent the tribunes and other ambitious individuals from dominating the voting, and to prevent even the people from abusing its power.

The government of Rome was admirable. From the time of its creation, its constitution was such that any abuse of power could always be corrected: whether by the spirit of the people, by the force exerted by the senate, or by the authority of certain magistrates.

Carthage perished because when it became necessary to end certain abuses, it would not tolerate even Hannibal himself to correct them. Athens fell because its errors were perceived as pleasant, rather than as calling for corrective action. In our time, those Italian republics that pride themselves on the longevity of their governments should understand that they are in fact remarkable only for the length of time that they have allowed faults to go uncorrected. It must be said that the degree of liberty they enjoy is less than that of the Romans at the time of the decemvirs.[22]

The government of England is more wisely constituted. It contains a body that continually examines the functioning of both the government as a whole and itself.[23] Its errors are such that they never go long uncorrected. Indeed, they are often useful in that they spur the spirit of vigilance in the nation.

In a word, a free government, that is, one always in a state of agitation, cannot survive if it cannot correct its faults by its own laws.[24]

CHAPTER IX
Two Causes of Rome's Downfall[1]

While Rome's domination was limited to Italy, it was easy for the republic to maintain itself. Every soldier was at the same time a citizen; every consul raised an army, and when his successor did so, it was not the same citizens who were called to serve. Since the number of troops was not excessive, care was taken to admit into the militia only those who had enough property to wish to preserve the city's existence.[2] Finally, the senate observed closely the conduct of its generals and thus prevented them from even thinking of any act contrary to their duty.

But when the legions passed beyond the Alps and the sea, the soldiers gradually lost their character as citizens, for they had to be left to fight a number of campaigns in the countries they were subduing. And the generals, as they came to control armies and kingdoms, became aware of their power, and could no longer obey.

The soldiers came to recognize only their general, on whom they placed all their hopes. Rome itself began to recede from their view. They were no longer the soldiers of the republic, but those of Sulla, Marius, Pompey, and Caesar. Rome could no longer know whether he who headed an army or a province was its general or its enemy.

As long as the Roman people was not corrupted by its tribunes, to whom it could grant no more than its own power, the senate could easily defend itself. For its part, its action was constant, whereas the people alternated between the extremes of impetuosity and passivity. But when the people could give its favorites a formidable authority abroad, all the wisdom of the senate became futile, and the republic was lost.

Free states do not endure as long as others. The reason is that their misfortunes and successes both contribute to their loss of liberty, whereas in a state where the people is not free, successes and misfortunes both confirm its servitude. A wise republic should hazard nothing that might make it subject to either good or bad fortune; the only good to which it should aspire is its own indefinite continuance.

If the great size of its empire ruined the republic, the size of the city itself contributed just as much to its downfall.[3]

Rome had conquered the entire universe with the aid of the other Italian peoples, to whom it, at different times, had given a variety of privileges.[4] Most of these peoples were not at first very much concerned about sharing the rights of Roman citizens, and some of them preferred to keep their own usages.[5] But when these rights were those of universal sovereignty, when it became the case that one counted for nothing in the world, in the event that one was not a Roman citizen, whereas one was everything with that title – at that point, the peoples of Italy resolved either to die or to become Romans. Since they were unable to achieve their end by either intrigue or petition, they took up arms. All along the coast of the Ionian sea, they revolted, and the other allies followed them.[6] Forced to fight those who were, so to speak, the hands with which it had put the rest of the universe in chains, Rome was lost. On the point of being reduced to the limits of its own walls, it shared as much of its rights as were demanded with those allies who still remained faithful.[7] Then it gradually accorded the same privileges to all the rest.

Thereafter, Rome was no longer that city distinguished by a people with a single spirit, the same love for liberty, the same hatred of tyranny. The people's jealousy of the senate's power and the prerogatives of the great, had always been mixed with respect; such jealousy came to nothing more than the love of equality. But after the peoples of Italy became Roman citizens, each city brought its own genius, its special interests, and its dependence upon some great protector.[8] The fabric of the city was torn into pieces; it no longer formed an integral whole. Since citizenship was attained only as the result of a fiction, since there were no longer the same magistrates, the same walls, the same gods, temples, and tombs, Rome was no longer viewed with the same eyes, did not inspire the same love of country as in the past; and those modes of feeling that once had been unique to the Romans, ceased to exist.

Ambitious individuals brought to Rome cities, and even nations, to trouble the voting, or to secure it for themselves. The assemblies were now indistinguishable from conspiracies; a troop of men bent on nothing more than sedition was dignified by the title of comitia. The authority of the people, its laws, the people itself –

all these became so chimerical, and anarchy reached such propor-
tions, that it became impossible to know whether the people had
or had not enacted an ordinance.[9]

The historians never tire of repeating that internal divisions ruined Rome.[10] What they fail to see is that these divisions were
necessary, that they had always existed, and should have continued to exist. It was the excessive size of the republic that alone
created the evil, that transformed popular tumults into civil wars.
It was highly necessary that there be internal divisions at Rome.
These warriors, so proud, so audacious, so terrible abroad could
not be very moderate at home. To demand that the citizens of a
free state be audacious in war and timid in peace is to ask for the
impossible. As a general rule, it may be assumed that whenever
everyone is tranquil in a state that calls itself a republic, that state
is no longer free.

What constitutes union in a political body is difficult to determine. True union is a harmony in which all the parts, however
opposed they may appear, concur in attaining the general good of
the society, just as dissonances in music are necessary so that they
may be resolved in an ultimate harmony.[11] Union may exist in a
state where apparently only trouble is to be found, that is, a
harmony that produces happiness, which alone is true peace.[12] It
results from the same sort of process as that of the universe whose
parts are connected by the action of some and the reaction of
others.

But underlying the unanimity of Asiatic despotism,[13] that is,
every government where power is not checked, there is always a
more serious type of division. The tiller of the land, the soldier,
the merchant, the magistrate, the noble are related only in the
sense that some of them oppress the others without meeting any
resistance. If this be union, it can be so not in the sense that
citizens are joined to one another, but rather that sense in which
corpses are united when buried in a mass grave.

It is true that a point was reached when the republic could no
longer be governed by the laws of Rome. But it has always been
the case that those good laws responsible for the expansion of a
small republic, turn out to be a burden once it has succeeded in
expanding far beyond its former bounds.[14] This occurs because the
nature of these original laws was such as to produce a great people,
rather than to govern it.

There is a great difference between good laws and expedient

laws, between those that enable a people to become the master of others, and those that enable it to maintain that power once it has been acquired.

There is at present a virtually unknown republic, which silently and secretly adds to its power daily.[15] It is certain that if it attains that expansion for which its wisdom destines it, that republic will be forced to change its laws. When this happens, it will be due not to the work of a legislator, but to the process of corruption.

Rome was made to grow at the cost of its neighbors, and for that its laws were excellent. Furthermore, no matter what its government, whether under the power of the kings, the aristocracy, or the people, Rome never ceased to engage in enterprises that required skill in the management of great matters. It always succeeded. Its superiority in wisdom over other states was not that of a day, but long-term; it continued to display the same superiority over them in periods of poor, moderate, and great fortune. Rome neither experienced prosperity without profiting to the full; nor misfortunes without turning them to advantage.

Rome lost its liberty because it achieved its distinctive mission (*ouvrage*) too soon.

CHAPTER XVIII
The New Maxims Adopted
by the Romans[1]

Sometimes it was the cowardice of the emperors; often the weakness of the empire that led to attempts to buy off those peoples who threatened invasion.[2] But peace cannot be purchased, for he who has sold it is put into an even better position to force another transaction of the same kind.

It is better to run the risk of a war that will turn out badly than to give money in order to have peace. A ruler will always be respected so long as it is known that he can be conquered only after overcoming formidable resistance.

What is more, such compensations have a way of turning into

the periodical payment of tributes. What is given freely at the beginning, then becomes compulsory, and is regarded as a permanent right. When an emperor refused payment to some people, or wished to reduce what had been given, they became mortal enemies. To take one among a thousand examples, the army Julian had led against the Persians was pursued during its retreat, by Arabs to whom he had refused to pay the customary tribute.[3] After this, during the reign of Valentinian, the Germans were offered presents smaller than those to which they had become accustomed. This angered them, and these northern peoples, who even then put so much store on points of honor, revenged this pretended insult by a cruel war.

All these nations[4] that surrounded the empire in Europe and Asia came to absorb bit by bit the wealth of the Romans. Just as the Romans had grown because all other rulers had brought to them all their gold and silver,[5] so now the Romans dwindled as they sent their gold and silver away.

The errors committed by statesmen are not always due to decisions freely made. Often such errors are but the necessary outcome of an existing situation, and one set of disadvantages leads to further disadvantages.

As has already been seen, the army became a great source of expense to the state. Soldiers had three types of benefits: their pay, their compensation after having served, and other occasional gifts. Often these were converted into rights by military men who held in their hands people and ruler alike.

The impossibility of meeting these expenses led to the search for an army that would cost less. Thus treaties were made with barbarian nations that had neither the luxurious style of life, nor the same spirit, nor the pretensions of the Roman soldiers.

Another advantage of this practice derived from the fact that the barbarians could fall upon a country without warning, since they required no preparations for war. This made it difficult to levy troops in the ordinary way for the defense of the attacked provinces. The Romans would then turn to another body of barbarians, always ready to take money, to pillage, and to fight. For the moment this met the Romans' needs, but subsequently they had as much trouble with their auxiliaries, as with their original enemies.

The early Romans never had armies with more auxiliary troops than Romans.[6] Although their allies were, properly speaking, their subjects, the Romans never cared to have that relationship with any nations more belligerent than they themselves.

But toward the end of their history, they not only failed to maintain this proportion of auxiliary troops, but filled their own ranks with barbarian soldiers.

Thus they established usages quite the contrary of those that had made them masters of the world. Formerly their policy had been to reserve the art of war for themselves, while barring their neighbors from it; at this time they destroyed it among themselves, while establishing it among others.

Here, in a word, is the history of the Romans: by following their original maxims, they conquered all other peoples. But after such success, their republic could no longer be maintained. It became necessary to change the form of government. Their new maxims, contrary to those with which they had begun, were applied to the new form of government. This caused the Romans to fall from their former greatness.

It is not fortune that rules the world. On this point, consult the Romans who enjoyed a series of consecutive successes when their government followed one policy, and an unbroken set of reverses when it adopted another. There are general causes, whether moral or physical, which act upon every monarchy, which advance, maintain, or ruin it. All accidents are subject to these causes. If the chance loss of a battle, that is, a particular cause, ruins a state, there is a general cause that created the situation whereby this state could perish by the loss of a single battle. In a word, the principal trend carries along with it the outcome of all particular accidents.[7]

. . .

The Romans arrived at their domination of other peoples, not only by their command of the art of war, but also by their prudence, wisdom, perseverance, by their love of glory and homeland (*patrie*). After these virtues disappeared under the emperors, the art of war remained.[8] Because of it, the Romans, despite the weakness and tyranny of their rulers, were able to keep what they had acquired earlier. But when corruption made itself felt even in the army, Rome became the prey of all other peoples.

An empire founded by arms must be maintained by arms. But just as it is impossible for its citizens to imagine how a state in trouble can emerge from its plight, so it is impossible for the inhabitants of a state that is at peace and is considered strong to believe that this situation will ever change. Thus the army comes to be neglected. It is thought that from the military, nothing is to be hoped, and everything feared. Hence not infrequently, attempts are even made to weaken it.

It was an inviolable rule of the first Romans that anyone abandoning his post, or leaving behind his arms in combat, was put to death. Julian and Valentinian reestablished ancient practice on this point. But the barbarians in the pay of the Romans were incapable of such discipline. Like the Tartars today, they were accustomed to flee and fight again, to seek pillage rather than honor.[9]

The discipline of the first Romans was such that generals were known to condemn to death their own sons for having won an unauthorized victory. But when the Romans were put into service in the same formations as the barbarians, they contracted that spirit of independence which characterized those nations. The account of Belisarius's wars against the Goths reveals a general whose orders were almost always disobeyed by his subordinates.

Even in the furor of the civil wars, Sulla and Sertorius preferred to perish rather than to do anything that would benefit Mithridates. In later times, whenever a minister or other prominent person thought that the entry of the barbarians into the empire might serve his avarice, vengeance, or ambition, he would offer it to them to ravage.[10]

No states need revenue more than those that are growing weaker. Thus taxes must be increased precisely when there is least capacity to pay them. It was not long before the exaction of taxes in the Roman provinces became intolerable.

The story of these horrible extortions must be read in the pages of Salvian.[11] Pursued by tax-farmers, citizens had no other alternatives than to flee to the barbarians or to offer their own freedom to the first taker.

This serves to explain the patience with which the Gauls submitted to the revolution that established so crushing a distinction as to create two nations: one noble, the other base. When the barbarians attached so many citizens to the soil, that is, made them serfs, they introduced almost no practice any crueler than what had previously existed.[12]

THE SPIRIT OF THE LAWS[1]

Montesquieu's Introduction[1]

The first four books of this work can be understood only by those who note that what I call virtue in republics is the love of one's native land (*la patrie*),[2] that is, the love of equality.[3] Such virtue is neither moral nor Christian, but political. It is the spring that moves republican government, just as honor is the spring that moves monarchy. Thus I have given the name of political virtue to the love of one's *patrie* and of equality. My ideas are new; I have been obliged to find new words, or to give new meanings to old ones. There are those who have failed to grasp this. To me they attribute absurd notions that would be considered revolting in every country in the world, because men in every country seek to be moral.

There is a very great difference between saying that a certain quality, a spiritual state, or virtue, is not the spring that moves a government, and saying that it is nowhere to be found in that government. If I say that this wheel, this cog are not the spring that makes this watch go, does it follow that they are not in the watch? It is so far from being true that the moral and Christian virtues are excluded from monarchy, that there is even place there for political virtue. In a word, honor exists in a republic, although political virtue is its spring; political virtue exists in a monarchy, although honor is its spring.

Finally, the good man (*l'homme de bien*), discussed in Book III, chapter V, is he whose goodness is not Christian, but rather political in the sense I have given.

Such a man loves the laws of his land and is moved to act by them. In this edition, I have put all such matters in a new light by further refining my ideas, and, in most places where I had used the word virtue, the text now reads political virtue.

Preface

If I have given offense by my treatment of any subject among the infinite number discussed in this book, this has not been due to ill will on my part. I am not by nature given to finding fault. Plato thanked Heaven that he was born at the time of Socrates; I am no less grateful for having been born a subject of the government under which I live, for having been so placed that I may obey those whom Heaven has caused me to love.

I request one favor, which I fear may not be granted me: do not judge the work of twenty years on the basis of a single rapid reading; approve or condemn the book as a whole, rather than by a few of its phrases. There is no better way to discover its author's design than through the design of the work he has written.

I began my inquiry by examining men; I have continued to believe that in the infinite diversity of their laws and *moeurs*, they have not been guided only by their fantasies.[1]

I have established certain principles, and seen how easily particular cases fall under them. The histories of all nations are nothing but the consequences of these principles. Every particular law is connected to another, or else derives from a more general law.

When I have had to consult the works of the ancients, I have sought to understand the spirit in which they were written. Otherwise I might have considered as similar cases that in fact differed; I might have missed those differences that separate cases ostensibly similar.

I have derived my principles, not from my prejudices, but from the nature of things.[2]

Many of the truths contained here cannot be understood until the reader sees the chain that connects them to other truths. The more he reflects upon the details, the more he will feel the certainty of the principles. But I have not included every last detail. Who could do so without producing deadly boredom?

The reader will find none of those striking phrases that seem to characterize writing today. For once put into perspective, all such efforts crumble. Usually they are the work of a mind that attacks only one aspect of a problem while ignoring all the rest.

What I write is not intended to censure arrangements established anywhere in the world. Here every nation will find the justification for its maxims. From this follows naturally the conclusion that proposals for change ought to come only from men of such exceptional genius that they can understand everything about the constitution of a state.

Whether the people is enlightened is no small matter. The prejudices of magistrates originate in those of their nation. In times of ignorance, men are untroubled by doubt even when they perpetrate the greatest evils; in times of enlightenment, they tremble even when they do the greatest good. If enlightened, they perceive ancient evils, and the means of correcting them. But they also see what evils may follow from attempts at reform. They allow an evil to continue if they fear that worse would result from attempts to correct it; they leave what is good alone when they doubt that anything better is possible. When such men examine the parts of a state, they do so only to understand the whole better; when they examine all the causes that affect a state, they do so only to learn what results follow from them.

I should consider myself the most fortunate of men if I could provide everyone with new reasons for loving his duties, his country, his laws; if I could make everyone appreciate his good fortune in living in his country, in having his present government, in occupying his present position.

I should consider myself the most fortunate of men if I could aid those who rule to know better what they ought to prescribe; if I could aid those who obey to find new pleasures in their obedience.

I should consider myself most fortunate if I could make it possible for men to cure themselves for their prejudices. By prejudices I mean, not what makes men ignorant of certain things, but what makes them ignorant about themselves.

It is when we seek to instruct others that we can best practice that general virtue which teaches us to love everyone. Man is a flexible being, who in society bows to the thoughts and impressions of others. He is equally capable of learning what is his own true nature once it has been made clear to him; and of losing even his awareness of having a nature, if this knowledge were to be concealed from him.

I have begun and abandoned this work any number of times. On a thousand different occasions, I have taken pages[3] and thrown them to the winds. Every day I have felt my paternal hands fall.[4] I followed my objective, but without forming any fixed plan. I could identify neither rules nor exceptions to them; I found the truth only to lose it. But once I discovered my principles, everything I had been seeking came to me, and in the course of twenty years, I have seen my work begin, grow, advance, and come to its end.

Any success that may be achieved by this book, I must in large part ascribe to the majesty of its subject. Nevertheless, I cannot believe that it contains nothing of genius. I have read what has been written before me by so many of the greatest men of France, England, and Germany. But although filled with admiration, I did not lose courage. I have been able to say along with Correggio,[5] "And I too am a painter."

BOOK I
Laws in General

Chapter I
The Relationship of Laws to Beings of Different Kinds

Laws, in the broadest meaning of the term, are the necessary relations that derive from the nature of things. In this sense all beings have their laws. The Supreme Being[1] has his laws, the material world has its laws, those beings superior in intelligence to man have their laws, animals have their laws, man has his laws.

Some have argued that a blind fatality has produced everything we perceive in the world.[2] But what is more absurd than the contention that a blind fatality could produce intelligent beings?

There is, then, a primordial reason; and laws are the relations between it and the different sorts of being, as well as the relations of these beings to one another.[3]

God's relationship to the universe is both that of Creator and Preserver; the laws He has followed in creation are those He follows in preservation. He acts according to these rules because He knows them; He knows them because He has made them; He has made them because they are related to His wisdom and power.

Since we see that the world, formed by the movement of matter, and lacking intelligence, continues to exist, its movements must be governed by invariable laws. Could another world than this be imagined, it too would have to have constant rules, or else it would be destroyed.

Thus the creation, which might appear to be an arbitrary act, presupposes rules as invariable as the fatality dear to atheists. It would be absurd to say that the Creator could govern the world without these rules, since without them the world would no longer continue to exist.

These rules are in an invariable relation to one another. Between two moving bodies acting upon each other, motion is received, increased, diminished, or lost in proportion to their respective mass and velocity. Every diversity is uniformity; every change, constancy.

Individual intelligent beings may possess some laws of their own making; but they are also subject to other laws in which they have had no part. Before there were intelligent beings, they were possible. Thus relations among them were possible, and consequently, laws as well. Before laws were made, there were relations of possible justice. To say that there is nothing just or unjust other than what is committed or forbidden by positive laws,[4] is the same as saying that before a circle is traced all its radii are not equal.

Hence it must be acknowledged that the relations of equity precede the positive laws that establish them: as, for example, supposing that there were societies of men, it would be right to conform to their laws; supposing that intelligent beings were to receive some benefit from another being, they ought to be grateful for it; supposing that one intelligent being were to create another, the one created ought to remain in that original state of dependence; supposing that one intelligent being were to injure another, he would merit the same in return, and so on.

But the intelligent world is far from being as well governed as the physical world. For although the intelligent world also has its laws that by nature are invariable, it does not follow them without deviation as does the physical world its laws. The reason for this is that individual intelligent beings are limited by their nature, and hence are subject to error. On the other hand, because of their nature, they act by themselves. Thus they do not always observe their original laws, and do not always obey even those they made for themselves.

It is not known whether animals are governed by the general laws of motion or by some particular motion. Be that as it may, their relation to God is no more intimate than the rest of the material world, and what they experience through their senses is useful to them only in the relation they have to themselves or to other beings like themselves.

It is by the attraction of pleasure that they preserve both individual beings and the species to which they belong. Animals have natural laws because they are united by sensation; they do not have positive laws because they are not united by knowledge. Nevertheless, they do not invariably follow their natural laws; these are better observed by vegetables, which have neither knowledge nor sensation.

The animals possess none of our supreme advantage, but they do have some that we lack. Altogether without our hopes, they have none of our fears; subject like us, to death, they are not aware of it; and yet for the most part they preserve themselves better than we do, and do not make such bad use of their passions.

As a physical being, man is, like all other bodies, governed by invariable laws. As an intelligent being, he never ceases violating those laws established by God and changing the others he has himself made. He must guide himself; yet he is a limited being. He is subject to ignorance and error, like all finite intelligences; even the little he knows slips from him. As a creature dominated by sensation, he is subject to a thousand passions. Such a being might at any moment forget his creator; God has reminded man by the laws of religion. Such a being might at any moment forget himself; philosophers have reminded him by the laws of morality. Made to live in society, he might forget his fellows; legislators have recalled him to his duties by political and civil laws.

Chapter II
The Laws of Nature

Prior to all laws mentioned above are the laws of nature, so called because they derive exclusively from the constitution of our being. In order to learn what they are, it is necessary to consider man before the establishment of society.[5] The laws of nature are received in that state.

Among the laws of nature, the first in importance, although not in order, is that which by impressing on our minds the notion of a creator, draws us towards him. In the state of nature, man would have the faculty of knowing before he had acquired knowledge. Clearly, the first ideas conceived by man would not be speculative:

he would concern himself with the preservation of his being before investigating its origins. Such a person would feel only his weakness; his timidity would be very great. If this must be confirmed by reference to experience, consider the wild men[6] who have been found in forests; anything will make them tremble and flee.

In such a state, every man would feel himself an inferior; he could scarcely imagine himself an equal. No one would seek to attack anyone else; peace would be the first law of nature.

It is unreasonable to impute to men, as does Hobbes, the desire to subjugate one another. The idea of sovereignty (*l'empire*) and domination is so complex and depends upon so many other ideas, that it could not be the first to occur to men.

Hobbes asks, "If men are not by nature in a state of war, why are they always armed? Why do they lock their houses?"[7] But does he not attribute to men, before the establishment of society, what could not happen until after its establishment? Only then do they find motives for attacking and defending one another.

To the sense of his weakness, man would soon add that of his needs. Thus another natural law would be that which would prompt him to seek nourishment.

I have said that fear would lead men to flee one another. But encouraged by all the indications that such fear was universally shared, they would soon come together. Besides, they would be drawn by the pleasure felt by one animal when approached by another of the same species. And to this would be added the attractions that have their origin in differences of sex. A third law would follow from their natural inclination for one another.

In addition to whatever men feel originally, they succeed in acquiring knowledge. Thus they possess a second tie that does not exist for other animals. They have, then, another new motive for uniting; the desire to live in society is the fourth law of nature.

Chapter III
Positive Laws

As soon as men are in a state of society, they lose their sense of weakness.[8] The equality that once existed among them comes to an end, and the state of war begins.

As each society comes to feel its strength, this creates a state of war among nations. Within each society, individuals become aware of their strength (*force*), and seek for themselves the major advantages of their society. This creates a state of war among them.

Laws are established among men by these two forms of the state of war. Men may be considered as inhabitants of a planet so large that it necessitates a number of different peoples, which have laws governing their mutual relations. Taken together, they make up the law of nations (*le droit des gens*). Men may be considered as members of a society that ought to be maintained. In this capacity, they have laws dealing with the relationship of those who rule to those who are ruled; this is called public law (*droit politique*).[9] There is still another legal relationship of the citizens to one another; this is civil law (*droit civil*).

The law of nations by its nature [*naturellement*] is founded on the principle that nations, without prejudicing their true interests, in time of peace ought to do one another all the good they can, and in time of war, as little injury as possible.

The object of war is victory; that of victory, conquest; that of conquest, preservation. From this principle and that which precedes it, derive all those rules which make up the law of nations.

All countries (*nations*) have a law of nations. Even the Iroquois, who eat their prisoners, have one.[10] They send and receive ambassadors, they are acquainted with the rights of war and peace. The only trouble with their law of nations is that its principles are false.

In addition to the law of nations, which applies to all societies, each of them has a public law (*droit politique*). Without a government, no society can continue to exist. "The combining of all power held by individuals (*La réunion de toutes les forces particulières*)," as Gravina has well observed, "constitutes what is called the political state (*l'état politique*)."[11]

The common power (*la force générale*) may be in the hands of a single person, or of many. Some have thought that because nature has established the power of the parent, the most natural government is that of a single person.[12] But the example of paternal power proves nothing. For if the power of the father is an argument for rule by a single man, then, in the event of the father's death, the power inherited by his brothers, or after the death of the brothers, the power inherited by their children, is an argument for government by the many. Political power (*puissance politique*) necessarily involves the union of several families.

There is a better way of deciding the extent to which a government is natural, and that is its conformity to the genius of the people for which it was established.

The power of individuals (*les forces particulières*) cannot be united without the conjunction of all their wills. "The union of these wills," as Gravina again observed very justly, "is what is called the civil state (*l'état civil*)."

Law in general is human reason, to the extent that it governs all the peoples of the earth. The political and civil laws of each nation ought to be only particular cases of the application of human reason.[13]

Laws ought to be so appropriate to the people for whom they were made that it would be highly unlikely that the laws of one nation could suit another.

Laws should be relative to the nature and principle of the government that is established, or that one would like to establish. Such a relationship ought to be present, whether they constitute a government as do public laws (*loix politiques*), or maintain a government, as do civil laws (*loix civiles*).

Laws should be relative to the physical characteristics (*au physique*) of the country, to the climate, whether freezing, burning, or temperate; to the quality of the terrain, to its location and extent; to the style of life of its inhabitants, whether farmers, hunters, or shepherds; the laws should be relative to the degree of liberty permitted by the constitution; to the inhabitants' religion, inclinations, riches, number, commerce, mores (*moeurs*), and customs (*manières*).[14] Finally, the laws are related to one another; their origins are related, as is the intent of the legislator, and the order of things on which they were established. They must be considered from all these points of view.

This is what I shall undertake to do in this work. I shall examine all these relationships. Taken together they comprise what is called *The Spirit of the Laws*.

I have in no way distinguished political from civil laws (*les loix politiques des civiles*). For my purpose is to treat not laws, but their spirit. Since that spirit consists of the various relationships that laws may have to things, my concern has been not so much with the natural order of laws, as with these things and their relationships to laws.

First I shall examine those relationships that exist between laws and the nature and principle of each type of government. Since nothing influences the laws more than such principles, I shall take care to clarify them. If I only can establish the principle in each case, the laws will be seen to flow from it, as though the principle were their literal source. Then I shall pass to other relationships, which appear to depend more upon circumstances peculiar to each situation.

BOOK II
Laws that Derive Directly from the Nature of the Government

Chapter I
The Three Types of Government and
Their Respective Natures

The three species of government are republican, monarchial, and despotic. To discover their nature, nothing more is necessary than to inspect the ideas of them held by the uneducated. I presuppose three such definitions, or rather, facts: "in a republican government either the people as a body or else only a part of the people hold the supreme power"; "in a monarchical government a single person governs, but by fixed and established laws"; "in a despotic government, on the contrary, a single man, unrestrained by law or other rules, dominates everything by his will and caprices."[1]

This is what I call the nature of each type of government. Now it is necessary to determine what laws follow directly from this nature, and consequently are primary and fundamental.

Chapter II
Republican Government and the Laws
that Follow from Democracy

Whenever the people as a body holds supreme power in a republic, this is a democracy. Whenever the supreme power is in the hands of one part of the people, this is called an aristocracy.

The people in a democracy is in some respects the monarch; in others, the subject.

It can be the monarch only by casting those votes that are the wills of its members. Then the will of the sovereign is the sovereign himself. Thus the laws fundamental to this type of government are those that establish who is eligible to vote. In a democracy it is crucial to have fixed rules determining how the right to vote is to be given, who is to exercise this power, who is to receive it, and what matters are to be decided by vote. This is just as important as it is to know in a monarchy who is the monarch and how he ought to rule.

Libanius says, "At Athens death was the penalty for any stranger who took part in the assembly of the people."[2] This was because the offender had usurped the right reserved to those participating in sovereignty.

It is essential to fix the number of citizens who may participate in assemblies. Otherwise it would be uncertain whether all the people had spoken, or only one part of it. At Sparta the number was fixed at ten thousand. Rome was destined to rise from insignificance to grandeur, to experience all the vicissitudes of fortune. At one time, almost all its citizens were outside its walls; at another, all Italy and much of the rest of the world were inside them. The number of citizens was never fixed,[3] and this was among the principal causes of its ruin.

The people, which holds the sovereign power, ought itself to do everything it can do well; that which it cannot do well must be done by its ministers.

The people may be said to have ministers only when these have been named by the people itself. Thus it is a maxim fundamental to this type of government that the people must name its ministers, that is, its magistrates.

If monarchies need the direction of a council or senate, the same is even more true of democracies. But if this body is to have the confidence of the people, it must be elected by them. This may be done directly, as did the Athenians; or indirectly, by a magistrate chosen for this purpose by the people, as the Romans did on occasion.

The people is admirably fitted to choose those it is to entrust with some part of its own authority. Then it has only to determine its choice on the basis of things it cannot ignore and facts known to everyone. It knows very well whether someone has fought many battles, and what success he has had in them; it is thus quite capable of electing a general. The people knows when a judge devotes himself to his office, gives general satisfaction, and has never been found corrupt; that is enough for choosing a praetor. The people is impressed by the magnificence or wealth of a citizen; that suffices for choosing an aedile. All such matters involve facts more easily learned in a popular assembly than by a monarch in his palace. But can the people manage a [complicated] matter of state, recognize the times, places, moments of greatest opportunity? No, it cannot.

Anyone doubting the people's natural capacity to discern merit has only to consider that long series of astonishingly good choices made by the Athenians and Romans. Surely these cannot be attributed to chance.

It is a matter of record that the Roman people, although given the right to elect plebeians to office, could never bring itself to do so. Similarly the law of Aristides had permitted the people of Athens to elect magistrates from any class whatever. Yet, Xenophon writes, there never was a case when the lowest part of the people (*le bas peuple*) demanded officers from those classes that might endanger their security or glory.[4]

Just as most citizens who have enough ability to choose others lack enough to be elected themselves, so the people, although capable of calling others to account for their administration, cannot by itself administer the state's business.

This must be carried on at a pace that is neither too fast nor too slow. But the people is either too energetic or insufficiently so. Sometimes with its hundred thousand arms, it overturns everything; sometimes with its hundred thousand feet, it creeps as slowly as so many insects.

In a popular state, the people is always divided into certain classes. The great legislators have distinguished themselves by their skill in making such divisions. These have always determined the duration and prosperity of democracies.

In deciding the composition of classes, Servius Tullius took the spirit of aristocracy as his criterion. In Livy[5] and in Dionysius of Halicarnassus,[6] we see how he put the right of suffrage in the hands of the principal citizens. He had divided the people of Rome into 193 centuries, which formed six classes. The rich, who were fewest, he put into the first centuries; those less rich, who were more numerous, into all the centuries that followed; thus throwing the very poor, who outnumbered all the rest, into the last century. Since each century[7] had but one vote, it was wealth and resources rather than numbers that decided elections.

Solon divided the people of Athens into four classes. In the spirit of democracy, he wished[8] to determine, not those eligible to vote, but those eligible to hold office. Recognizing the right of every citizen to vote, he further permitted members of all four classes to choose judges. But magistrates could be selected only from the first three classes, that is, from those well off.

Fundamental to all republics are the laws that establish who are eligible to vote. No less fundamental is the method of voting itself.

The nature of democracy prescribes voting by lot; that of aristocracy, voting by a choice among candidates.

Voting by lot is a method that offends no particular individual; it gives every citizen a reasonable hope of serving his country.

Yet it contains an inherent defect. The great legislators have all distinguished themselves by the means they have used to minimize the damage done by the lot and to compensate for it.

In Athens, Solon provided that all military positions be selected by choice from among the candidates; that senators and judges be elected by lot.

He decreed that those civil magistrates who had to administer large sums of money should be selected by choice; that all other magistrates be elected by lot.

At the same time he wished to minimize the damage done by the lot. Thus he provided the following rules: only those who presented themselves as candidates could be elected by lot; victors would then be examined by judges;[9] anyone could accuse them of being unworthy to hold office.[10] In this way, he combined the lot with selection by choice among candidates. It was further provided that after a person had finished his term as magistrate, he had to undergo another examination of his conduct in that capacity. Under such conditions, those citizens unqualified for office must have been most reluctant to present themselves as candidates for election by lot.

Likewise fundamental to a democracy is the law determining the conditions for casting ballots. It is of the utmost importance whether balloting is public or secret. In one of the later phases of the Roman Republic laws were enacted that made balloting secret. Cicero wrote[11] that these laws[12] were among the most important causes of the republic's fall. Yet since various republics follow quite different practices, I ought to state here my assessment of them.

There can be no doubt that when the people votes, it should do so in public;[13] this ought to be regarded as another law fundamental to democracy. For it is necessary that the lower classes (*le petit peuple*) be enlightened by those of higher rank, that the precipitous qualities of the lower classes be held in check by the grave example of certain notables. Hence, by making the ballot secret in the Roman Republic, all was lost; it was no longer possible to enlighten the populace when it took the wrong track. The contrary is true when the body of nobles votes in an aristocracy,[14] or when the senate votes in a democracy.[15] Since in both cases it is most important to prevent the rise of intrigues (*les brigues*), there cannot be too much secrecy.

Intrigue in a senate is dangerous; it is no less so in a body composed of nobles. But intrigue is quite another thing for the people, whose nature is to act by passion. In states where the people has no part in government, it can become as passionate about an actor as it would be about public affairs, were it allowed to participate in them. A republic is ruined when there are no more intrigues. This occurs when the people is corrupted by bribery: it then becomes cold and calculating, it becomes absorbed with money and ceases to care about public affairs. Unconcerned with the government and what is proposed to it, the people quietly awaits its payments.

Still another law fundamental to democracy is that the people alone enacts laws. Yet there are a thousand occasions when it is necessary that the senate have the power to legislate. It is frequently appropriate that a law be tried before it is made permanent. On this point, the constitutions of Rome and Athens were excellent. The senate's decrees[16] had the force of laws during the period of a year; they did not become permanent until ratified by the people's consent.

Chapter III
Laws that Follow from the Nature of Aristocracy

In an aristocracy, sovereign power is lodged in the hands of a certain number of persons. These both make laws and carry them out. The rest of the people has no more power in regard to them than do the subjects of a monarchy in regard to their ruler.

Here voting by lot is inappropriate, since it would produce only inconveniences. For this is a government in which the most humiliating distinctions are established by law. Such distinctions could not be made less odious by use of the lot; under an aristocracy, it must always be the nobleman who is envied, and not the magistrate.

When the nobility is numerous, there must be a senate to regulate those matters which the body of nobles is incapable of deciding, as well as to prepare this body for those matters it does decide. In this case, it may be said that aristocracy of a kind resides in the senate, democracy in the body of the nobles, while the people is nothing.

In an aristocracy, it is an excellent idea to raise the people by some indirect means from its position of powerlessness. Thus the bank of St. George at Genoa is in large part administered by the most prominent members of the people.[17] This arrangement gives the people a certain influence upon the government, from which all its prosperity derives.

Senators should not have the right to choose replacements for those seats that are unfilled; such an arrangement would perpetuate abuses. At Rome, which in its early years was a kind of aristocracy, the senate did not fill vacant seats, new members were named by the censors.[18]

In a republic the sudden rise of a citizen to extraordinary power produces monarchy, or more than monarchy. Under monarchical government, the laws have provided for, or been accommodated to the constitution; the very principle of the government checks the ruler. But when a citizen of a republic gains extraordinary power,[19] the damage done is greater, because being unanticipated by the law, there exists no way of checking it.

The exception to this rule comes in cases when a state's constitution is such that it necessitates a magistrate possessing extraordinary power. Such was Rome with its dictators; such is Venice with its state inquisitors. These are terrifying offices designed to restore the state to liberty by violence. But what is the source of the differences between the magistracies of these two republics? It stems from the fact that Rome defended the remains of its aristocracy against the people while Venice employs state inquisitors to maintain its aristocracy against the nobles. It follows that at Rome, the dictatorship could only be of short duration, since there the people acted with impetuosity, rather than cold-blooded calculation. It was necessary that a magistracy of this kind should act in a strikingly impressive way since its purpose was to intimidate, rather than to punish the people. It was also proper that the dictator be created to deal with a particular emergency, and that his unrestricted authority be limited to that alone. For he was elevated to this position only because the situation was altogether unanticipated. Venice, on the contrary, needs a permanent magistracy, for there schemes may be begun, continued, suspended, and resumed; the ambition of a single person becomes that of a family, and the ambition of a single family, that of many. A secret office is needed, since the crimes punished by it are hatched in secrecy and silence. This inquisition has to watch over everyone, for its purpose is not to remedy known disorders, but to prevent even those that are unknown. Finally, the Venetian institution was established to punish suspected crimes; the Roman used threats rather than punishment, even for crimes that were openly avowed.

In all magistracies, it is necessary to compensate for the greatness of a power by the brevity of the office's duration. Most legislators have limited tenure of office to a year: a longer term would be dangerous; a shorter one, contrary to the nature of the function (*chose*). Who would wish to govern in such a way, even in his own domestic affairs? At Ragusa[20] the chief magistrate is changed every month; the other officers, every week; and the governor of the castle, every day. But this can take place only in a small republic[21] bordering upon formidable powers that might easily corrupt such insignificant magistrates.

The best aristocracy is that in which the part of the people which does not share political power is so poor and few in number, that those who do dominate have no interest in oppressing the rest. Antipater[22] established a law that no Athenian with less than two thousand drachmas could vote. In this way, he formed the best possible aristocracy, for this requirement was so small as to exclude very few, and certainly no one of any note.

Aristocratic families, therefore, ought to be, as much as possible, members of the people. The more an aristocracy resembles a democracy, the more perfect it is; the more it resembles a monarchy, the more imperfect.

The most imperfect of all is when that part of the people which obeys is in a state of civil slavery to that part which commands. This is the case with the aristocracy of Poland, where the peasants are slaves to the nobility.

Chapter IV
Laws that Follow from the Nature of Monarchical Government

Intermediary powers, although subordinate to and dependent upon the ruler, constitute the nature of monarchical government, that is, one in which a single person governs by fundamental laws.

These intermediary powers I call subordinate and dependent, for in a monarchy, the ruler is indeed the source of all power, political and civil. These fundamental laws necessarily presuppose intermediary channels through which power flows. For if a state is governed only by the ever-changing and capricious will of a single person, nothing can be fixed, and there can be no fundamental laws.

The most natural of such subordinate intermediary powers is that of the nobility. In a sense, the nobility is one part of the essence of monarchy, whose fundamental maxim is: "without a monarchy, no nobility; without a nobility, no monarchy."[23] There are, of course, despots, but these are something else.

In certain European states, there are those who contemplate the abolition of all judicial functions exercised by those who are lords (*seigneurs*) by feudal tenures.[24] The authors of this proposal have failed to notice that this has already been done by the Parliament of England. Abolish in a monarchy the privileges of the feudal lords, of the clergy, of the nobility, and the cities (*les prérogatives des seigneurs, du clergé, de la noblesse, et des villes*), and you will soon have either a democratic state or a despotism.

For many centuries the courts of a great European state have been striking at the patrimonial jurisdiction of the feudal lords (*seigneurs*) and at the jurisdiction of the church. Without wishing to censure judicial officers of such wisdom, we must nevertheless leave it to the public to decide how much the constitution will be changed as the result of these efforts.

Although far from infatuated with the privileges of the clergy, I should like to see their jurisdiction settled once and for all. The question is not whether they received such jurisdiction rightfully, but whether as a matter of law it belongs to them; whether this jurisdiction is a part of the country's laws, or is subordinate to them; whether between two powers recognized as independent, the conditions should not be reciprocal; and whether it is not equally the duty of a good subject to defend the jurisdiction of the prince and to maintain the limits prescribed upon his authority from time immemorial.

The power of the clergy is as dangerous in a republic, as it is appropriate to a monarchy, especially one verging on despotism. Now that Spain and Portugal have been deprived of their laws, what would become of them, if it were not for the church, which alone checks arbitrary power. The power of the church is good as a barrier when no other is available. Since despotism inflicts the most dreadful evils upon human nature, anything that limits despotism is good. Even an evil may thus be transformed into a benefit.

Just as the ocean, which threatens to inundate the earth, is checked by weeds and the smallest pebbles on its shore, so monarchs, whose power seems unbounded, are checked by the smallest obstacles, and allow their natural pride to be modified by protests and petitions.

In order to increase their liberty, the English have abolished all the intermediary powers that constituted their monarchy. They have good reason to guard their liberty, for were they to lose it, they would become one of the most enslaved peoples on earth.[25]

Mr. Law, because he understood neither the constitution of a republic nor that of a monarchy, was among the greatest promoters of despotism yet seen in Europe.[26] Besides the innovations made by him, so sudden, so unprecedented, so bizarre, he wished to abolish all intermediary ranks and political bodies. He was dissolving[27] the monarchy by his chimerical reimbursements, and seemed intent upon buying up the constitution itself.

In a monarchy, it is not enough to have intermediary ranks; there must also be a body that is a depositary of laws (*un dépôt des lois*).[28] This can only be done by those political bodies that announce laws when they are made and recall them to the public's attention when they are forgotten. The ignorance natural to the nobility, its inattentiveness, its scorn for civil government, all create the need for a body that concerns itself with calling attention to laws that otherwise remain a dead letter. The ruler's council is not an appropriate depositary of laws. By its nature, it is the depositary of the momentary will of the ruler, not of laws fundamental to the constitution. In addition, the ruler's council is always changing; it is neither permanent nor numerous; it does not enjoy the same confidence the people feel for a political body. Hence in difficult times, it is capable neither of enlightening the people, nor of leading them back to proper obedience.

Despotic states, which have no fundamental laws, have no such depositary of laws. This is the reason why religion has so much power in despotic countries. In them it is a kind of depositary and a force working for continuity. If it is not religion that plays that role, it is performed by those customs revered in place of laws.

Chapter V

Laws that Follow from the Nature of the Despotic State

From the nature of despotic power, it follows that the single person who holds it should pass it over to another individual who puts it to use. Anyone whom his five senses inform continually that he is everything, and others, nothing, is naturally lazy, voluptuous, and ignorant. Hence he neglects public affairs. But were he to entrust his power to many others, there would be disputes among them. Each contender would form a cabal to support his claim to be the despot's first slave; the ruler would then have to return to administering the state. It is simpler, therefore, for him to abandon his power to a vizier,[29] whose authority will be the same as his own. The establishment of a vizier is a law fundamental to the despotic state.

It is recorded that a pope, struck by the sense of his own incapacity, made infinite difficulties about agreeing to his election.[30] Finally, he did accept and handed over to his nephew everything that was to be decided. Pleased with himself, he said, "I should never have believed that this office is so easy." The same is true of oriental rulers. They are dumbfounded when first they are placed upon the throne. For they have just emerged from a sort of prison where their eunuchs have enervated their hearts and minds, and often kept them ignorant of even their rank. But once they have chosen a vizier, and have abandoned themselves in their seraglio to the most brutal passions; once they have, in the midst of their slavish court, followed their most stupid caprices; then they can say to themselves that they would never have believed that their office was so easy.

The more an empire grows, the greater becomes its ruler's seraglio, and therefore, the greater his intoxication by its pleasures. Thus it is the rule in such states, that the more peoples to be ruled, the less the despot thinks of government; the greater the matters to be decided, the less he deliberates over them.

BOOK III
The Principles of the Three Governments

Chapter I
What Distinguishes the Nature of a Government from Its Principle

After having examined those laws which follow from the nature of each government, I must turn to those that originate in its principle.

There is this difference[1] between the nature of government and its principle: its nature is what makes it what it is; its principle is what makes it act. The first is its peculiar structure; the second, the human passions that set it in motion.

For laws ought to relate to the principle of each type of government just as much as they do to its nature. Those principles must therefore be investigated. This is what I propose to do in this book.

Chapter II
The Principle of Each Government

I have already stated that the nature of a republican government consists in supreme power being held by either the people as a collective body, or by certain families. The nature of monarchical government is that sovereign power is in the hands of the prince, who, however, exercises it according to established laws. The nature of a despotic government is that a single person rules by his own will and caprice. Nothing more is needed to determine the respective principles of these three types of government; they follow naturally from what has already been said. I shall begin with republican government, and first discuss democracy.

Chapter III

The Principle of Democracy

No great probity is required for the support or maintenance of either a monarchical or despotic government. The force of laws in monarchy and the threat of the prince's power in despotism direct or repress everyone. But in a popular government, still another spring is necessary and that is virtue.

What I have stated here is confirmed by all history and conforms closely to the nature of things. For it is clear that in a monarchy, where he who executes the laws judges himself to be above them, there is less need of virtue than in a democratic government, where the person who executes the laws perceives himself as subject to them, and feels their weight.

It is no less clear that a monarch who, through bad advice or negligence, ceases to execute the laws, may easily remedy this evil; he has only to change his council or himself correct any such negligence. But the state is ruined if the laws are no longer being executed in a democratic government. For this can happen only after the republic has been corrupted.

What a spectacle the English made of themselves in the last century when they attempted with such little success to establish a democracy. The government was continually changing. For those who directed public affairs had no virtue; ambitious, they were irritated by the success of that one person among them who had dared the most.[2] The aspirations of one faction could be restrained only by those of another. The people, astonished, searched for democracy, and found it nowhere. Finally, after many changes, shocks, and reactions, it became necessary to seek refuge by returning to that form of government which had been proscribed.

When Sulla wished to restore liberty to Rome, that city was no longer fit for it.[3] Rome had only the feeble remains of virtue. Since even this continued to diminish, Rome, instead of being awakened by Caesar, Tiberius, Caius Claudius, Nero, and Domitian, became increasingly enslaved.[4] Whatever blows were struck had as their target not tyranny, but one or another tyrant.

Those Greek statesmen who lived under democratic government knew of no support for it other than virtue. Today, statesmen can tell us only of manufacturing, finances, wealth, and even luxury.

When virtue no longer exists, ambition enters those hearts capable of it, and avarice becomes universal. The objects of desire are changed. What once was loved is loved no more: citizens who formerly considered themselves as free because of their laws now wish to be free from them. Every citizen is like a slave in flight from the house of his master. What used to be accepted as a maxim of equity is now called rigor; what once was considered a rule is now called constraint; what once was considered the attention [of the law-abiding] now is called fear.[5] Avarice, which used to mean acquisitiveness now connotes frugality. Formerly, private wealth was the source of public funds; now public funds are treated as the inheritance of private persons. The republic is turned into an empty shell, and its former force is transformed into nothing more than the power of a few citizens and the license of all.

During the period when Athens was so gloriously triumphant, it had no more men under arms than when it suffered the disgrace of being enslaved. Athens had twenty thousand citizens[6] when it defended the Greeks against the Persians, when it contended for empire with Sparta, when it invaded Sicily. It had twenty thousand citizens when Demetrius of Phalereum had them counted,[7] as though they were slaves in a marketplace. When Philip dared to attempt the domination of all Greece,[8] when he appeared at the gates of Athens, it had even then lost nothing but time. Yet we may read in Demosthenes how difficult it was to awaken Athens; it feared Philip, not as the enemy of its liberty, but of its pleasures.[9] This city, which had withstood so many defeats, which had risen again after having been destroyed, was defeated at Chaeronea, and remained so for all time. What good did it do Athens that Philip sent back its prisoners, since they were not really men. Henceforth it would be as easy to triumph over the forces of Athens as it had once been difficult to triumph over its virtue.

How could Carthage have managed to maintain itself? When Hannibal, after having been made praetor, attempted to keep the magistrates from plundering the republic, they complained about him to the Romans. What a wretched people! They wished to be citizens, but not to share the burdens of a state. They were willing to receive title to their riches from the hands of those who would destroy them. Soon Rome insisted upon having three hundred of the principal citizens as hostages; next it obliged Carthage to surrender its arms and ships; finally Rome declared war. From what Carthage did in despair when disarmed[10] can be inferred what it might have achieved with its virtue at the time when it still had all its forces.

Chapter IV

The Principle of Aristocracy

An aristocratic government requires virtue, as is the case in a democracy. But it is true that virtue is not so much an absolute prerequisite of aristocracy as of democracy.

In an aristocracy the people, who bear the same relation to the nobility as do subjects to a monarch, is kept in order by laws made by the nobles. The people in an aristocracy, therefore, needs virtue less than the people in a democracy. But how is the nobility to be kept in order? They who are meant to execute the laws against their colleagues, will immediately perceive that they are acting against themselves. From the very nature of the aristocratic constitution, it follows that virtue is necessary in the nobles as a body.

Inherent in an aristocratic government is a certain force unknown to democracy. In an aristocracy, nobles form a body which by exercising its privilege to serve its own special interest, restrains the people. Thus the mere existence of such laws provides sufficient motivation for the nobles to carry them out.

It is as easy for a body of nobles to restrain others, as it is difficult to restrain itself.[11] The nature of the aristocratic constitution is such, that it seems both to subject the nobles to the law and to exempt them from it.

For such a body can restrain itself in two ways only: either by a virtue so great that the nobility puts itself in some measure on a level with the people, a step that may lead to the foundation of a great republic; or by a lesser virtue, which consists of a certain type of moderation that makes nobles consider all members of their body approximately equal, a position upon which their preservation depends.

Moderation is, therefore, the very soul of this government, and by this I mean a moderation which derives from virtue, not that which has its origin in the cowardice and indolence of the soul.

Chapter V

Virtue Is Not the Principle of Monarchical Government

In monarchies, when great things are to be done, they are made to depend as little as possible upon virtue. As in the best machines, skill consists of using the smallest possible number of movements, springs, and wheels.

The existence of the monarchical state does not depend upon

love of country, desire for true glory, self-denial, the sacrifice of those interests dearest to us, or upon any of the heroic virtues displayed by the ancients, but known to us only by the accounts of them we have heard.

In monarchy, laws replace all the virtues, which are here superfluous. The state excuses you from any obligation to be virtuous; in its eyes an action committed without anyone noticing it, in a sense has no legal consequences.

Although by their nature all crimes are public, nevertheless a distinction is generally made between those crimes which are truly public and those crimes which are private, and are so called because they damage an individual more than the whole of society.

For in republics, private crimes are more public; that is, they violate the constitution of the state more than the interests of individuals. In monarchies, public crimes are more private; that is, they violate the interests of individuals more than the constitution of the state itself.

I beg my readers not to be offended by what I have said here, for I am but following all the histories. I know very well that virtuous princes are not rare; what I have said is that in a monarchy it is extremely difficult for the people to be virtuous.[12]

Historians of all ages have reached the same conclusion about monarchs' courts; it should be remembered that peoples everywhere have agreed that courtiers have a wretched character. These conclusions are not matters of speculation, but derive from sad experience.

In all times and places, the character of most courtiers has been, I believe, the same: ambition combined with idleness, meanness mixed with pride, the desire of riches without work, aversion to truth, flattery, treason, bad faith, failure to carry out commitments, scorn for all the duties of a citizen, fear of the prince's virtue, the hope that his weakness will prevail, and going even beyond all that, the perpetual ridiculing of virtue. It is unlikely that when the leading men of a state are dishonest, that the rest will be honest; that when deceit is customary for those at the head of the state, that the rest will be satisfied with being dupes.

But what should be done if by chance there should be found among the people, someone unfortunate enough to be honorable (*honnête*)?[13] Cardinal Richelieu, in his *Political Testament*, insinuates that a monarch ought not to employ such a person.[14] So true is it that virtue is not the spring of this form of government! Certainly without being altogether absent, virtue does not move this government.

Chapter VI

What Makes Up for Virtue in Monarchical Government

With all due speed, I hasten to finish this subject, lest I be suspected of writing a satire against monarchical government. This is not the case, for if this form of government lacks one spring, it has another. This is *honor*, the prejudice felt by every person and rank, which replacing the political virtue previously referred to, everywhere acts as its equivalent. In monarchical government, honor may inspire the most glorious actions; it may, when joined to the force of the laws, lead to the proper end of government like virtue itself.

Thus in well-regulated monarchies, while almost everyone is a good citizen, there are but few good men. For to be a good man (*homme de bien*),[15] it is necessary to intend to be so,[16] and to love the state more for itself than for any personal advantages it may produce.

Chapter VII

The Principle of Monarchy

A monarchical government presupposes, as has been said, distinctions, ranks, and even a nobility based on birth. The nature of honor is to demand privileges and distinctions; it, therefore, by its very nature, belongs to this form of government.

In a republic, ambition is pernicious. In a monarchy it has good effects; it gives life to that type of government. Its advantage lies in that it is not dangerous, because a monarchy can continue to restrain it.

This form of government may be said to resemble the system of the universe itself, in which there is a force that constantly pushes all bodies away from the center, and a power of gravitation that attracts these bodies to it. Honor sets all the parts of the body politic in motion, and by its very action connects them; thus every individual moves towards the public good, while he has been thinking only of promoting his own interests.

It is true that, philosophically speaking, it is a false honor that links all the parts of the state. But even this false honor is as useful to the public as true honor could possibly be to private persons.

The power of honor can be seen from the fact that it obliges men to perform the most difficult actions, requires fortitude as well, and this without any other compensation than that of glory.

Chapter VIII
Honor Is Not the Principle of Despotic States

Honor is in no way the principle of despotic states. Since in them all men are equal, no one may be preferred to any other. Since all men are slaves, no distinction may be made among them.

Besides, honor has its own laws and rules, which it cannot compromise; it is determined by its own caprice and cannot accept the caprice of another. Hence honor is found only in those states where the constitution is fixed, and which has known laws.

How could a despot permit honor? Honor depends upon scorning life; the despot has power only because he can deprive men of life. How could honor tolerate the despot? Honor has fixed rules and even its caprices are regularized; the despot has no rule, and his caprices destroy all others.

Honor, unknown in despotic states where often there is not even a word to express it,[17] is the prevailing principle of monarchies. There it gives life to the whole body politic, to the laws, and even to the virtues.

Chapter IX
The Principle of Despotic Government

A republic requires virtue; a monarchy, honor; a despotic government, fear. There, virtue is not at all necessary; honor, dangerous.

In it the immense power of the ruler passes in its entirety to those to whom he confides it. Men capable of setting a high value on themselves would be equally capable of making revolutions. It is necessary, therefore, that fear destroy courage, and wipe out even the most modest ambitions.

A government where power is checked can, to the extent that it wishes, relax its springs without any danger. It maintains itself by its laws and by its own strength. But in a despotic government, when the prince momentarily relaxes his threatened use of force; when he momentarily is deprived of the capacity to wipe out all those who hold positions of leadership,[18] all is lost. For the spring of government, fear, no longer exists, and the people no longer have a protector.

Apparently it was for this reason that the cadis[19] held that whenever the grand seigneur limited his own authority by word or oath, he was not obliged to observe it.[20]

Under despotism, it is necessary that the people be judged by laws and the notables by the caprice of the prince, so that the head of the lowest subject be safe and the pasha's head always in danger.[21] Such governments are so monstrous that it is impossible to discuss them without horror. The sophi of Persia, dethroned in our time by Merveis, saw his regime ruined even before that conquest, because he had not shed enough blood.[22]

History tells us that the horrible cruelties of Domitian so terrified his governors, that the people were able to reestablish themselves somewhat during his reign.[23] It is in this way that a flood which overflows one side of the countryside, leaves untouched fields on the other side, where the eye can see fine meadows from afar.[24]

Chapter X
Differences in Obedience to Moderate and Despotic Governments

In despotic states the nature of government demands unconditional obedience. Once the will of the ruler is known, it ought to produce its effect as infallibly as that produced when one ball strikes another.

There is no reconciliation, modification, accommodation, coming to terms, seeking equivalents, no conferences, discussions, remonstrances, no consideration of proposals for something different but equal or better [to what has been decided by the ruler]. Here man is a creature who obeys the will of another creature.[25]

Nor is anyone permitted either to express his fear about a future danger, or to excuse his own lack of success by the caprice of fortune. The lot of man, like that of beasts, becomes nothing but instinct, obedience, and punishment.

Under this type of government, it is futile to oppose to the will of the sovereign those sentiments natural to man: respect for one's father, love for children and for women, laws of honor, the state of one's health. Here when an order is received, it must be obeyed immediately.

In Persia, when the king has condemned someone, no one is permitted to mention him again, or to request his pardon. Even if the ruler were drunk or out of his mind, his order must be carried out.[26] For otherwise he would contradict himself, and that the law does not permit. This mode of thought has been characteristic of

Persia in all periods of its history: the order given by Ahasuerus to exterminate the Jews, could not be revoked. Thus it was necessary to give the Jews permission to defend themselves.

Nevertheless, there is one thing which on occasion may oppose the will of the ruler,[27] and that is religion. Men will abandon their parents, they will even kill them, if the ruler so orders; but men will not drink wine even if he wills and orders them to do so. The laws of religion provide the supreme rules because they bind the sovereign as well as his subjects. But the same is not true of the laws of nature; [in despotic government] the prince is no longer considered to be a man.[28]

In monarchical and moderate states, power is limited by its very spring, that is, honor which rules like a monarch over both the king and the people. Here there is no resort to the laws of religion, a courtier would feel himself ridiculous in referring to them. But appeal is constantly made to the laws of honor. From them stem consequent adjustments in obedience to the original command. By its nature honor is capricious; to obey in a state whose principle is honor is to follow such caprices.

Although the mode of obedience is different in these two types of government [monarchy and despotism], power is the same in both. No matter what the direction taken by the ruler, he turns the scale, has his way, and is obeyed. The decisive difference [between these two forms] is that in a monarchy, the prince has been educated, and that his ministers are infinitely more able and experienced in public affairs than their counterparts in a despotic state.

Chapter XI
Reflections on the Preceding Chapters

Such are the respective principles of these three forms of government. What has been said does not imply that in any given republic, virtue in fact exists, but that it ought to. Nor does the previous argument prove that in a given monarchy, honor predominates, any more than fear is invariably the principle of every despotic state. Rather the point is that these principles ought to actuate each of the types of government to which they are appropriate. Otherwise the government will be imperfect.

BOOK IV

The Laws Governing Education[1] in a State Ought to Be Relative to Its Principle of Government

Chapter I

Laws that Govern Education (*Des Lois de l'Education*)

The laws governing education are the first to affect us. Since these laws prepare us to be citizens, every private family ought to be ruled according to the design of that greater family which includes them all.

If the people as a whole is directed by a single principle, so too will be the private families that are its constituent parts. Thus each type of government will have different laws governing education. In monarchies, the object of such laws will be honor; in republics, virtue; in despotism, fear.

Chapter II

Education in Monarchies

In monarchies, education begins, not when children enter those public institutions where they receive instruction, but rather when they enter the world. This is the school called honor, that omnipresent teacher who ought to guide us wherever we go.

It is in the world that we constantly see and hear three things: that our virtues ought to stem from a particular kind of nobility; our *moeurs* from a particular kind of candor; our *manières* from a particular kind of politeness.

The virtues taught in monarchies always depend less upon what one owes to others than upon what one owes to oneself; less upon what draws us toward our fellow-citizens than upon what distinguishes us from them.

In monarchies, men's actions are judged, not by whether they are good, but by whether they appear attractive (*belles*); not by whether they are just, but by whether they appear grand; not by whether they are reasonable, but by whether they appear extraordinary.

Honor operates in such a way that when it deems an action noble, it may just as easily do so as a judge weighing what is legitimate, or as a sophist justifying what has been done.

Honor permits seduction both by those in the grip of love's passion and by those who think only of conquest. This explains why *moeurs* are never so pure in monarchies as in republics.

Honor equally condones deceit by noble characters and by those who deal with matters of great consequence, such as politics, where cunning is not counted against those practicing it.

Nor does honor forbid adulation, except when its object does not possess a great fortune, and the person practicing it is aware of his own low status (*basesse*).

As for *moeurs*, I have already said that in monarchies, education produces a certain kind of candor. Thus truth in conversation is esteemed. But is this for the sake of truth? Not at all. Truth is esteemed because those who speak it produce the impression of being bold and free. Such a person appears to care only whether matters are as he has stated, and to be indifferent about the effect of his statement.

This is why appreciation for this sort of candor is directly related to contempt for the sort practiced by the people, who esteem only truth and simplicity.

Finally, education in monarchies requires a certain politeness of *manières*. Men, who are born to live together, are also born to please one another. Anyone who altogether neglected the social proprieties would so shock those with whom he lives, would so discredit himself that he could achieve nothing.

But politeness does not usually owe its origin to so pure a source. It arises from the desire to distinguish oneself from others. It is pride that makes us polite; we flatter ourselves by displaying *manières* of a sort that proves we are not of low status, that we have not lived with that kind of person who has always been shunned.

In monarchies, politeness is made an integral part of the ruler's court. One man, excessively great, makes all others small. Hence that regard one owes to everyone; hence that politeness, which flatters those who practice it as much as those who are its object. For such politeness makes it clear that one belongs to the court, or deserves to.

To take on a courtly air is to abandon one's own grandeur in favor of that borrowed grandeur which pleases the courtier more. A courtly air gives him a certain disdainful modesty that produces a considerable effect. Yet the courtier's pride diminishes imperceptibly in proportion to the distance separating him from the source of his greatness.

At court there is a delicacy of taste that extends to everything, a delicacy that comes from the constant use of the superfluities made possible by a great fortune, from the variety of pleasures, and the fatigue they produce; from the multiplicity, the very confusion of caprices, which have only to be thought agreeable to assure their acceptance.

These are the things with which education operates in order to produce what is called a man of honor (*l'honnête homme*), who possesses all the qualities, all the virtues requisite in this form of government.[2]

In monarchy, honor is everywhere inescapable. It affects every mode of thought and every mode of feeling; it directs even the principles of action.

This bizarre sense of honor defines both the content and form of the virtues; it adds rules of its own invention to all those already prescribed to us. It extends or limits our duties according to its own whim, without regard to whether these duties derive from religion, politics, or morality.

Nothing in a monarchy comes before those prescriptions of the laws, religion, and honor which mandate obedience to whatever the ruler may will. Yet this same principle of honor dictates that the ruler ought never to command any action that would dishonor us, and this because to do so would make us incapable of serving him.

Designated to assassinate the duke of Guise, Crillon instead offered his services to Henry III for open combat against the duke. After the massacre at St. Bartholomew, Charles IX ordered the governors of every province in France to massacre the Huguenots. Vicomte d'Orte, the commander at Bayonne, wrote to the king:[3] "Sire, among the inhabitants of this city and the soldiers stationed here, I could not find even one who was willing to act as executioner. These are good citizens and brave soldiers. They and I beseech your majesty to make use of our arms and lives in matters to which we can apply ourselves." Such great and generous courage excluded as impossible the performance of so base an act.

Nothing is recommended more highly to the nobility by honor than to serve their monarch in war. And, indeed, this is in their eyes, the most distinguished profession, because its dangers, its successes, and even its misfortunes are the road to grandeur. Yet even in prescribing this, honor insists upon applying its own law to whatever cases may arise. If honor is affronted, then it demands or permits withdrawal [from making war].

Honor requires that those subject to it regard themselves as under no obligation either to accept office or to refuse it. And honor places this liberty above [material] fortune.

Thus honor has its supreme laws, to which education is obliged to conform.[4] Foremost among them are the requirements that we may set a value upon our fortunes, but are forbidden absolutely to set any upon our lives.

The second is that, once we have been raised to a rank, we should never do or permit anything that might seem to suggest that we regard ourselves as inferior to that rank.

The third is that those things prohibited by honor are most rigorously forbidden when the laws do not make similar provision; and that those things demanded by honor are most insisted upon when the laws are silent.

Chapter III

Education under Despotic Government

Just as the purpose of education in monarchies is to ennoble men's hearts, so its purpose in despotic states is to debase them. In despotic states education must be servile. Even those holding power benefit from such an education, for no one can be a tyrant without at the same time being a slave.

Absolute obedience presupposes ignorance in the person who obeys; ignorance is presupposed as well in the person who commands. For he need not deliberate, doubt, or reason; he has only to will.

In despotic states, each house is a government apart. Education, which [elsewhere] comes from living with others, is here very restricted: all it does is to put fear into mens' hearts, and to acquaint them with a few, very simple religious principles. Here learning would be dangerous; emulation, fatal. As for the virtues, Aristotle found it impossible to believe that there is any distinctive one that could be achieved by slaves.[5] This would limit greatly the scope of education under despotism.

Thus education is in one sense nonexistent. Everything previously known must be wiped out, so that something may be taught. It is necessary first to make a man into a bad subject in order to create a good slave.

For why should effort go into educating a good citizen, if all that he can do is to share in the public misery? If he loved his country, he would be tempted to collapse the springs of its government. If he did not succeed, he would perish. If he did succeed, he would risk the ruin of himself, his ruler, and his government.

Chapter IV
What Distinguishes the Effects of
Ancient from Modern Education

Most ancient peoples lived under governments that had virtue for their principle. When this existed in its full vigor, they performed actions unknown in our time, and which astound our petty souls.

Their education had another advantage over ours: it was never contradicted. In the last year of his life, Epaminondas said, heard, saw, did the same things as he had done at the age when he had begun his education.

Today we receive three educations, which differ or even conflict: that of our parents, that of our teachers, and that of the world. What the last tells us reverses all the ideas received during the first. In part, this stems from the contrast that exists [in our society] between the obligations of religion and of the actual world. Such a contradiction was unknown to the ancients.

Chapter V
Education in a Republican Government

It is in a republican government that the whole power of education is required. In despotic governments, fear arises spontaneously from threats and punishments; in monarchies, honor is favored by the passions, and favors them in turn, but political virtue is self-renunciation, which is always very painful.

This virtue may be defined as the love of one's country and its laws. Such a love, demanding the constant preference for public over self-interest, is the source of all the subordinate virtues. These come to nothing more than this evaluation of the public interest as the highest good.

Such love is peculiar to democracies. Only in them is government entrusted to every citizen. For government is like everything else in this world: if it is to be preserved, it must first be loved.

No one has ever claimed that kings do not love monarchy or that despots hate despotism.

In republics, everything depends upon establishing such love. To inspire it ought to be the concern of education. The surest means of instilling love of country among children is for their fathers themselves to possess it.

Usually parents are able to pass on their knowledge to their children; they are even better able to pass on their passions.

If that does not occur, this is because the work of the family has been effaced by the impressions received from the world outside.

Young people do not degenerate; this occurs only after grown men have already become corrupt.

[Chapters VI–VIII are omitted.]

BOOK V
The Laws Provided by the Legislator Ought to Be Relative to the Principle of Government

Chapter I
The Idea of This Book

We have just seen that principles of education ought to be relative to the principle of each type of government. The same is true of the laws given to the society as a whole. The relationship between the laws and this principle stretches all the springs of government, and the principle in turn receives new strength from the laws. Thus in physics, an action is always followed by a reaction.

We are going to examine this relationship in each type of government, and shall begin with the republican state, which has virtue as its principle.

Chapter II
What Is Meant by Virtue in a Political State[1]

Virtue in a republic is a very simple thing: it is love of the republic, it is a feeling, and not a consequence of knowledge. Thus in such a state, virtue may inspire the lowliest man as much as the highest. Once the people have acquired good maxims [to guide their conduct], they hold to them longer than those regarded as men of honor (*les honnêtes gens*). Corruption rarely begins with the people. It is often the case that their limited knowledge attaches them all the more strongly to what is already established.

Love of country leads to good mores (*moeurs*); good *moeurs*, to love of country. The less we are able to satisfy our private passions, the more we can devote ourselves to those passions connected with the public good. Why are monks so attached to the rules of their orders? It is because of precisely that aspect of these rules which makes them unendurable. Their rules deprive them of all those things on which passions are usually based; therefore all that is left is their passion for the rules that afflict them. The more austere they are, the more they restrain their natural inclinations; the more intense become those passions left to them.

Chapter III
What Love of the Republic Means in a Democracy

In a democracy, to love the republic is to love democracy; to love democracy is to love equality.

Again, to love democracy is to love frugality. Democracy ought to provide everyone with the same happiness and the same advantages, the same pleasures and the same expectations. This can be done only by frugality on the part of all.

In a democracy, love for equality so limits ambition that the only desire, the only happiness permissible is that of rendering greater services to one's country than do all its other citizens. They cannot all render the same service, but they all have an equal obligation to render what they can. From birth on, one contracts so immense a debt to one's country, that it can never be discharged.

Thus in a democracy, distinctions among citizens are created by the principle of equality, even when citizens are honored for great services already rendered their country, or for their superior talents.

The love of frugality limits the citizen's desire for possessions to concern for providing what is required by his family, and something more for his native land. Riches give a citizen power he cannot use in his own behalf. Were he to do so, he would no longer be an equal. Nor can he enjoy the pleasures that riches will buy, for this would violate equality just as much.

Well-ordered democracies, by establishing frugality within private families, have made possible public expenditures. This was the case with Athens and Rome, where the means for magnificence and excess were created by this very frugality. Just as religion requires purity of those making offerings to the gods, so the laws require frugal *moeurs* of citizens so that they may make their contribution to their native land.

The good sense and happiness of individuals depend to a considerable extent upon their talents and wealth being neither too great nor too small. If a republic by its laws, has formed many such moderate persons, they will be wise, and it will govern itself wisely; because the individuals composing it are happy, it will be very happy.

Chapter IV
How Love of Equality and Frugality Is Inspired

Love of equality and frugality are greatly stimulated by the very existence of these qualities in a society which has established them by law.

In monarchies and despotic states, no one aspires to equality. Not even the idea occurs; everyone aspires to superiority. People of the very lowest rank only wish to rise in order to become masters of others.

The same is true of frugality. It can be loved only by those who practice it. Those corrupted by pleasure will scarcely be those who love the frugal life. Had it been natural and common for them to do so, Alcibiades would not have excited universal admiration.[2] Nor will frugality be loved by those who envy or admire the luxury enjoyed by others. Obsessed by either the wealth of the rich, or the misery of those like themselves, such men detest their own wretched situation. Yet they neither know nor love what could put an end to their discontent.

Thus the maxim is true which holds that if equality and frugality are to be loved in a republic, those virtues must previously have been established by law.

Chapter V
How Laws Establish Equality in a Democracy

Some ancient legislators such as Lycurgus and Romulus, divided up the land equally. This can take place only when a new republic is established, or else when an ancient republic becomes so corrupted that a state of mind develops in which the poor believe themselves obliged to seek, and the rich to accept, such a remedy.

If a legislator, when making a division of this kind, does not at the same time enact laws to support it, then the constitution he has established will be short lived. Inequality will return through the opening left by the law, and the republic will be ruined. . . .

In a democracy, although real equality is the soul of the state, it is nevertheless so difficult to establish that exactitude on this point ought not to be carried to the extreme. It is enough to place citizens by a census[3] within categories that reduce differences or fix them at a given level. After that it must be by specific laws that inequalities are compensated for by taxes imposed upon the rich, and by relief given to the poor. Only moderate wealth can give or suffer such adjustments. Men of great wealth regard as an insult everything not assigned them on the basis of their claims to superiority in power and honor.

Every inequality in democracy ought to be derived from the very nature of democracy and from the principle of equality itself. For example, it may be feared that in a democracy those who need regular work in order to live may be impoverished by serving as a magistrate, or that they might neglect its functions; that artisans might be made too proud, that an excessive number of freed slaves might become more powerful than the original citizens. In such cases, equality among citizens[4] may be denied by democracy for the utility of democracy. But this equality which is denied is only apparent. For a man ruined by his tenure of office will be in a worse condition than other citizens; such a man, obliged to neglect his functions, will reduce other citizens to a condition worse than his own, and so on.

Chapter VI

How Laws Ought to Maintain Frugality in Democracies

In a well-ordered democracy, it is not enough that the shares of land be equal; they must also be small, as was the case with the Romans. "May God forbid," said Curius to his soldiers, "that a citizen regard as small, a piece of land that can feed a man."[5]

Just as equality of wealth supports frugality, so frugality supports equality of wealth. Although different, these two things are so constituted that one cannot continue to exist without the other. Each is at once cause and effect. If one disappears from a democracy, the other always follows it.

It is true that when a democracy is based upon commerce, it may well happen that individuals may have great wealth without corrupting *moeurs*. For the spirit of commerce is accompanied by frugality, economy, moderation, labor, wisdom, tranquillity, order and restraint. It follows that as long as this spirit lasts, the riches produced by it can have no bad effects. But trouble begins when excessive wealth destroys this spirit of commerce. It is then that all at once are created those disorders due to inequality, which up to this time had not been felt.

If the spirit of commerce is to be maintained, the principal citizens must themselves be involved in it; this spirit must exist in pure form, without any compromise with any other; all laws must favor it; and this by the provision that wealth be divided in proportion to increases in commerce. Thus every poor citizen will be taken care of so that he can work on the same basis as all others, while every rich citizen will be reduced to circumstances so moderate that he will have to work if he wishes either to conserve what he has or to add to it.

In a commercial republic, it is wise to have a law of inheritance that provides all children with an equal share in their father's estate. The consequence of this is that however great the father's fortune, his children are always less wealthy than he had been. Thus they are impelled to avoid luxury and to work as hard as he had done. All this applies only to commercial republics; in those of any other kind, the legislator must take quite different measures.[6]

In Greece there were two types of republics: one military, like Sparta; the other, commercial, like Athens. In the first, citizens were not permitted to practice any occupation; in the second, efforts were made to instill a love of work. Solon made it a crime for anyone not to practice an occupation, and required that every citizen account for how he made his living. Indeed, in a well-ordered democracy, whose citizens ought to spend for only the necessities of life, these ought to be available to everyone. Who else could provide them?

Chapter VII
Other Means of Encouraging Democracy's Principle

Not every democracy can divide up its land into equal parts. In some circumstances such an arrangement might be impracticable, dangerous, and even incompatible with the constitution. There is no obligation always to take extreme measures. If in a given democracy, it appears that to divide the land would not preserve the *moeurs*, but would produce the opposite effect, then other means ought to be sought.

If a permanent body is established to regulate *moeurs* and this is a senate recruited on the basis of age, virtue, seriousness, and eminent services, its members, exposed to public view like the images of the gods, will inspire feelings that will penetrate into the hearts of every family.

Above all, this senate must attach itself to ancient institutions in such a way that neither the people nor the magistrates ever abandon them.

As for *moeurs*, there are great advantages in maintaining ancient ways (*coutumes*). Corrupt peoples rarely do great things; they seldom establish societies, found cities, create laws. On the contrary, only a people of simple and austere *moeurs* can establish such institutions. Hence it is usually the case that to remind men of their ancient maxims is the way to restore them to virtue.

Besides, even if some change (*révolution*) has occurred and the state has been given a new form, this was made possible only by infinite suffering and labor, qualities seldom found in a society characterized by idleness and corrupt *moeurs*. Those who have made the change wish to enjoy its benefits, and this is not likely to be the case unless they establish good laws. Thus ancient institutions are a consequence of reforms; new governments, of abuses. When a government has long endured, it becomes worse as the result of an almost imperceptible decline; only by great effort can it once again become good. . . .

Nothing contributes more to the maintenance of *moeurs* than the extreme subordination of the young to the old. On both sides, this relationship will produce restraint: the young because of their respect for the old; the old because of their respect for themselves.

Nothing gives more force to laws than the extreme subordination of citizens to public officers. Xenophon wrote:[7] "The great difference separating Sparta from other city-states was due to Lycurgus. His supreme achievement was to make its citizens obey the laws. When summoned by a magistrate, they come running. But at Athens a rich man would be reduced to despair if he thought himself subordinate to a magistrate."

Again, paternal authority is most useful for maintaining *moeurs*. As has already been remarked, in a republic there is no force as repressive as those found in other forms of government. What is lacking must be supplemented by the laws; they do so by the use of paternal authority.

Roman fathers had the power of life and death over their children;[8] Spartan fathers had the right to punish even other men's children.

When the Roman Republic perished, so too did parental authority. In monarchies where such purity of *moeurs* is not requisite, everyone is subject to the power of the magistrates.

Roman laws, which accustomed the young to being dependent, established a long period of being legally a minor. Perhaps we are wrong to take over this usage. In a monarchy, there is no need for so much constraint.

In a republic, this same subordination might make it necessary, as with the Romans, for the father as long as he lived, to continue as the master of his children's estates. But this is not part of the spirit of monarchy.

Chapter VIII

How, in an Aristocracy, the Laws Ought to Be Relative to the Principle of Government

In an aristocracy, if the people is virtuous, the state will enjoy a prosperity much like that produced by popular government; in this way it will become powerful. But rarely is there much virtue where men's fortunes are as unequal as they are likely to be in aristocracies. Hence the laws must encourage, to the greatest extent possible, a spirit of moderation, and seek to restore that equality which the constitution necessarily removes.

The spirit of moderation is what is called virtue in an aristocracy, where it holds the place of equality in a democratic state.

If the pomp and splendor that surround kings supply a part of their power, modesty and simplicity of *manières* are a source of strength for aristocratic nobles.[9] When they do not insist upon any distinctions, when they mix with the people, dress like them, share pleasures with them, the people forgets its weakness.

Each type of government has its own nature and principle. Thus aristocracy ought not take on the nature and principle of monarchy, which would happen if the nobles were to have personal prerogatives distinct from those of the group (*corps*) to which they belong. Privileges ought to be reserved for the senate; respect ought to be enough for senators.

In aristocratic states, there are two main sources of disorders: excessive inequality between those who govern and those who are governed, and the same degree of inequality among the different members of the ruling group (*corps*). From these two types of inequality arise those hatreds and jealousies which the laws ought to prevent or terminate.

Inequality of the first kind is found principally when the privileges enjoyed by the notables confer honor upon them only by shaming the people. Such was the result of the Roman law forbidding patricians to marry plebians.[10] Its only effect was to make the patricians at once haughtier and more odious. In their harangues, the tribunes made the most of the opportunities thus furnished them.[11]

Such inequality will also be created if the citizens differ in their respective liability to taxes, a situation that may be created in four ways: when the nobles reserve to themselves alone the privilege of paying nothing, when they commit fraud to avoid taxes,[12] when they themselves collect taxes under the pretext of compensation for the positions they hold, and, finally, when they make the people pay tribute [monies] which they share among themselves. This last case is rare. When it does occur, such an aristocracy is the harshest of governments.

During the time that Rome inclined toward aristocracy, it successfully avoided these disadvantages. Magistrates did not receive any compensation from their office. The notables of the republic were taxed like anyone else; they paid even higher taxes; and in some cases, they alone were taxed. Finally, far from dividing among themselves the state revenues, all that they could withdraw from the public treasury, all the wealth that fortune provided them, they distributed to the people, whom they hoped would forgive the notables their honors.[13]

It is a fundamental maxim that public gifts to the people are as pernicious in a democracy as they are beneficial in an aristocracy. In a democracy, they destroy the spirit of the citizen; in an aristocracy, they restore it to him.

If no revenues are distributed to the people, they must at least be convinced that such funds are well administered. To allow the people to see the results of public taxation is to allow them to enjoy its benefits. That golden chain displayed in Venice, the wealth carried in Roman triumphs, the treasures guarded in the temple of Saturn, were truly the riches of the people.

In an aristocracy, it is above all essential that the nobles do not themselves levy taxes. In the Roman state, the first order never became involved with raising taxes; instead it made the second order responsible for doing so. In time even this had great disadvantages. Were the nobles to raise taxes in an aristocracy, all their subjects would be at the mercy of those holding public office. There would be no higher court to check such power. Those nobles appointed to remove abuses would instead profit from them. The nobles would be like those rulers of despotic states who are free to confiscate property whenever it pleases them.

The profits made in this way would soon be regarded as a family heritage which avarice could increase at pleasure. The collection of taxes would fall off; the public revenues would be reduced to nothing. It is in this way that some states, without receiving any visible setbacks, have been so weakened as to surprise their neighbors and astound their own citizens.

[In an aristocracy], nobles should be forbidden to engage in commerce. With their unlimited credit, they would create all sorts of monopolies. Commerce is a profession of men on equal terms. The worst of despotic states is that in which the ruler is a merchant.

The laws of Venice[14] forbid nobles from engaging in commerce, which might bring them, however innocently, exorbitant wealth.

The laws ought to make use of the most efficient means to ensure that the nobles render justice to the people. If the nobles have not established a tribune [of the people], they should themselves act as such a tribune.

Every kind of barrier to the execution of the laws is fatal to aristocracy, and tyranny will soon succeed it.

At all times the laws ought to repress that pride which arises from domination. There must be, once and for all, a magistrate capable of putting fear into the hearts of the nobles, as did the ephors in Sparta and the state inquisitors in Venice, both of which were offices bound by no set procedures. This type of government needs to have violent means at its disposal. A mouth made of stone[15] is open to any informer in Venice. It might be called the mouth of tyranny itself.

Such tyrannical officers in an aristocracy resemble censors in a democracy, who, by the nature of their office, are no less independent. In fact, censors must never be liable for the actions they have taken during their tenure of office, for they must always be given confidence, and never discouraged. In this regard the Romans were admirable. All other magistrates might be required to justify their official conduct,[16] but never censors.[17]

Two things are pernicious in an aristocracy: either extreme poverty or extreme wealth on the part of the nobles. To prevent their becoming poor, it is above all necessary to compel them to pay their debts without delay. In order to keep their wealth at a moderate level, wise and subtle precautions must be taken, not confiscations (agrarian laws, abolition of all debts), which are the source of endless evils. . . .

Finally, the laws must not recognize the distinctions created by vanity among families on the pretext that some of them are more noble or ancient. All such matters must be relegated to the status of petty squabbles among individuals.

Sparta ordered all such things well. Even the most cursory inspection will reveal how the ephors were able to overcome the weaknesses of the kings, the notables, and the people.

Chapter IX

How, in a Monarchy, Laws Ought to Be
Relative to Its Principle

Since honor is the principle of this type of government, the laws ought to be related to it.

They must operate in such a way as to support that nobility, of which honor is, so to speak, both the child and father.

They must make the nobility hereditary, not to serve as the boundary between the power of the ruler and the weakness of the people, but as the tie that binds them together. . . .

All these privileges must be peculiar to the nobility, and must never pass to the people. Otherwise the principle of government will be violated and the power of the nobility will be reduced to that of the people.

The laws must favor every kind of commerce compatible with the constitution,[18] so that the people, without ruining themselves, may satisfy the never-ending wants of the king and his court.

The laws must regulate the collection of taxes, so that this does not become more of a burden than the taxes themselves.

The first result of heavy taxes is additional labor, then comes exhaustion, and, finally, a spirit of indolence.

Chapter X
Prompt Action in Monarchies

Monarchical government has one great advantage over republican: since public business is guided by a single person, the executive power can operate more speedily. But since speed can degenerate into haste, the laws ought to impose some delay. Laws not only ought to support the nature of each constitution, but also to provide remedies for those disadvantages which may result from that same nature.

Cardinal Richelieu would have monarchies eliminate those thornlike bodies (*les épines des compagnies*) which make endless difficulties about everything.[19] Even if despotism had not ruled that man's heart, it still would have dominated his thought.

Those bodies which serve as the depositaries of the law never obey better than when they move slowly.[20] It is in this way that they bring to the ruler's affairs that sort of reflection which can scarcely be expected either from courtiers ignorant of the state's laws, or from royal councils which always move too hastily.[21]

What would have become of the finest monarchy in the world if its magistrates had not, by their delays, their complaints and entreaties, limited the exercise of its kings' powers, even when applied to the most virtuous of their causes? For these monarchs, had they consulted only their own generous souls, would have without calculating bestowed excessive rewards upon those who had served them with a similarly uncalculating courage and fidelity.

Chapter XI

The Excellence of Monarchical Government

Monarchical government has one great advantage over the despotic. By its very nature, the monarchy requires that below the ruler there be several orders (*ordres*) which uphold the constitution.[22] Thus the state is made more permanent; the constitution, more stable; and the safety of those who govern, more assured.

Cicero[23] believed that what saved the republic was the establishing of tribunes. "In fact," he said, "there is nothing more terrible than the use of force by a people without a leader. A leader senses that a matter must be resolved by him, and so he takes thought about it. But the people in their impetuosity are unaware of the peril into which they are rushing." This reflection is applicable both to a despotic state, which is a people without tribunes; and to a monarchical state, in which the people may be said to have tribunes.

Indeed it is everywhere obvious that when rebellion occurs in a despotic government, the leaderless people always carry matters as far as they can. The disorders they create are extreme, while in monarchies the opposite is true: matters are seldom carried to excess. The leaders of the intermediary bodies fear for themselves, they are afraid of being abandoned; the intermediate dependent powers[24] do not wish the people to gain too much of an advantage. Rarely are all the orders in a [monarchical] state entirely corrupted. The ruler depends upon these orders for support; the seditious neither wish nor hope to overthrow the state, cannot and will not overthrow the monarch.

In such circumstances, men of wisdom and authority intervene; compromises are made, differences reconciled, corrective measures taken. The laws regain their vigor and once again make themselves heard.

Thus all the histories of our country are full of civil wars, but not revolutions; those of despotic states are full of revolutions, but not civil wars.

Those who have written the history of civil wars in certain states, even those who have fomented them, provide ample proof of how little monarchs have to fear from those [intermediary] groups to whom they entrust the authority necessary to perform their services. Even when they err, such groups aspire to follow both the laws and their duties; and rather than put themselves in the service of the seditious, they restrain the rage and impetuosity of the rebels.[25]

Cardinal Richelieu, recognizing, perhaps, that he had subdued too much the orders that comprise the state, looked instead for support from the virtues of the monarch and his ministers.[26] From them he demanded so much that only an angel could possess so much concentration, wisdom, firmness, and knowledge. It is not likely that from now to the time when monarchies no longer exist, we shall see such a king and such ministers.

Just as a people living under a good civil government are happier than those who wander lawless and leaderless through the forests, so the monarchs who live under the fundamental laws of their state are happier than despots who have nothing of this kind to moderate either the passions of their people or those of their own heart.

Chapter XII
The Same Subject Continued

There is no point in looking for magnanimity in despotic states, for the ruler cannot display a greatness he does not himself possess. Glory is here absent.

It is in monarchies that subjects gather around a king to receive light from him; each of them has, so to speak, more space, and can exercise those virtues which impart to the soul not independence, but grandeur.

Chapter XIII
The Idea of Despotism

When the savages of Louisiana want fruit, they cut down the tree at its base and gather the fruit.[27] Despotic government operates in the same way.

Chapter XIV
How, in a Despotic Government,
the Laws Are Relative to Its Principle

The principle of despotic government is fear. A timid, ignorant, cowed people does not need many laws.

In such a state, everything ought to revolve around two or three ideas. Hence there is no need to add any new ones. When you teach an animal, you take great pains not to let him change his trainer, his task, or his pace. You make an impression upon his brain by two or three movements, and no more.

When the ruler has been confined [to his seraglio] he cannot leave this voluptuous abode without great annoyance to his keepers. They cannot bear to see his person and power pass into hands other than their own. Such a ruler rarely makes war in person, and does not dare even to allow his subordinates to do so for him.

Such a ruler, unaccustomed to encountering any resistance in his palace, is infuriated by anyone taking up arms to oppose him. Thus he is usually dominated by anger or revenge. Besides, he cannot possess any notion of true glory. Under such governments wars are waged with all their natural fury, and in them the law of nations has less scope than elsewhere.

Such a ruler has so many defects that he must be afraid to expose his natural stupidity. If he remains hidden, his true condition will be unknown. Fortunately, in such countries, men are such that they can be governed by nothing more than a name.

When Charles XII was at Bender, he met with some resistance from the Swedish senate. He wrote that he would send one of his boots to rule over it. Had this boot governed, it would have done so in the same way as a despotic king.

If the ruler is a prisoner, he is considered to be dead, and another mounts the throne. Those treaties made by the prisoner are void, his successor will not acknowledge them. Indeed, since he is at once the laws, the state, and the ruler, when he ceases to rule, he is nothing; were he not to be considered dead, the state would be destroyed.

Among the things that most persuaded the Turks to make a separate peace with Peter I was the fact the Muscovites told the vizier that another ruler had been placed on the throne in Sweden.[28]

The preservation of the state is identified with that of the ruler, or rather with the palace to which he is confined. Anything that does not directly menace the palace or the capital city makes no impression on minds so ignorant, arrogant, or prejudiced. They cannot follow, foresee, or even conceive that events are connected. Politics must be very limited, both in its springs and in its laws, and political government be made as simple as civil government.[29]

Everything is reduced to reconciling political and civil government with domestic government, the officers of the state with those of the seraglio.

Such a state is best off when it can regard itself as alone in the world, when it is surrounded by deserts, and separated from peoples it calls barbaric. Since it cannot rely upon its militia, it ought to destroy a part of itself.[30]

Since the principle of despotic government is fear, its goal is tranquillity. But this is not peace; but the silence which falls upon cities about to be occupied by the enemy.

Since strength lies, not in the state, but in the army that founded it, the state cannot defend itself without the army. But this poses a formidable threat to the ruler. How, then, is the security of the state to be reconciled with that of the ruler's person?

Observe how the government of Moscow strives to emerge from despotism, which it finds even more of a burden than does its people. It has suppressed its elite guards, made less severe punishments for crimes, established courts; it has even come to learn what laws are, and to provide instruction for its peoples.[31] But there are causes, particular to this state, which will probably lead it back to the very evil it is seeking to escape.

In these [despotic] states, religion has more influence than anywhere else; it is fear added to fear. The peoples of the Mohammedan empires in part derive from their religion their extraordinary veneration for their rulers.

It is religion that tempers slightly the Turkish constitution. Its subjects, although untouched by any sense of honor that might attach them to the glory and greatness of the state, nevertheless do acquire some attachment to it from the force and principle of religion.

No despotic government damages itself more than one in which the ruler declares himself the owner of all land, and the heir of all his subjects. What results is the complete neglect of agriculture, and, in addition, if the ruler engages in commerce, the ruin of every kind of industry.

In such states, nothing is repaired or improved.[32] Houses are built only to keep alive those who erect them; [irrigation] ditches are not dug, nor trees planted; everything is taken from the land, and nothing returned: the land lies uncultivated, and the whole country is turned into a desert.

Would the avarice and cupidity of the great be diminished by laws abolishing title to ownership of the land and succession to estates? Not at all; rather such laws would stimulate avarice and cruelty. Believing that they possess no property other than that gold and silver which they manage to steal or conceal, the notables are driven to devise a thousand oppressive methods.

What may prevent utter ruin [in a despotic state] is the existence of some usage (*coutume*) that moderates the ruler's avidity. Thus in Turkey, the ruler contents himself with taking three percent of what is inherited[33] by men of the people. Even so, the ruler (*grand seigneur*) bestows most of the land upon his armed forces, and does so in any way his whim dictates. He confiscates everything left by the officers of the empire, and whenever a man dies without male heirs, the ruler receives title to the property, while the female heirs are limited to the income from it. Hence it follows that titles to most of the land are held in the most precarious way.

According to the law of Bantam,[34] the king takes all inheritances, and in them are included the wife, children, and home of the deceased. To evade the cruelest provisions of this law, children must be married off at the age of eight, nine, or ten, or even younger. In this way they can escape the misfortune of being treated as part of their father's estate.

In states without fundamental laws, succession to the throne cannot be fixed. The next wearer of the crown is chosen by the ruler, from either inside or outside his own family. It would be futile to establish by law that the eldest son be the heir; the ruler could always choose someone else. His successor is declared by the ruler himself, by his ministers, or by a civil war. This provides one more reason why a despotic state is more likely to be dissolved than a monarchy.[35]

When every prince of the royal house is eligible for the succession, whoever gains the throne then has his brothers strangled, as in Turkey; blinded, as in Persia; driven mad, as is the custom with the Mongols; or else, if none of these precautions are taken, as in Morocco, the death of a ruler produces a frightful civil war.

According to the constitutions of Moscow,[36] the czar may choose whomever he wishes to succeed him, from either inside or outside the royal family. Such an arrangement causes a thousand revolutions, and makes the throne as insecure as the succession is arbitrary. Since nothing is more important for the people than to know the order of succession, the best principle is that which is most impressive, such as birth or the sequence of births. When matters are so ordered, conspiracies are ended, and ambition stifled; there is no need to dominate the mind of a weak ruler, or to force a dying one to express his choice.

When succession is provided for by a fundamental law, only one prince is heir to the throne, and his brothers have no justification, real or apparent, for disputing his precedence. There no longer is any need to conjecture about the particular preference of the father or to attempt to realize his wishes. Hence there is no longer any question of arresting the king's brother and having him put to death than there is of treating any other subject in this way.

But in despotic states, where the brothers of the king are both his slaves and his rivals, prudence requires that the safety of their persons be safeguarded, especially in Mohammedan countries, where the religion regards victory or success as a judgment of God. Thus no one is sovereign by right, but only in fact.

Ambition is much more inflamed in those states where the princes of the royal line know that if they do not gain the throne they will be imprisoned or put to death. In countries like our own, such princes enjoy a condition that satisfies, if not their ambition, at least their more moderate desires.

The rulers of despotic states have always abused marriage. Usually they take several wives, especially in Asia, that part of the world where despotism has been, as it were, naturalized. They have so many children that they can scarcely have any more affection for them than the children have for one another.

The reigning family resembles the state: it is too weak, while its chief is too powerful; in appearance it is great, but actually it comes to nothing. Artaxerxes[37] put all his children to death for having conspired against him. It is unlikely that fifty children would conspire against their father; it is even less likely that they would have done so simply because he refused to turn over his concubine to his eldest son. It is easier to believe that what was involved was some intrigue typical of the seraglios of the Orient, where cunning, malice, and deceit hidden by darkness, reign in silence; where an old ruler, who becomes more idiotic every day, is the foremost prisoner of his own palace.

After everything that has been said here, it might appear that human nature would never cease rebelling against despotic government. But despite the love men have for liberty, despite their hatred of violence, most of the world's people are subject to despotic rule. That is easily understood. To construct a moderate government requires that powers be combined, regulated, moderated, and set in motion. Ballast must be placed in one power to make it capable of resisting another. This can be done only by a masterpiece of legislation which rarely occurs by chance, and which prudence is seldom given the opportunity to attain. By contrast, [the simplicity] of despotic government is striking and obvious; it is uniform throughout, and since only the passions are required for its establishment, anyone is capable of that.

Chapter XV
The Same Subject Continued

In warm climates, where despotism usually prevails, the passions make themselves felt at an early age, and also are extinguished;[38] the mind develops early; the dangers that arise from dividing fortunes are less acute; there is less possibility for individuals to achieve distinction; less communication between young people confined to their homes; they marry earlier, and hence may be considered adults earlier than in our European climates. In Turkey, boys come of age at fifteen.[39]

[In such climates], there can be no such thing as the handing over of his estate by a bankrupt[40] to satisfy his creditors. Under a government where no one's fortune is assured, loans are made to a person rather than to an estate.

Such handing over of an estate is naturally permitted in moderate governments,[41] and above all, in republics, because of the greater confidence in the probity of its citizens. This is also due to the mildness [of the law] inspired by a form of government that everyone seems to have chosen for himself.

Had the legislators of the Roman Republic recognized such bankruptcy,[42] they would have avoided many seditions and civil discord; they would have had to endure neither the dangers caused by such evils, nor the consequent risks taken in the effort to remedy them.

Poverty and the insecurity of property in despotic states make usury natural. Everyone raises the value of his money in proportion to the danger he sees in lending it. In these unhappy countries, destitution enters from all sides; all resources dry up, including even that of borrowing money.

The result of this is that a merchant cannot undertake large transactions; he lives from day to day. If he orders too great a quantity of merchandise, he would lose more by the interest he would be obliged to pay than he could gain by the sale of the goods. Also, despotic states leave no scope for laws regulating commerce; what passes for such legislation can be reduced to simple maintenance of order.

A government cannot be unjust without putting some power in the hands of its agents; it is impossible that they not profit from their position. Embezzlement is, therefore, natural in such governments.

Since there is nothing unusual about such a crime under despotism, confiscation of property is here a useful instrument. It eases the condition of the people, for the money obtained in this way otherwise would have to be exacted with difficulty by the ruler from his exhausted subjects. Nor is he limited [in his use of confiscation] by any concern for preserving families; none of them matters to such a ruler.

In moderate governments, precisely the opposite is true. Here confiscation of property would make title to property uncertain, it would impoverish innocent children, would destroy an entire family when the actual object in view was to punish a single guilty individual. In republics, confiscations, by depriving a citizen of what he needs to subsist, would have the evil effect of destroying equality, which is the very soul of this type of government.[43]

. . .

Chapter XVI
The Delegation (*Communication*) of Power

In despotic government, when power is passed from one set of hands to another, nothing is held back. The vizier is the despot himself, while every subordinate officer is the vizier. In monarchical government, power is not applied so directly; the monarch, when he delegates his power, moderates it.[44] For when he distributes his authority, he never does so without reserving to himself more than what he gives to others.

Thus in monarchical states, however dependent the governors of cities may be upon the governor of their province, they are even more dependent upon their monarch; however dependent the officers of subordinate units may be upon their general, they are even more so upon the monarch.

In most monarchies, there is the wise and established practice that all those who hold more than a little authority are not permitted to have any connection with the militia. The consequence is that since they derive their authority only from the explicit will of the monarch, who may or may not wish to employ them, they are in one sense in the public service, and in another, not.

This is incompatible with despotic government. For if there were men in such a state, who, although not actually in the government's service, nevertheless held prerogatives and titles, this would make it possible for men to be great on their own account. And this would be contrary to the nature of the government.

If the governor of a city were independent of the pasha, compromises would be constantly necessary if they were to agree. This would be absurd in a despotism. What is more, if such an individual governor were in a position not to obey his pasha, how could this officer be held to answer for his province with his head?

In despotic government, authority cannot be balanced; and this is as true of the most minor magistrate, as of the despot himself. In moderate governments, the law is everywhere reasonable and everywhere known, and thus can be followed even by the magistrates of lowest rank. But under despotism, the law is nothing more than the will of the ruler. Even if the despot were wise, how could a magistrate follow a will unknown to him? He has no choice but to follow his own.

Nor is that all. Since the law is nothing more than what the ruler wills, since he can will only what he knows, there must be an infinite number of people who perform acts of will for him in just the way he himself does.

Finally, since the law is nothing more than what the ruler wishes at any given moment, those who perform acts of will for him must be as unpredictable as he himself.

[Chapter XVII is omitted.]

Chapter XVIII

Rewards Given by the Sovereign

In despotic governments, where, as we have said, no one is moved to act except by hope of the conveniences of life, a ruler who would confer rewards has nothing to give but money. In a monarchy, where honor alone predominates, the ruler would reward only by conferring marks of distinction, were it not for the fact that distinctions of honor cannot be enjoyed without luxury of a kind that creates [expensive] wants. The ruler, therefore, compensates for these wants by granting honors that lead to wealth. But in a republic, where virtue reigns, a motive that suffices by itself and precludes all others, the state provides rewards only by public recognition of virtue.

As a general rule, in either a monarchy or republic, great rewards are a sign of decadence because they prove that the respective principles of these governments have become corrupted. In the first, the idea of honor no longer has any force; in the second, the distinctive virtue of citizens has decayed.

The worst Roman emperors were those who provided the most lavish rewards: for example, Caligula, Claudius, Otho, Nero, Vitellius, Commodus, Heliogabalus, and Caracalla. The best emperors, like Augustus, Vespasian, Antoninus Pius, Marcus Aurelius, and Pertinax, were frugal. Under good emperors, the state returned to its principles; from the treasury of honor came compensation for the lack of other kinds of treasure.

Chapter XIX
The Three Types of Government and Their Respective Principles: Some Further Consequences

I cannot conclude this book without making some further applications of my three principles.
[Two questions are omitted.]

Third Question: Should both civilian and military offices be put into the same hands? In a republic, these offices should be joined; in a monarchy, separated. In a republic, it would be very dangerous to restrict the bearing of arms to a special profession, distinct from those which exercise civilian functions. In a monarchy, it would be no less dangerous to assign these two functions to the same person.

In a republic, a citizen takes up arms only in his capacity as defender of his country and its laws; it is because he is a citizen that he temporarily turns himself into a soldier. If these two roles were separated, anyone under arms who thought of himself as a citizen, would instead be made to feel that he is nothing but a soldier.

In a monarchy, soldiers are interested only in glory, or at the very least, honor or wealth. Civil offices ought never be assigned to such men. On the contrary, they ought to be kept under the control of civilian magistrates. Such an arrangement would prevent the same body of men from gaining the confidence of the people at the same time that they had the power to abuse it.[45]

Consider the example of a nation, which is a republic disguised in the form of a monarchy.[46] That nation fears nothing more than the creation of a separate profession for those who make war. For there the soldier remains always a citizen, or even a magistrate so that these functions may serve as a pledge to their country (*patrie*), and that they may never be forgotten.[47]

Just such a distinction between civilian and military offices was created by the Romans after the fall of the republic. Nor was this arbitrary. It was an effect that came from changing the Roman Constitution; it followed from the nature of monarchical government. And what was only begun by Augustus,[48] subsequent emperors[49] were forced to complete. This was necessary in order to hold military government in check.

This principle was not at all understood by Procopius, when he was competing with Valens for the control of the empire. For at the very time that Procopius conferred upon Hormisdas, a prince of the Persian royal family, the office of proconsul,[50] Procopius restored to that office the power it had once had of supreme command over all troops within its area. Of course Procopius may have had special reasons for doing what he did. [But] a man who is seeking supreme power cares less for the interest of the state than for his own interest.

Fourth Question: Is it appropriate that public offices be sold?[51] In despotic governments, they ought not to be sold, for the ruler must have the power to install or remove his subjects instantaneously.

Such venality of office is good in monarchical states, because it impels men to do as a family profession, what would not be undertaken through the motive of virtue; because it assigns every man his duties, it contributes to the permanence of the orders that comprise the state. Suidas[52] remarked with much justice that Anastasius, by selling all public offices, made the empire into a kind of aristocracy.

Plato[53] could not tolerate such venality. "This is exactly," he wrote, "as though a person were made a pilot or sailor because of his money. Is it possible that this rule should be bad in every other profession in life, but good only for leadership in a republic?" But Plato's concern is with a republic based upon virtue; our concern here is with monarchy. And under this form, chance will supply better choices for office than will the ruler. For in a monarchy, if offices are not put up for sale according to a public procedure, then they will be sold in some other way by courtiers, who at once lack resources and are consumed by avid desires. Thus chance will provide those better fitted for employment than would choice by the ruler. Finally, in a monarchy, this way of advancement through wealth inspires and maintains industriousness,[54] a quality much needed in this type of government.

BOOK VIII
Corruption of Principle in the Three Governments

Chapter I
General Idea of This Book

The corruption of every type of government almost always begins with the corruption of its principles.[1]

Chapter II
Corruption of the Principle of Democracy

The principle of democracy is corrupted in two ways: when a democracy loses the spirit of equality; when the spirit of equality becomes extreme, that is, when everyone wishes to be the equal of those he has chosen to command him. Then the people, no longer capable of enduring the power it has itself delegated, wishes to do everything itself: to replace the senate in deliberation, the magistrates in execution, and the judges in their function.

When this is the case, there can no longer be any virtue in a republic. When the people wishes to exercise the functions of their magistrates, these are no longer respected. When the deliberations of the senate no longer carry any weight, there can be no esteem for its members, and, consequently, for the old. When there is no respect for the old, there can be none for fathers; husbands will receive no deference; masters, no submission. Everyone will come to love such lawlessness; to command will be felt to be as onerous as to obey. Women, children, slaves will submit to no one. There will no longer be any *moeurs*, love of order, or even virtue.

In his "Banquet," Xenophon has given an accurate picture of a republic, the people of which has abused equality. Each guest gives in turn his reason for being pleased with his lot. "I am content," says Charmides, "because I am poor. When I was rich, I had to court false accusers, for I knew well that I was more liable to be harmed by them than the contrary. The republic was always asking some new tax from me, but I never dared go elsewhere. Since I have become poor, I have acquired authority; no one threatens me, rather it is I who threaten others. I can leave or stay, as I wish. Already the rich leave their places so that I may occupy them. Now I am a king, before I was a slave. Once I paid the republic taxes, today it supports me. I no longer fear losing [what I have], but instead live in the hope of acquiring more."[2]

The people fall into such misfortune when those they trust, because they are themselves corrupt, seek to corrupt the people. In order to conceal their own ambition, these [leaders] speak of nothing but the people's greatness; in order to conceal their own avarice, they flatter that of the people.

Corruption will increase both among the corruptors and those who are already corrupted. The people will divide up the public funds among itself. Having added the management of public affairs to its [original] idleness, it now wishes to add luxurious amusements to its poverty. But given its idleness and luxury, nothing but the public treasury will serve its needs.

Nor will it be surprising to see [the people] selling its votes. In order to give anything very much to the people, it is necessary to extort even more. But this can be done only by overthrowing the republic. The greater the apparent advantages derived from its liberty, the nearer approaches the time when [the people] will lose it. There arise petty tyrants who have all the vices of a single tyrant. Soon, not even what remains of liberty can be supported, and a single tyrant emerges. The people lose everything, including the advantages acquired during its corruption.

Thus democracy has to avoid two types of excess: the spirit of inequality, which leads to aristocracy, or to the rule of a single person; and the spirit of extreme inequality, which leads to despotism under one ruler, since such rule always ends with conquest.

It is true that those who corrupted the Greek republics did not always become tyrants. This was because they were more attached to eloquence than to the art of war. In addition, all the Greeks felt an implacable hatred for those who subverted a republican government. It was for this reason that anarchy degenerated into the annihilation [of the state], rather than turning itself into tyranny.

But Syracuse, situated in the midst of many small oligarchies converted into tyrannies,[3] and also possessing a senate[4] almost never mentioned by its historians, suffered from evils far exceeding those usually produced by corruption. This city was always in a state either of license[5] or of oppression. It suffered no less from its liberty than from its servitude, for both would sweep across it like violent storms. Despite its power in relation to other states, even the smallest force exerted by a foreign power was enough to cause its overthrow. The people of Syracuse, which was enormous in population, was always confronted by this cruel alternative: either to choose a tyrant or itself to become one.

Chapter III
The Spirit of Extreme Equality

The spirit of true equality is as far removed from that of extreme equality, as is heaven from earth. The spirit of true equality consists, not in creating a situation in which everyone commands, or in which no one is commanded, but rather in our obeying or commanding only our equals. It does not seek to avoid having a master, but rather to have only its equals as its masters.

It is indeed true that in the state of nature, men were born equal, but they could not remain so. Society makes them lose this equality, and it can be regained only by resort to the use of the laws.

There is this difference between a democracy which is well ordered, and one which is not: in the first, men are equal only as citizens; in the second, they are also equal as magistrates, senators, judges, fathers, husbands, or as masters.

Virtue by its nature is closely allied to liberty, but virtue is no nearer to extreme liberty than it is to servitude.

Chapter IV
Particular Cause of the People's Corruption

When the people contribute much to some great success, they become so proud that they can no longer be led. Jealous of their magistrates, they become jealous of the offices they hold; enemies of those who govern, they extend their enmity to the constitution itself. Thus its victory over the Persians at Salamis corrupted the republic of Athens;[6] thus its defeat of the Athenians ruined the republic of Syracuse.[7]

The republic of Marseilles never experienced such great transitions from subjection to grandeur. It both governed itself wisely and maintained its principles.

Chapter V

Corruption of the Principle of Aristocracy

Corruption occurs in aristocracy when the power of the nobles becomes arbitrary. In this case, there can no longer be any virtue either in governors or in the governed.

When the ruling families observe the laws, this is a monarchy ruled by many monarchs. This arrangement is by its nature very good indeed, for almost all these rulers are linked by the laws. But when the ruling families do not observe the laws, this becomes a despotic state ruled by many despots.

In this case, the republic exists only in regard to the nobles, and applies only to the relationships among them. The governing body is a republic; the body governed, a despotic state. No two bodies could be more divided from each other.

Corruption reaches its extreme point when the power of the nobles is made hereditary,[8] for then it becomes almost impossible for them to be moderate. If the nobles are few, their power increases, but their security decreases. If the nobles are many, their power decreases, but their security increases. When power increases while security diminishes, a point is reached resembling that of the despot, whose power is as excessive as his danger is great.

If there is a large number of nobles in a hereditary aristocracy, the government will be less violent. But since this creates a situation in which little virtue is likely to be found, the nobles will fall into a spirit of nonchalance, idleness, abandon. And this means that the state no longer will have strength or its spring.[9]

If an aristocracy's laws are such that they make the nobles more sensitive to the perils and fatigue of command than to its pleasures, the state can maintain the strength of its essential principle. The same holds true if the state is confronted by a situation in which it has something to fear, so the security can come only from within, while uncertainty threatens from outside.

Since a certain type of confidence constitutes the glory and security of a monarchy, the contrary follows that republics must be in fear of something.[10] Fear of the Persians maintained the laws of Greece. Carthage and Rome intimidated each other, and were each strengthened. It is strange but true that the more security states enjoy, the more easily they become subject to corruption, like water that is too stagnant.

Chapter VI

Corruption of the Principle of Monarchy

As democracies are subverted when the people usurps the functions of the senate, the magistrates, and the judges, so monarchies become corrupted when constituted bodies (*corps*) are gradually deprived of their prerogatives, or towns of their privileges.[11] In such cases, democracies move toward the despotism of all; monarchies, toward the despotism of a single person.

"What destroyed the Ch'in and Sui dynasties," writes a Chinese author, "was the decision of their rulers to depart from the ancient practice of restricting themselves to a general inspection [of how their empires were being governed], the only function worthy of a sovereign, and instead to govern personally without any intermediaries."[12] This Chinese writer here reveals the cause of corruption in almost all monarchies.

Monarchy is lost when a king believes that he better displays his power in transforming the order of things than in conforming to them; when he deprives some of their natural functions and bestows them upon others; when he cares more for his fantasies than for his judgment.

Monarchy is lost when a king, centering everything upon himself, summons the state to his capital, the capital to his court, and the court to his own person.[13]

Finally, monarchy is lost when a king is mistaken about his authority, his situation, and the love of his people, when he does not recognize that a monarch ought to feel secure, just as a despot ought to think himself in danger.

Chapter VII

The Same Subject Continued

The principle of monarchy is corrupted when its supreme honors become but the marks of supreme servitude, when the notables are deprived of the respect rendered them by the people, and made into the vile instruments of arbitrary power.

This principle is corrupted even more when honors have been made incompatible with honor, when it has become possible for men to be rewarded for infamy[14] by the highest honors.

The principle of monarchy is corrupted when the monarch

transforms his justice into severity; when, like the Roman emperors, he wears a Medusa's head on his breast;[15] when he himself assumes that menacing and terrible look which Commodus ordered to be given to statues of himself.[16]

The principle of monarchy is corrupted when extraordinarily base persons become vain about the grandeur surrounding their servitude, when such persons believe that because they owe everything to their ruler, they owe nothing to their native land (*patrie*).

But if it is true (as experience has always shown) that as the monarch's power increases, his security decreases, surely it is high treason against him to corrupt this power to the point of transforming its nature.[17]

Chapter VIII
The Danger of Corrupting the Principle of Monarchical Government

The greatest disadvantage (*l'inconvénient*) occurs, not when a state passes from one moderate form of government to another, as from republic to monarchy, or from monarchy to republic, but when a state falls and is precipitated from a moderate government into despotism.

Most European peoples are still governed by *moeurs*. But if despotism is allowed to become sufficiently severe, either by a prolonged abuse of power, or by a major military conquest, neither *moeurs* nor climate would be able to check it. Thus in this beautiful part of the world, human nature would suffer, at least for some time, those insults inflicted upon it in the other three parts of the earth.[18]

Chapter IX
How the Nobility Is Ready to Defend the Throne

The English nobility buried itself in the debris of the throne while defending Charles I. And earlier when Philip II made the word, liberty familiar to the French, the crown was always supported by that nobility which considered itself bound by honor to obey its king, although it considered sharing power with the people as the ultimate degradation.

The ruling house of Austria has never relaxed its efforts to oppress the Hungarian nobility. Little did that house know how well it would be served by that nobility. That house sought to extort nonexistent wealth from them, but failed to see what sort of men these were. When a number of rulers banded together to divide up the states that had made up the Austrian domain, all its parts remained immobile and powerless, and fell in a heap, so to speak. Only this Hungarian nobility showed any sign of life. It was outraged, forgot all past wrongs, and went to war. For it believed that its glory lay in perishing and in forgiving.[19]

Chapter X

Corruption of the Principle of Despotic Government

The principle of despotic government is in the process of being corrupted because it is corrupt by nature. Other governments perish because accidents occur which violate their respective principles; despotic government is ruined by its own inherent defect when accidents fail to keep its principle from corrupting itself. Despotic government may be maintained only when it is forced to conform to some order, or to submit to some rules by circumstances deriving from climate, religion, from the setting, or genius of its people. Such things constrain its nature without changing it. For its ferocity remains, although tamed for a time.

Chapter XI

The Natural Effects of Principles When Good or Corrupted

Once the principles of a government have been corrupted, the most excellent laws become defective and work against the state; but when its principles are sound, even defective laws produce excellent effects. For the power of the principle overrides everything else.

The Cretans wished to maintain the restraints of law upon their leading magistrates. The device they used was most unusual, that of insurrection. A number of citizens would revolt,[20] put the magistrates to flight, and force them to reenter private life. Such actions were considered to conform to law. Such an institution, prescribing sedition as a means of preventing abuse of power, would seem to be well calculated to destroy any republic whatever. But it had no such effect upon Crete, and for the following reason:[21]

When the ancients wished to cite that people with the greatest love of its native land (*patrie*), they invariably invoked the Cretans. "Native land (*patrie*)," wrote Plato,[22] "a name so dear to the

Cretans." Their term for it was that used by a mother to express the love she feels for her children.[23] For love of native land (*patrie*) corrects everything else.

The laws of Poland also provided for insurrection. But the disadvantages produced by it are ample proof that only the Cretans could use successfully such a remedy.

The efficacy of Greek gymnastics depended in the same way upon the merit of the principle of government. "The Spartans and Cretans," wrote Plato,[24] "inaugurated famous academies of gymnastics, and these were responsible for the great roles played in the world by their respective cities. At first there was fear of immodesty, but this gave way to a recognition of the public utility [of gymnastics]." At the time of Plato, these were indeed admirable institutions,[25] because their object, the art of war, was of the greatest importance. But when the Greeks were no longer actuated by virtue, these academies had pernicious effects even upon the art of war. Now men entered the arena, not for training, but for corruption.[26]

Plutarch tells us[27] that in his time, the Romans believed that such gymnastics were responsible for the servitude into which the Greeks had fallen. Precisely the contrary was true, for it was the servitude of the Greeks that had corrupted gymnastics. At the time of Plutarch,[28] the parks where men fought in the nude, and the games that simulated combat, turned young Greeks into cowards, led them into a sordid love, and made of them nothing but clowns. But at the time of Epaminondas, training in wrestling was responsible for the Theban victory at Leuctra.[29]

There are but few laws that lack merit when a state still is animated by its principles. As Epicurus said of riches: "It is not the liquor which has become corrupted, but the vase that contains it."

Chapter XII
Continuation of the Same Subject

. . .

Once a republic has become corrupted, none of the resultant evils can be put right except by getting rid of the corruption, and restoring the original principles. Any other attempted remedies will be futile, or add to existing evils. While Rome still was faithful to its principles, the monopoly of judges by senators produced no abuses. But after Rome became corrupt, no satisfactory arrangement was possible, no matter what body was entrusted with this function. Senators, knights, public treasurers, taken singly, or in combinations of two or all three together, worked as badly as did any other possible body. Knights had no more virtue than did senators; state treasurers, than knights; nor were these last any better than the centurions.

After the Roman people succeeded in gaining a part in the election of patrician magistrates, it might have seemed probable that those who flattered the people would become the arbiters of government. This did not happen. This same people which had opened up these magistracies to plebeians, always elected patricians. Because it was virtuous, it was magnanimous; because it was free, it disdained power. But after having lost its principles, it became the case that the more power gained by the people, the fewer accommodations it made. This continued to the point where, having become its own tyrant and slave, the people lost the strength of liberty and fell into the weakness of license.

[Chapter XIII is omitted.]

Chapter XIV
How the Slightest Change in the Constitution Ruins Its Principles

Aristotle reports that Carthage was a very well-ordered republic.[30] Polybius tells us that at the time of the Second Punic War,[31] Carthage suffered from the disadvantage of the senate having lost almost all its authority.[32] Livy informs us that when Hannibal returned to Carthage, he found that the magistrates and other principal citizens were turning the public revenues to their own profit, and abusing their authority.[33] Thus the virtue of the magistrates disappeared along with the authority of the senate, for everything flowed from the same principle.

The prodigious effects of the censorate at Rome are well known.[34] Yet the time came when it was felt to be a burden. Nevertheless, it was continued, for the Romans were still in a state of luxury, rather than of corruption. It was Claudius who weakened the censorate and in this way tipped the balance in the direction of corruption. When this occurred, the censorate[35] abolished itself, so to speak. First troubled, then revived when insisted upon, temporarily abandoned, the censorate was entirely inoperative until the time when it became futile, the time, that is, of Augustus and Claudius.

Chapter XV

Those Means Most Efficacious for Preserving the Three Principles

My argument cannot be understood without reference to the four books that follow.

Chapter XVI

The Distinctive Characteristics of a Republic

By its nature a republic has but a small area, otherwise it cannot easily continue to exist. In a large republic, there are large fortunes, and, therefore, but little moderation in the minds of men. Its resources are too considerable to be entrusted to a citizen; interests become increasingly individual. In it, a man may first come to feel that he can be happy, great, glorious without his native land (*patrie*), then that he can only be great standing by himself upon the ruins of his native land (*patrie*).

In a large republic, the common good is sacrificed to any number of other considerations; it is subject to exceptions; it comes to depend upon accidents. In a small republic, the public good is more keenly felt, better known, closer to every citizen; abuses are spread less widely, and consequently, are less tolerated.

What enabled Sparta to endure so long was that after all its wars, it remained within its territory. Its sole end was liberty; the sole advantage of its liberty, glory.

The *esprit* that animated the Greek republics was that of contentment, both with the extent of their territories, and with their laws. Athens became ambitious, and transmitted this spirit to Sparta. But in both cases, their ambition was directed more toward commanding free peoples than slaves; more toward leading than breaking their union. All was lost upon the creation of monarchy, a government characterized by a spirit rather more inclined to expansion of territory.

Except in extraordinary circumstances,[36] only a republican government can last within a single town. The ruler of such a small state will be led by its nature to seek to oppress his subjects because although his power is great, he has but few means either of enjoying it or of making himself respected. Thus he will harry his people. On the other hand, such a ruler might easily be conquered either by a foreign power or even a domestic force. For the people could at any time assemble and unite against him. When the ruler of a town is expelled from it, the contest is over; when a ruler of many towns is expelled from one of them, the contest has only begun.[37]

Chapter XVII
The Distinctive Characteristics of Monarchy

A monarchical state ought to be of moderate size. If it were small, it would be a republic. If it were very large, the notables of the state would have considerable resources of their own. Far from the eyes of the ruler, each of them would have his own court apart from that of the ruler, and would be also protected by both the laws and the *moeurs* against prompt retaliations. Thus the notables might cease to obey because they would have nothing to fear from a punishment at once too slow and too far removed.

Thus Charlemagne had no sooner formed his empire, than he was forced to divide it. A number of smaller kingdoms had to be created, either because those who governed his provinces would not obey him, or because he wished to be in a better position to make them do so.

After the death of Alexander, his empire was divided up. How could the great of Greece and Macedonia obey orders after each of them had been free and independent, or at least commanders of the victorious armies spread over so vast a domain?

After the death of Attila, his empire was dissolved. It had contained so many rulers, who, once freed from constraint, could not again be made to resume their bondage.

Only the immediate establishment of unlimited power can prevent the dissolution of empire. But this is a second catastrophe, as though the initial act of aggrandizement were not enough.

Rivers flow and merge with the sea; monarchies lose themselves in despotism.

[Chapter XVIII is omitted.]

Chapter XIX
The Distinctive Characteristics of Despotism

A great empire presupposes despotic authority on the part of its ruler. Speed in executing his decisions must compensate for the distance separating him from his domains; fear must be used to prevent negligence on the part of the distant governor or magistrate; the law must be concentrated within a single person. And the law must change continually, as those accidents arise which multiply in a state in direct proportion to its size.

Chapter XX
What Follows from the Preceding Chapters

It is natural that small states be governed as republics; those of moderate size, as monarchies; and that great empires be dominated by despots. Thus it follows that if the principles of the existing government are to be preserved, its territorial limits must be limited to its present dimensions. To the extent that the state contracts or expands itself, its spirit will change as well.

Chapter XXI
The Chinese Empire

Before concluding this book, I shall reply to an objection that may be made to everything I have said up to this point.

Our missionaries describe the vast empire of China as an admirable government, which is actuated by a principle that combines fear, honor, and virtue. Thus I may seem to have made a useless distinction when I set out the principles of the three types of government.

I fail to see what honor can mean to peoples who do nothing except when threatened by beatings.[38]

Furthermore, that virtue of which we hear so much from our missionaries diverges greatly from the accounts of our merchants, who can testify to the mandarins' extortions.[39] My authority this time is the great Lord Anson.[40]

Besides, there is the evidence of those letters of Father Parennin, which deal with the proceedings brought by the emperor against certain princes of royal blood who displeased him by their conversion.[41] What these letters reveal is a plan of tyranny followed without deviation, and insults to human nature inflicted according to rule, that is, in cold blood.

In addition, we have the letters of Mairan and the same Father Parennin, which deal with the government of China. After a few rational questions and answers, the mystery is dispelled.

May it not have been the case that our missionaries were deceived by the appearance of order? Impressed by the constant exercise of a single person's will, for they are themselves governed in just this way, they were no less delighted to find [such a government] in the courts of Indian kings. Since the only purpose of the missionaries' visits was to introduce great changes, it is easier for them to convince these princes that they can do whatever they will than to persuade their peoples that they can endure anything.[42]

Finally, even in error, there may be some element of truth. It may be that special, even unique circumstances, cause the Chinese government to be less corrupted than it ought to be. Certain causes, derived for the most part from the nature of the climate, have overcome moral causes in this country, and produced extraordinary results.

The climate in China is unusually favorable to the propagation of the human race. The fecundity of women there is unequaled anywhere else in the world. Even the cruelest tyranny does not put a stop to the increase of population. The ruler cannot say, as did Pharaoh, "Let us oppress them wisely." He is more likely to be reduced to Nero's wish that all mankind should have but one head. Despite tyranny, China, because of the force exerted by its climate, will always continue to be populous, and thus triumph over tyranny.

Like all countries where rice is grown,[43] China is subject to frequent famines. When its people is starving to death, it disperses in order to seek the means of survival. Everywhere bands are formed of three, four, five thieves. Most of them are immediately exterminated; others grow, and then are exterminated in turn. But when there are so many provinces, so distant from one another, some one of these bands may meet with success. It maintains itself, grows stronger, becomes an army, and then marches directly upon the capital, where its leader seizes the throne.

Because of the nature of things, a bad government is here punished immediately. Because so enormous a people lacks subsistence, disorder spreads with great rapidity. In other countries, it is difficult to remedy abuses because their effects are not easily perceived; their rulers are not warned so rapidly or strikingly as in China.

The emperor does not feel, as do our rulers, that if he governs badly, he will be less happy in the life to come, and less powerful and wealthy in this life. The emperor knows that if his government is not good, he will lose both his empire and his life.

Despite the exposure of children, the population of China continues to grow,[44] and an enormous effort is necessary if adequate subsistence is to be produced. This requires incessant attention on the part of the government. Its constant concern is that everyone be able to work without fear of being deprived of what he produces. This government ought to be less civil than domestic.

Here is the origin of these regulations that have been so much discussed. In China there was an attempt to make the laws rule along with despotism. But whatever is joined to despotism loses all strength. When overwhelmed by its misfortunes, this despotism had sought to enchain itself [by laws]. But it armed itself with its chains and became even more terrible.

Thus China is a despotic state, the principle of which is fear.[45] Perhaps, at its beginning, when the empire was not so large, the government was less despotic. But today this is not the case.

BOOK IX
The Relation of Laws to the Power of Defense[1]

Chapter I
How Republics Provide for Their Security

If a republic is small, it will be destroyed by a foreign power; if it is large, it will destroy itself by some internal defect.

Both democracies and aristocracies, whether good or bad, are equally liable to these two disadvantages. The evil is in the thing itself; no form can provide a remedy against it.

Thus it is most likely that men would have been obliged to live forever under the government of a single person, had they not conceived a type of constitution that combines all the internal advantages of republican government with the power of monarchy in foreign affairs. I refer to the federative republic (*la république fédérative*).

This form of government is an agreement by which a number of political units (*plusieurs corps politiques*) consent to become citizens of that larger state they wish to form. This is a society of societies, which constitutes a new one capable of increasing even further by addition of any others that may care to join this union.

It was because of such associations that Greece as a whole was able to flourish so long. It was by such associations that the Romans attacked the rest of the world, and only such associations enabled the rest of the world to withstand Rome. And when Rome attained the high point of its power, it was by associations beyond the Danube and the Rhine, associations created by dread, that the barbarians were able to resist.

It is this form of association that has caused Holland,[2] Germany, and the Swiss leagues to be considered by Europe as republics that will last forever.

In the past, associations of cities were more necessary than they are now. A city that lacked power was exposed to greater dangers. Conquest could deprive it, not only of the executive and legislative powers, as is now the case, but also of everything else that counts as property.[3]

A republic of this kind, capable of resisting force from the outside, can maintain its greatness without internal corruption. The form of such a society forestalls any disadvantage whatever.

Any part attempting to usurp [supreme power] could not succeed to the same extent in all the members of the confederation. If it became too strong in one, this would alarm all the rest. If it subjugated one part, that which remained free could resist with forces independent of those already conquered and could overwhelm the would-be conqueror before it could complete its work.

In the case of an uprising in any one of the federated states, the others could put it down. Were abuses to occur in one part, the others could put it right. Such a state could be destroyed on one flank and not on the other. The confederation could be dissolved while its members remain sovereign.

Because such a state is made up of small republics, it can enjoy good government within each of them while possessing through the power of association all the advantages in foreign relations of large monarchies.

Chapter II
A Confederation Ought to Be Composed of States of the Same Nature, and Is, Above All, Suited to Republics

The Canaanites were destroyed because they were small monarchies that had not formed a confederation to join in common defense. Indeed, the nature of small monarchies is not suited to confederation.

The federative republic of Germany is made up of free cities and small states ruled by princes. Experience demonstrates that as a confederation it is inferior to those of Holland or Switzerland.

The spirit of monarchy is war and aggrandizement; the spirit of republics is peace and moderation. Only by some forced expedient can these two types of government be made to remain together in a federative republic.

. . .

Chapter III
Other Prerequisites of a Federative Republic

In the Dutch republic, no province may form an alliance without the consent of the others. Such a law is excellent and indeed necessary in a federative republic. Because no provision of this kind is to be found in the German constitution, all sorts of misfortunes beset its members because of the imprudence, ambition, or avarice of any one of them. A republic that is united by a political confederation, gives up all powers to that confederation and retains none.

. . .

Chapter IV
How Despotic States Provide for Their Security

Republics provide for their security by uniting, despotic states by separating and then keeping to themselves, so to speak. They sacrifice one part of their country, ravage their frontiers and turn them into deserts. In this way, the heart of the [despotic] empire is made inaccessible.

It is an axiom of geometry that the greater the area of bodies, the less the relative circumference of each. Thus this practice of laying waste frontiers is more tolerable in large states than in those of moderate size.

Such a state damages itself as much as could a cruel enemy. But [it can stop at any time, while] an enemy could not be made to do so.

The despotic state preserves itself by another kind of separation as well. This consists of putting distant provinces in the hands of a ruler who is its vassal. The Mogul, [the king of] Persia, the emperors of China have such arrangements; the Turks are well off because of having put between themselves and their enemies the

Tartars, the Moldavians, the Wallachians, and in the past, the Tran-
sylvanians.

[Chapter V is omitted.]

Chapter VI
Defensive Power of States in General

For a state to exert its full force, its size must be such that the
proper relation exists between the speed with which attacks may
be launched against it and its capacity to take effective counter-
measures. Since the attacker at the beginning can appear on every
side, the defender must be able to meet him at all these points.
Therefore, the size of the state must be of a moderate extent so
that it is in the proper proportion to the speed nature has given to
man to enable him to move from one place to another.

France and Spain have precisely the requisite size. Their forces
can be transported easily from one place to another; armies may
be joined and move rapidly from one frontier to another. Thus
they need not fear those operations which require some time for
their execution.

In France, by admirable good fortune, the distance of the capital from the frontiers is in proportion to their respective weakness.
Thus the monarch can view each part of his country to the extent
that it is exposed to danger.

. . .

The real power of a ruler consists, not so much in his capacity
to conquer, as in the difficulty encountered by anyone seeking to
attack him, in the immutability of his situation, so to speak. But
when states seek to add to their territories, they expose themselves
as never before to attack.

It follows that just as monarchs ought to be wise enough to add
to their power, they ought to be prudent enough to limit it. While
removing the disadvantages of being too small, they ought to be
aware at all times of the disadvantages of great size.

Chapter VII
Reflections

A great prince who ruled for so long a time was often accused by
his enemies of having conceived and put into operation a project

for subjecting all other states.[4] This accusation of seeking universal monarchy was based, rather more, I believe, on their fears than on good reasons. Had he succeeded, nothing would have been more fatal to Europe, to his own traditional subjects, to himself, to his family. Heaven, which knows what is truly advantageous, served him better by [ordaining] his defeats, than it would have done by providing him with victories. Instead of making him the only king in Europe, it did him the greater favor of making him the most powerful.

The subjects of this ruler, when abroad, are never impressed except by what they have left behind at home.[5] When leaving their country, they consider glory as their highest good, but when in distant lands, they view it rather as an obstacle to their return. This people is made distasteful by its good qualities because these seem to be combined with scorn [for all others]. It can bear up under wounds, dangers, exhaustion, but not the loss of its pleasures; it loves nothing as much as gaiety, and can console itself for the loss of a battle if given a derisive song about the commanding general. Such a people could never have persevered in this enterprise [of universal monarchy], which, if unsuccessful once, would have been so for all time.

Chapter VIII
When a State's Power of Defense Is Inferior to Its Offense

It was the lord of Coucy who told King Charles V that, "The English are never weaker, nor more easily conquered than in their own country." The same was said of the Romans, and experienced for themselves by the Carthaginians. And the same fate awaits every power that sends its armies far away in order to reunite by the power of discipline and the armed forces those who are divided among themselves at home by their political or civil interests. The state is weakened by the original disorder which persists, and even more by the remedy for it.

The maxim coined by the lord of Coucy forms an exception to the general rule against undertaking wars in distant countries. And this exception proves the rule because it operates only against those who have themselves violated the rule.

Chapter IX
The Relative Power of States

All grandeur, all force, all power are relative. Care must be taken by any [state] seeking to increase the sum of its grandeur not to diminish it in relation to that possessed by others.

Toward the middle of Louis XIV's reign, France attained the high point of its grandeur, relatively speaking. Germany had not as yet had monarchs as great as those who have since appeared. The same held true of Italy. Scotland and England had not yet been constituted as a single monarchy. Nor had this happened in the case of Spain, where Aragon was still separated from Castile, weakening not only themselves, but also the other parts of Spain, which remained disunited. As for Moscow, it was no better known in Europe than was the Crimea.

Chapter X
Weakness in Neighboring States

A state next to another in decline (*dans sa décadence*) ought to take particular care not to precipitate its neighbor's ruin. For no situation could be more fortunate for a ruler than having a neighbor to receive all the onslaughts and insults of fortune. Rarely does a state in so fortunate a situation add to the sum of its power without losing something relative to that of other states.

BOOK XI
Laws that Comprise Political Liberty: Their Relation to the Constitution

Chapter I
General Conception

I distinguish those laws that comprise political liberty considered in relation to the constitution, from those laws that comprise liberty in relation to the individual citizen. The first type of laws will be the subject of this book; the second will be examined in the next book.

Chapter II
Different Meanings Given to the Word Liberty

No word has been given more different meanings, no word has made such varied impressions upon the minds of men as that of liberty. Some have taken it to mean their capacity to depose at will a person to whom they have given tyrannical power; others to mean the capacity to elect someone they ought to obey; still others to mean the power to bear arms, and thus to be able to use violence; and finally, there are those who understand it as the privilege to be governed only by a man of their own nation, or by their own laws.[1] A certain people believed for a long time that liberty consisted of the privilege of wearing a long beard.[2] Some have reserved the term for one form of government and refused it to all others. Those who had relished republican government claimed that liberty belonged to it alone; the same was done by those who had enjoyed monarchical rule.[3] Finally, everyone has applied to the term, liberty, to that form of government, which conforms to his own customs or inclinations. In a republic, the evils about which one complains are produced by means that are neither evident nor constant, and the laws seem to carry more weight than their executors. Thus liberty is usually considered a characteristic of republics, but not of monarchies. Finally, since in democracies, the people seems to be able to do almost everything it wishes, liberty has been considered a characteristic of that type of government as well. This is to confuse the power of the people with its liberty.

Chapter III
What Liberty Is

It is true that in democracies the people apparently does whatever it wishes. But doing what one wishes is not political liberty. In a state, that is, a society where laws exist, liberty can consist only in being able to do what one ought to will, and in not being constrained to do what one ought not to will.

We must distinguish independence from liberty. Liberty is the right to do everything the law permits. If a citizen could do what the law prohibits, he would no longer possess liberty because all others would have the same power.

Chapter IV
The Same Subject Continued

Neither democracy nor aristocracy is free by nature.[4] Political liberty exists only in those governments where power is moderated (*les gouvernements modérés*). Even in them, liberty is not always found. Political liberty exists only when there is no abuse of power. But all experience proves that every man with power is led to abuse it; he will continue to apply his power until he discovers what are its limits. Indeed, even virtue itself must be kept within bounds.

To prevent the abuse of power, things must be so ordered that power checks power. A constitution may be so framed that no one is compelled to do what is not made obligatory by law, nor forced to abstain from what the law permits.

Chapter V
The Objectives of States

Although all states share the same general objective, which is to preserve themselves, nevertheless each of them has its own particular purpose. Aggrandizement was the objective of Rome; war, of Sparta; religion, of the laws of Israel; commerce, of Marseilles; public tranquillity, of Chinese laws;[5] navigation, of the laws of Rhodes; natural liberty, of savage regimes; in general, the pleasures of the ruler under despotism; the glory of the king and his state under monarchy; the independence of every individual is the objective of Polish legislation, and its consequence, the oppression of all.[6]

There is also a nation that has political liberty as the direct object of its constitution. We shall proceed to examine the principles upon which this nation bases its liberty. If they are sound, then liberty will be reflected there, as in a mirror.

To discover whether political liberty is established by a constitution, requires no great effort. If, once located, it can be recognized, why look further?

Chapter VI
The English Constitution[7]

In every government, there are three sorts of powers: the legislative; the executive, in regard to those matters determined by the laws of nations; and the executive, in regard to those matters determined by the civil law.

By virtue of the first, the ruler or magistrate makes laws, either temporarily, or for all time, as well as correcting or abrogating those already in existence. By virtue of the second, he makes war or peace, sends or receives ambassadors, ensures security, and makes provision against invasion. By virtue of the third power, he punishes crimes, or passes judgment upon disputes arising among individuals. This is called the judicial power; the second, simply the executive power of the state.[8]

For a citizen, political liberty is that tranquillity of mind which derives from his sense of security. Liberty of this kind presupposes a government so ordered that no citizen need fear another.

When both the legislative and executive powers are united in the same person or body of magistrates, there is no liberty. For then it may be feared that the same monarch or senate has made tyrannical laws in order to execute them in a tyrannical way.

Again, there is no liberty, if the power to judge is not separated from the legislative and executive powers. Were the judicial power joined to the legislative, the life and liberty of the citizens would be subject to arbitrary power. For the judge would then be the legislator. Were the judicial power joined to the executive, the judge could acquire enough strength to become an oppressor.[9]

All would be lost if the same man, or the same body, whether composed of notables, nobles, or the people, were to exercise these three powers: that of making laws, that of executing public decisions, and that of judging crimes or disputes arising among individuals.[10]

In most European kingdoms, the government is limited (*modéré*), because the ruler, who possesses the first two powers, leaves the exercise of the third to his subjects. But among the Turks, where all three powers are united in the sultan's person, a frightful despotism prevails.

In the Italian republics, where all three powers are combined, there is less liberty than in our monarchies. What is more, to maintain themselves, these republics require means just as violent as those used by the Turkish government. One proof of this is the state inquisitors;[11] another, the box into which any informer at any time may drop his letter of accusation.

Consider what can happen to a citizen of such republics: the same body of magistrates has, as executor of the laws, all the power it has given itself in its legislative capacity. It can plunder the state by what it decides in general (*ses volontés générales*); and, since it also has the judicial power, it can destroy any individual citizen by what it decides in his particular case (*ses volontés particulières*).

Here all power is united. Although there is none of the external pomp habitual to the despotic ruler, nevertheless such power makes itself felt at every moment.

It is no less true that those rulers who have wished to become despots have always begun by uniting in their own persons all the magistracies (*toutes les magistratures*); and, in the case of many European kings, all the great offices of their state.

I concede that the pure hereditary aristocracy of the Italian republics does not correspond exactly to Asiatic despotism. The number of magistrates sometimes makes the magistracy less severe; not all nobles can always join in the same designs; and the variety of tribunals serve to limit one another. Thus in Venice, it is the Supreme Council that has the legislative power; the *pregardi*, the executive; the *quarantia*, the judicial. But what is most unfortunate derives from the fact that all these tribunals are formed from magistrates who belong to the same social estate (*corps*), which virtually turns them into one and the same power.[12]

The judicial power ought not be given to a permanent senate, but should be exercised by persons drawn from the people as an estate (*corps*)[13] and this at certain times of the year, according to a procedure prescribed by law. The court formed in this way ought to last no longer than necessity requires.

In this way, the judicial power, so terrible to men, becomes, as it were, invisible and of no force (*invisible et nulle*) because it is attached neither to any estate (*état*) nor to any profession.[14] There are no judges constantly in public view; it is the office that is feared, not the individuals who hold it.

Thus it is even necessary that in indictments for grave crimes, the accused, in accordance with the law, should choose his judges, or, at least, be able to challenge enough of them that those remaining may be considered to have been chosen by him.

The other two powers might rather be assigned to magistrates or permanent bodies (*corps*), because their jurisdiction does not extend to any individual. One of these powers is nothing more than the general will (*la volonté générale*) of the state; the other, nothing more than the execution of that general will.[15]

But although the makeup of tribunals ought not to be fixed, the same ought not be true of their judgments, which should be determined only by the precise text of the law.[16] If judgments came to nothing more than the individual opinion of the judge, men would live in society without knowing precisely what were the obligations they had contracted.

The accused ought not to be made to think that he has fallen into the hands of those inclined to do him violence. Thus it is not too much to require that his judges be either of the same rank (*condition*) as himself, or his peers (*pairs*).[17]

If the legislative power allows the executive power the right to imprison those citizens who can provide security for their good behavior, then there is no longer any liberty.[18] This would not be the case if such citizens were arrested in order to bring them to trial without delay under an indictment for a crime defined by law as subject to capital punishment. For then they would really be free, since they would be subject only to the power of the law.

But if the legislative power thinks itself endangered by a secret conspiracy against the state, or by communication with a foreign enemy, then it may for a short and limited time permit the executive power to arrest suspected citizens, who would be losing their liberty temporarily in order to preserve it for all time.[19]

And this is the only reasonable means that may be substituted for the tyrannical magistracy of the ephors and the state inquisitors of Venice, who are also despotic.[20]

In a free state, every man who is considered a free citizen ought to be governed by himself. Hence the people as an estate (*corps*) ought to have the legislative power. However, since that is impossible in large states and subject to many disadvantages in small ones, the people must do by its representatives everything it cannot itself do.

Everyone knows much better the needs of his city than those of other cities; he is a better judge of his neighbors' capacities than those possessed by their other compatriots. Members of the legislative body should not be drawn, therefore, from the nation in general. What is more appropriate is that the inhabitants of every place of importance elect a representative.[21]

The great advantage of representatives is their capacity to discuss public business. For this the people [as a body] are quite unfitted, and this is among the greatest disadvantages of democracy.

It is not at all necessary that representatives, whose constituents have given them general directions, await as well specific directions on each issue, as is done in the diets of Germany. It is true that this way of proceeding would turn the words of deputies into something closer to the voice of the nation. But this would occasion infinite delays and turn every deputy into the master of every other. Thus, in the most urgent circumstances, all the nation's force might be arrested by the caprice of a single person.

Sidney has well observed that when the deputies represent a body or estate of the people (*un corps du peuple*), as in Holland, they ought to be accountable to their constituents. When the deputies represent boroughs (*bourgs*), as in England, the situation is not the same.

In the separate districts, all citizens ought to have the right to choose their representative by election. The only exception concerns those whose condition is so base that they are considered to have no will of their own.[22]

Most ancient republics suffered from this great defect: the people had the right to take decisions involving action (*prendre des résolutions actives*) of a kind that required participating in the subsequent execution of such decisions. And of this they are quite incapable. They should enter into government only to the extent of choosing representatives, something which is very much within their reach. Although few men can assess precisely the qualifications of candidates for office, nevertheless everyone can know in general whether or not the person he chooses is better informed (*éclairé*) than other candidates.

Nor ought the representative body be chosen to take some decision involving executive action by itself (*quelque résolution active*), for which it is not fit. Rather it ought to be chosen to make laws, or to see whether the laws it has already made have been well executed, both matters for which it is very well fitted, and indeed, can be done by no other body.

In every state there are always some people distinguished from the rest by their birth, wealth, or honors. If combined indiscriminately with the people, so that everyone counted equally, such common liberty would constitute slavery [for the distinguished]. Nor would they have any interest in defending this common liberty, because under it most decisions would go against them. Thus their share in legislation ought to be in proportion to the other advantages they enjoy in the state. And this can be assured only when they constitute on the one side, a body (*corps*) that has the right to check the people's actions, and, on the other, when the people have the right to check their actions.[23]

In this way, the power to legislate will be entrusted both to the body of nobles and to the body chosen to represent the people. Each will assemble and deliberate separately; each will have its own views and interests.

As for the three powers mentioned above, the judicial, in a sense, has no force (*est en quelque façon nulle*).[24] This leaves but two. They need a power so constituted that it can limit both of them. This can be done by that part of the legislative body which is composed of nobles, and is very well fitted to produce such an effect.

The body of nobles ought to be hereditary. In the first place, it is so by nature. What is more, it ought to be given a very considerable interest in maintaining its prerogatives, for these by their very existence are enough to provoke hatred and in a free state must always be in danger.

But a power based on hereditary principles may be led to attend to its own special interests and to forget those of the people. Hence in all matters where great profit can be extracted from corruption, as for example, when considering laws raising money, such a body of nobles should participate in legislation, not by its power to make laws, but only by its power to veto them.

What I call the power to make laws (*faculté de statuer*) is the right to ordain by itself (*le droit d'ordonner par soi-même*) and to amend what has been ordained by another. What I call the power to veto (*faculté d'empêcher*) is the right to void a decision taken elsewhere, the power held by Roman tribunes. And although the power to veto may be combined with the right to approve, yet such approval comes to nothing more than the declaration that no use will be made of the veto power. This is, therefore, the source of the other power [to approve].

The executive power ought to be in the hands of a monarch, because this part of government, which almost always requires rapid action, is better administered by one person than by many. On the other hand, whatever is determined by the legislative power is often better decided (*ordonné*) by many than by one.

If there were no monarch, if the executive power were entrusted to a number of persons taken from the legislative body, there would no longer be any liberty. For the two powers would be united, the same persons would sometimes in fact share, and always have the power to share, in both.[25]

If the legislative power were to go without meeting for a considerable time, there would no longer be any liberty. For one of two things would occur: either there would no longer be any legislative decisions, and the state would fall into anarchy; or else decisions would be taken by the executive power, which would thus become absolute.

It would serve no purpose to have the legislative body always in session. Not only would this be inconvenient for the representatives, it would also preoccupy the executive power, which would think, not of doing what it is meant to do, but rather of defending its prerogatives, and its right to execute [legislation].

Furthermore, were the legislative body continually in session, it might happen that new representatives would be chosen only to replace those who had died. In that case, if the legislative body were ever corrupted, there would be no remedy. When different legislative bodies succeed each other, the people, if it has a bad opinion of the one in power, may place its hopes upon the one that will succeed it. But if the legislative body always remained the same, then in the event that it were corrupted, the people with nothing further to hope from legislation, would either be overcome by fury, or fall into indolence.

The legislative body ought not to meet at its own initiative. For a body is not considered to possess a will until it is in session. If the decision to meet were not unanimous, then it would be impossible to determine which in fact is the legislative body, that part in session, or that part which is absent. Were it to have the power to adjourn itself, it might happen that it would never adjourn, and this would be dangerous in the event that it attempted to encroach upon the executive power. Besides, there are better and worse times for convening the legislative body. Thus it ought to be the executive power, which on the basis of what it knows about the circumstances, sets the time and duration of legislative meetings.

If the executive does not have the power to check the designs of the legislative, this body would become despotic. For if it could arrogate to itself all the power it wished, then it would annihilate all other powers.

But it does not follow that as a matter of reciprocity, the legislative ought to have the power to check the executive. For there are limits to what the executive power can do, and these derive from its very nature. It is unnecessary to set further bounds. Furthermore, the executive power is always exercised on short-term matters. The power of the Roman tribunes was defective because it could check not only the legislative, but the executive, and this caused great damage.

But if in a free state, the legislative power ought not to have the power to check the executive, it has the right and ought to have the means to investigate how the laws it has passed have been carried out. This is the advantage that such a government has over that of Crete and Sparta, where the *cosmoi* and ephors gave no account of their administration.[26]

Whatever the result of its investigation, the legislative body ought not have the power to judge the personal acts or official conduct of the individual entrusted with the executive power. His person ought to be sacred because it is necessary to the state that the legislative body not become tyrannical. From the moment that this person [the executive] is accused or judged, liberty is no more.[27]

In such a case, the state would be, not a monarchy but a republic that is not free. But whoever holds the executive power cannot abuse it without the aid of evil counselors, who, serving him as ministers, detest all laws, although these same laws may benefit them as men. These counselors may be investigated and punished, and this is an advantage of this government over that of Gnidus, under which the law did not permit calling the amimones[28] to account, even after their tenure of office was over.[29] Therefore the people could never obtain any satisfaction from these magistrates for the injustices they had committed.

In general, the judicial power ought not be joined to any part of the legislative. However, this principle is subject to three exceptions, all deriving from the individual interest of the defendant.

The great are always subject to envy. Were they to be judged by the people, they would be in danger of being deprived of that privilege guaranteed to even the most humble citizen of a free state, that of judgment by their peers. Nobles, therefore, ought to be tried, not in the ordinary courts of their nation, but in that part of the legislative body which is made up of nobles.

It sometimes happens that the law, which is at the same time enlightened and blind, is too rigorous in some cases. But the judges of the nation are, as I have already said, nothing more than the mouth which pronounces the words of the law. As such, they are inert and can moderate neither the force nor the rigor of the law.

It is that part of the legislative body, which, as I have just else-where called indispensable, is equally so in this regard. One part of its supreme authority is to modify the law in the direction of the [intended purpose of] law itself by mitigating its severity.

It might also happen that some citizen, acting in a public capacity, violates the rights of the people, and commits crimes that ordinary magistrates could not or would not punish. But in general, the legislative power is debarred from acting as a court and especially in such a case as this, when it represents the people, which is one of the interested parties. Thus the legislative power cannot do more than accuse. But before which body ought this to be done? Will the legislative power go and demean itself before the ordinary courts of law, which are inferior to it? Moreover, these courts are composed of men, who, like the legislative body itself, are drawn from the people. What is more likely than that the courts would be swayed by the authority of so great an accuser? No, in order to preserve both the dignity of the people and the security of the individual, that part of the legislature which represents the people must bring its charges before that part of the legislature which represents the nobles, a body with neither the same interests nor passions.[30]

Here is an advantage that this type of government has over most ancient republics, which were defective in that the people was at the same time both judge and prosecutor.

As has been said, the executive power ought to take part in legislation through its power to veto, without which it would soon be stripped of its prerogatives. But if the legislative power participates in executing what it has enacted, then the executive power will be just as much undone.

If the monarch were to participate in legislation by his power to make laws, there would no longer be any liberty. Nevertheless, if he is to defend himself, he must take part in legislation, and this by his power to refuse consent.

The change of government at Rome was caused by the fact that the power to refuse consent was reserved to the people rather than to the senate, which held one part of the executive power, or to the magistrates, which held the other.

Here, then, is the fundamental constitution of the government being discussed. Since the legislative body is made up of two parts, each is made dependent upon the other (*l'une enchaînera l'autre*) by their mutual power to reject legislation. Both will be connected by the executive power, which itself will be connected to the legislative.

These three powers ought to produce repose, or inaction. But since the nature of things requires movement, all three powers are obliged to act, and to act together.

Since the executive power participates in the legislative only by its power to refuse its consent, it cannot be allowed to participate in debate. It is not even necessary that it have the power to propose legislation, since it [already] possesses the power to reject decisions. Thus it can veto those proposals made against its will.

In some ancient republics, public affairs were debated by an assembly of all the people. It was natural that in such a body the executive power could introduce proposals and participate in discussing them. Otherwise, decisions would have been extraordinarily confused.

If the executive power took any part in raising money other than by consenting [to decisions made elsewhere], there would no longer be any liberty. For in this way, the executive would be legislating on the single most important point taken up by a legislative body.

If the legislative power were to raise money, not annually, but for all time, it would run the risk of losing its liberty because the executive power would no longer depend upon it. When such a right is held in perpetuity, it makes no difference whether it derived from oneself or from someone else. There would be the same result if the legislative power were to provide, not annually, but in perpetuity for the land and sea forces, the command of which it ought to confide to the executive power.

To prevent the executive power from being able to oppress, the armies confided to it must be made up from the people, and have its spirit, as was the case at Rome until the time of Marius. There are but two means adequate to this end: either those serving in the army should have enough property to answer to their fellow-citizens for their conduct and be enrolled for one year only as was done at Rome. Or else, if there be a body of troops constituted as a standing army, and made up of the most despicable parts of the nation, the legislative power must be able to dismiss them at its pleasure. And the soldiers ought to live together with the people, and not have any separate camps, barracks or fortresses.

Once an army has been established, it ought to depend, not directly upon the legislative body, but upon the executive power.

This follows from the very nature of the military enterprise, which consists more of action than of deliberation.

Men tend to place courage above timidity, action above prudence, force above discussion. An army will always despise a senate and respect its own officers. It will disregard orders emanating from a body whose members it believes to be timid, and therefore unworthy of commanding the army. Thus what happens is this: as soon as an army takes orders directly from a legislative body, the government will become dominated by the military. If the contrary of this has ever occurred, it has been due to extraordinary circumstances: the army has always been kept divided; or it has been composed of various units, each under the authority of a different province; or the principal cities occupy excellent positions, to which they owe their security, and thus there are no garrisons.

Holland is still more secure than Venice. If Holland's troops were to revolt, she could drown them, she could starve them out. For they are not quartered in cities that could furnish them with the supplies of food they need. Thus their means of subsistence is precarious.

If the army is under the authority of a legislative body, and special circumstances prevent the government from being dominated by the military, then two other undesirable things could happen rather than this one: either the army must destroy the government, or the government must greatly weaken the effectiveness of the army.

And to weaken the army in this way would be due to a cause certain to be fatal, and originating in the very weakness of the government.

The admirable work of Tacitus, *On the Manners and Customs of the Germans*, demonstrates that it is from them that the English have borrowed the idea of their political government.[31] This handsome system was discovered in the woods.

Since everything human must end, the state discussed here will lose its liberty and perish. Rome, Sparta, Carthage – all have perished. This state will perish when its legislative power becomes more corrupt than its executive.

It is not my concern to determine whether or not the English in fact enjoy such liberty. I need say no more than that it is established by their laws. Further than that I shall not look.

It is not my intent to depreciate other governments by this procedure, nor do I wish to assert that such extreme political liberty ought to be regretted by those who enjoy a moderate share of liberty. How could I say such a thing? For I have always believed that excess, even of reason, is not always desirable, and that men are almost always most comfortable with the mean, rather than the extreme.

Harrington, in his *Oceana*, has also sought to determine just how far the constitution of a state may carry liberty. But it may be said of him that he sought liberty without being able to recognize it when he saw it, that he built Chalcedon, although he had the shores of Byzantium before his eyes.[32]

Chapter VII
Monarchies Known to Us

The monarchies we know, as I have just stated, do not have liberty as their direct object. Rather they aim only at the glory of the citizens, the state, and the ruler. But from such glory results a spirit of liberty, which in states of this kind, may achieve things just as great, and contribute as much to happiness (*bonheur*) as liberty itself.

Here the three powers are not distributed and based on the model of the constitution just discussed. Each of these powers are disposed in ways peculiar to its government. This determines the extent to which they approximate to political liberty. If they do not [at all] approximate to it, then the monarchy will degenerate into despotism.

Chapter VIII
Why the Ancients Lacked a Clear Idea of Monarchy

The ancients had no notion of a government based on a body of nobles, and even less of a government based on a legislative body formed by the representatives of a nation. The Greek and Italian republics were cities, each of which had its own government, and convened its citizens within its walls. Before the Romans swallowed up all these republics, there were practically no kings to be found, whether in Italy, Gaul, Spain, or Germany. All were petty peoples or republics. Africa itself was subject to a great power; Asia Minor was occupied by Greek colonies. Thus there were no examples of representative bodies in cities, nor of assemblies in states. As for finding a ruler who governed by himself, one would have had to go as far as Persia.

It is true that there were federative republics. A number of cities would send deputies to an assembly. But what I am saying is that there were no monarchies so constituted.

Here is the first type of monarchy known to us. The Germanic nations which conquered the Roman Empire were, as is well known, free. This can be verified by reference to Tacitus in *On the Manners and Customs of the Germans*. The conquerors spread over the country; they lived for the most part in the fields, and hardly at all in towns. When still in Germany, the whole nation could be assembled. But they could no longer do so, once they had been dispersed after the conquest. Nevertheless, the nation had to deliberate on its business, as it had done before the conquest. This it did by representatives. Such was the origin of the Gothic form of government among us. It was at first a mixture of aristocracy and monarchy, and suffered from the defect that the common people (*le bas peuple*) was enslaved. It was a good government that had within itself the capacity to become better. The custom came into being of granting letters of enfranchisement. Soon the civil liberty of the people, the prerogatives of the nobility and of the clergy, the power of kings, were so harmonious that I do not believe that the world has ever seen a government so well limited (*tempéré*) as those in every part of Europe as long as that period lasted. And how extraordinary that the corruption of the government of a conquering people should have led to the best type of government that could ever have been imagined by man.

Chapter IX

Aristotle's Mode of Thought

When he came to the treatment of monarchy, Aristotle was clearly at a loss. He set up five species of it, and he distinguished them, not by the form of constitution, but by considerations which were either fortuitous, such as the ruler's virtues or vices; or extraneous [to any such analysis], such as whether a tyranny was established by usurpation or succession.

Aristotle ranked both the Persian Empire and the kingdom of Sparta as monarchies. But it is evident that one was a despotic state, and the other, a republic.

The ancients were incapable of framing any precise concept of monarchy, for they never understood how the three powers could be in the proper relationship within a government headed by a single person.

[Chapters X–XIX are omitted.]

Chapter XX
The Conclusion of This Book

I should like to investigate the distribution of the three powers in all limited (*modérés*) governments known to us, and to calculate on this basis the degree of liberty enjoyed by each of them. But it is not always necessary to exhaust a subject and leave the reader with nothing to do. I write, not so much to make people read, but rather to make them think.

BOOK XIV
The Relation Between Laws and the Nature of Climate

Chapter I
The General Idea [of This Part, Books XIV–XVIII]¹

If it is true that the character of the mind and the passions of the heart vary so much from one climate to another, then laws ought to be relative both to the variety of those passions and to the variety of mental characteristics.

Chapter II
How Men Differ from One Climate to Another

Cold air constricts the extremities of the body's external fibers.² This increases their elasticity and favors the return of the blood from the extremities to the heart. Cold air contracts these fibers,³ and thus adds to their force. Hot air, by contrast, relaxes and lengthens the extremities of the fibers, and thus diminishes their force and elasticity.

More vigor is found, therefore, in peoples who live in cold climates. The action of the heart and the reaction of the fibers' extremities function better; the humors are in better equilibrium; the blood moves more freely toward the heart, and reciprocally the heart is more powerful. This increased power is responsible for many consequences; for example, greater self-confidence, that is, more courage; a greater sense of superiority to others, that is, less desire for revenge; a greater sense of security, that is, more frankness, fewer suspicions, less cunning and trickery. To sum up, such differences must create very different sets of characteristics. When a man is put into a warm, closed space, he will suffer and become faint for the reasons I have just given. Under such circumstances, he will be little disposed to accept any bold venture. Indeed his weakness will make him despondent; he will fear everything because he knows that he is capable of nothing. The inhabitants of warm countries are timid in the same way as are the aged; those of cold countries are courageous in the same way as young people. If we consider our most recent wars,[4] those freshest in our memories, we can better see certain almost imperceptible effects of the sort that we should not be able to detect in more remote history. What emerges clearly is that when they had to fight in the countries of the south, the northern peoples performed in less glorious fashion than did their compatriots who displayed all their courage when they fought in their own climate.

. . . . The nerves come from every direction in our body and terminate in the skin. Each of them itself is a bundle of nerves. Usually it is not the whole nerve that is moved, but a tiny part of it. In hot countries where the tissue of the skin is relaxed, the ends of the nerves are expanded and exposed to even the weakest action of very small stimuli. In cold countries, the tissue of the skin is compressed, and the papillae compressed. The skin corpuscles are to some extent paralyzed; sensation reaches the brain only when it is extremely strong and originates from the whole nerve. But imagination, taste, sensitivity, and vivacity derive from an infinite number of minute sensations.

I have observed the outer part of a sheep's tongue, where to the naked eye, it appears to be covered with papillae. Using a microscope, I have seen small hairs, or a sort of down on these papillae. Between them were pyramids shaped like pincers toward their ends. It appears most probable that these pyramids are the principal organ of taste.

I froze half of this tongue, and observing it with the naked eye, I found the papillae to have shrunk considerably. There were even several rows that had sunk into their sheaths. When I examined the outer part with a microscope, no pyramids were visible. As the tongue became defrosted, observation by the naked eye revealed that the papillae could be seen to rise. With the microscope, corpuscles began to appear.

This observation confirms what I have been saying: in cold countries, the nervous papillae are less expanded; they sink deeper into their sheaths, and are sheltered from the action of external objects. Therefore sensations are felt less vividly.

In cold countries, there is but little sensitivity to pleasures; in temperate countries, there is more; in hot climates, sensitivity becomes extreme. Just as climates are distinguished by degrees of latitude, they may also be distinguished, so to speak, by degrees of sensitivity. In both England and Italy, I have seen the same opera played by the same performers, with altogether different effects upon audiences in the two countries. The first was so calm; the second, so transported that it seemed impossible that both effects could be produced by the same music.

. . .

From this sensitivity of organs in warm climates, it follows that the soul is subject to the sovereignty of everything related to the union of the two sexes. Here this is the supreme object.

In northern climates, the physical urge to love has barely the strength to make itself felt. In temperate climates, love is accompanied by innumerable additional appeals meant to stimulate; its attraction comes from what appears to be the passion of love, but in fact falls short of it. In hot climates, love is sought for its own sake; it is the only source of happiness (*bonheur*); it is life itself.

In southern countries, the body is a machine that is delicate, weak, but sensitive. In a seraglio, it gives itself over to an unending succession of pleasures that are stimulated and are satisfied. Or else, it will give itself over to a love that because it leaves women greater independence is exposed to infinite dangers. In northern countries, the body is a healthy and well-constructed machine that is, however, heavy. It finds its pleasures in whatever puts its humors into motion: the hunt, travels, war, wine. In the north will be found peoples who have few vices and not a few virtues; they have much frankness and sincerity. But if we move toward the south, we seem to be losing sight of morality itself. Here the most violent passions multiply the number of crimes; everyone seems to seek everything that gives him advantages over others in the pursuit of these very passions. In temperate countries, the inhabitants are inconstant in their *manières*, in both their vices and virtues. The climate lacks the determinate behavior to fix the inhabitants in one or another pattern.

A climate may be so hot as to deprive the body of all vigor. Then weakness overcomes the mind itself: there is no curiosity, no noble efforts, no generosity of feeling. All inclinations are passive; it is indolence that makes men happy here. Almost any punishment seems less onerous than the need to exercise the mind; and slavery becomes preferable to the moral effort required if one is to live one's life.

[Chapter III is omitted.]

Chapter IV
The Cause of the Immutability of Oriental Religion, *Moeurs*, *Manières*, and Laws

The oriental peoples have a certain indolence of mind reinforcing that sensibility which makes them so sensitive to every impression. Such indolence of mind and body makes them incapable of any action, any effort, any resistance. Their souls, once they have received an impression cannot be rid of it. For this reason oriental laws, *moeurs*, and *manières*, even if of no intrinsic importance, such as their mode of dress, remain today what they were a thousand years ago.

Chapter V
Bad Legislators Favor Vices Produced by the Climate; Good Legislators Oppose Them[5]

The Indians believe that repose and nonbeing (*le néant*) are the foundation of all things, and the end in which they culminate. Thus for the Indians, absolute lack of motion is the most perfect state, the objective of all their desires. To the Supreme Being,[6] they give the name of 'Unmoving.' The Siamese believe that supreme happiness consists of never being obliged to work a machine or to move a body.[7]

In countries where excessive heat enervates and enfeebles, repose is so delicious and movement, so painful, that this metaphysical system appears natural. Buddha,[8] who gave the Indians their laws, took his own sensations as his guide when he defined the human condition in an extremely passive way (*lorsqu'il a mis les hommes dans un état extrêmement passif*). But his teaching, which originated in the laziness produced by the climate, further encouraged it, and by so doing caused an infinite number of further evils.

Those who gave the Chinese their laws (*les législateurs de la Chine*) were more sensible when they treated men, not in terms of the peace they would enjoy in the life to come, but rather in terms of the action requisite for discharging their duties in this life.[9] Thus these legislators made Chinese religion, philosophy, and laws all eminently practical. The more physical causes incline men to inaction, the more moral causes ought to counter such effects.

[Chapters VI–VIII are omitted.]

Chapter IX
Means of Encouraging Industry

In Book XIX, I shall demonstrate that lazy nations are usually proud. But the effect can be turned against the cause; pride can be used to destroy laziness. In the south of Europe where men are so sensitive about their honor, it would be good to award prizes to those farmers (*laboureurs*) who have best cultivated their fields, and to those artisans who have most developed their skills. Such practices would be successful in almost every country. In our time, they have succeeded in making Ireland into one of the largest manufacturers of linen in Europe.

[Chapter X is omitted.]

Chapter XI
The Relationship of Laws to Sicknesses
Produced by Climate

. . .

The plague is a disease whose ravages are even more rapid [than syphilis, the origins of which Montesquieu had just attributed to the New World]. Its principal source is Egypt, from which it spreads to the rest of the world. In most European states, excellent precautions have been devised to prevent the spread of this disease, and in our time, an admirable means has been found to do so. Troops surround the infected part of the country and prevent all communication with the rest.

The Turks,[10] who take no comparable precautions, see Christians in the same town as themselves escape the plague while their own people die of it. The Turks buy the clothes of those who have been infected, wear them, and proceed as before. The doctrine of a rigid fate that directs everything, makes their magistrates into tranquil spectators who believe that because God has already done everything, nothing remains for them to do.

Chapter XII
Laws against Suicide[11]

There is no hint in any of the histories of the Romans that they ever killed themselves without cause. But the English commit suicide unaccountably, doing so amid even the happiest of circumstances. This action was for the Romans the consequence of their upbringing (*éducation*), being connected to their mode of thought and customs; among the English it is the consequence of a disease,[12] being connected with the physical state of the body, and independent of every other cause.

It appears that this disease is the result of some defect in the filtering of liquids contained in the nerves. The body, whose forces of motion cannot be exerted, becomes weary of itself. Although the soul feels no pain, it does experience some uneasiness about continuing to exist. Pain is a local sensation that induces in us the desire to see an end to it; the feeling that life is a burden is an evil that cannot be precisely located, but induces the desire to put an end to life itself.

It is clear that it is for good reasons that the civil laws of some countries brand suicide with infamy. But in England it cannot be punished without at the same time punishing the effects of madness.

Chapter XIII
Effects Resulting from the Climate of England

England is a nation so affected by this illness caused by the climate that its distaste for everything extends to life itself. Clearly the government best suited to men apt to find everything unendurable is that in which they cannot attribute their difficulties to a single person, and where it is the laws that govern and not men. Under such circumstances, they could not change the government without subverting the laws themselves.

And if the climate has also imparted to this nation a certain characteristic impatience, which makes it incapable of putting up with the same arrangements for very long, then it becomes even more obvious that the type of government just described is most appropriate for it.

This characteristic impatience is of itself no great matter, but can become significant when joined to courage.

It differs from that lack of seriousness which leads men to take up or drop projects without cause. It is closer to obstinacy, because it originates in a sense of misery so intense that it is undiminished even by the continual experience of suffering.

Such a characteristic in a free nation is most apt to disconcert the designs of tyranny,[13] which is always slow and feeble when it begins, and later becomes quick and powerful. Tyranny at first extends only a hand in aid; later it displays any number of arms when it turns to oppression.

Servitude is always preceded by sleep. But a people which is never at rest, which is constantly feeling every part of itself and finding nothing but pain, can hardly be lulled to sleep.

Politics is a fine smooth file,[14] which does its work slowly by wearing down resistance. For men such as those we have been discussing, the delays, the details, the sangfroid of negotiation are intolerable, and they are less successful in it than any other nation. Thus they lose by the treaties they make what they have gained by their arms.

BOOK XV

How the Laws of Civil Slavery Are Related to the Nature of the Climate

Chapter I
Civil Slavery

Slavery, properly so called, is the consequence of establishing the right of one man to own another, to become absolute master over his life and property. There is nothing good about the nature of slavery. It is useful neither to the master nor to the slave. The slave can achieve nothing as the result of being virtuous. As for the master, he acquires all sorts of bad habits from his relationship to his slaves. Without being aware of it, he becomes accustomed to behaving with a total absence of moral virtue; he becomes proud, hasty, severe, irascible, voluptuous, cruel.

In despotic countries, where men already live in a state of political slavery, civil slavery is more nearly tolerable than elsewhere. Under despotism, everyone ought to be content to be provided with subsistence and to be allowed to go on living. Thus it is little more of a burden to be a slave than to be a subject.

But in a monarchical government, where above all, human nature must not be put down and debased, there should be no slavery. In democracies, where everyone is equal, and in aristocracies, where laws ought to be designed so as to provide as much equality as the nature of this government permits, slavery is contrary to the nature of the constitution. For slavery serves only to give citizens that power and luxury they ought not to have.

Chapter II

The Origin of the Right of Slavery
According to the Roman Jurists[1]

One would never have believed that slavery was established because of pity, and this in three different ways.[2]

The law of nations allowed prisoners to become slaves in order to prevent their being put to death; Roman civil law allowed debtors to sell themselves in order to forestall severe treatment by their creditors; the law of nature (*le droit de nature*) requires that children who can no longer be fed by a slave father should be themselves enslaved.

Such arguments by the Roman jurists make no sense. It is untrue that killing in war is permissible. It becomes so only in case of necessity. But when one man has enslaved another, he cannot be said to have been subject to any necessity to kill him. For the fact is that he has not done so. War can confer only one right over captives, and that is to ensure that they can no longer harm victors. All the nations of the world[3] condemn murder in cold blood by soldiers once combat has ended.

Nor is it true that a man can sell himself. Sale implies a price. When a person sells himself, all his goods become his master's property. Thus the master gives nothing and the slave receives nothing.[4] It may be said that the slave would have a *peculium*.[5] But this *peculium* goes along with the person. If the law does not permit a man to kill himself because he thus robs his country of his person, then it is equally illicit to sell himself. The liberty of every citizen is a part of public liberty. In a democratic state, this liberty is even a part of sovereignty. To sell one's status as a citizen is an act so extravagant that it cannot be attributed to any man.[6] If liberty has a price for the buyer, it is beyond all price to the seller. The division of property (*biens*) is authorized by the civil law, which cannot, however, include in the notion of property any part of those very men who are to make the division. The civil law restores all former rights to anyone who has made a contract unjustly damaging to himself. Thus the civil law must restore all former rights to anyone who has made that contract which is most unjust and damaging.[7]

The third way [of becoming a slave according to Roman law] was by birth. This fails as did the previous two arguments in favor of slavery. For if a man cannot sell himself into slavery; he is even less able to sell his unborn son. If a prisoner of war may not be reduced to slavery, the same is even more true of his children.

It is permissible to put a criminal to death because the law that punishes him was made to protect him. For example, a murderer has enjoyed the benefits of the law by which he is condemned. Since it protected his life at all times, he has no ground for complaint against it. The same is not true for a slave. The law establishing slavery has never benefited him; in every case, it has worked against and never for him. And this violates the fundamental principle of all societies.

It may be said in reply that the law of slavery benefits the slave because his master provides him with sustenance.[8] Slavery, then, ought be restricted to those incapable of earning their living. But no one wishes such slaves. As for children, it is nature that has given their mothers' milk, and thus provided sustenance. What remains of their childhood is so close to the age when they possess the capacity to reciprocate by their services for any sustenance provided them, that their master cannot claim that he has earned any right over them by the food he has provided.

Furthermore, slavery is as contrary to the civil law as it is to natural law. What civil law could prevent a slave from running away? Since he is not a member of society, why should the laws of society concern him? All that can keep him [from flight] is the law of the family, that is, the law of his master.

Chapter III
Another Origin of the Right of Slavery

I should like to assert that it is also true that the law of slavery derives from the scorn felt by one nation toward another because their customs (*coutumes*) differ.

Lopez de Gama[9] relates "that the Spanish found near St. Martha several basketfuls of crabs, snails, grasshoppers, and locusts: which turned out to be what the local inhabitants ate. The conquerors made it a crime for the conquered to do so." This author admits that it was on this basis that the Spaniards claimed the right to enslave the Americans. What was more, the Americans were guilty of smoking tobacco and not wearing their beards as did the Spanish.

Knowledge makes men gentle; reason leads to humanity; but prejudices can only eradicate both these dispositions.

Chapter IV
Another Origin of the Right of Slavery

I should like to assert that it is also true that religion, in order to make its own propagation easier, bestows upon those who believe the right to reduce to slavery those who do not.

It was this mode of thought that encouraged the destroyers of America in their crimes.[10] On this idea was founded the right to reduce so many peoples to slavery. For these bandits who so fervently wished to be Christians without giving up their banditry, were very devout.

Louis XIII[11] was made extremely uneasy by the law that enslaved all the negroes in his colonies. But when told that this was the most efficacious way of converting them, he gave his consent.

Chapter V
Negro Slavery[12]

If I were ever forced to defend our right to make negroes our slaves, this is what I should say:

Since the European peoples have exterminated the Americans, they were obliged to make the Africans their slaves in order to clear such vast stretches of land.

Sugar would cost too much if it were not produced from that plant which is cultivated by slaves.

Since these are not only black from head to foot, but have flat noses as well, it is almost impossible to pity them.

It cannot be believed that a being so very wise as God could have placed a soul, let alone a good soul, in a body that is all black.

It is so natural to think color the essence of human nature, that the peoples of Asia, who make much use of eunuchs, employ the most emphatic means to deprive blacks of what they share with us.

The color of a man's skin may be determined by his hair. So important was this to the Egyptians, the world's best philosophers, that they put to death all red-haired persons falling into their hands.

Negroes prefer a necklace made of glass to one of gold, which is valued so highly by all civilized nations. What better proof could there be that negroes lack common sense?

It is impossible to suppose that such people are men. For were this the case, we might begin to suspect that we ourselves are not Christians.

Weak minds exaggerate too much the injustice done to Africans. Were it as great as they make out, surely the rulers of Europe, who are so given to making useless treaties, would have agreed to a general convention in behalf of mercy and pity.

[Chapter VI is omitted.]

Chapter VII

Another Origin of the Right of Slavery

Here is another origin of the right of slavery, and of even that cruel practice of slavery found among men.

There are countries where the heat so weakens the body and enfeebles men's courage that only the fear of punishment can oblige them to perform any onerous duty. Therefore slavery in such places is less offensive to reason. Since the master is as lazy in relation to his sovereign, as is the slave in relation to his master, here civil slavery is accompanied by political slavery.

Aristotle[13] wishes to prove that there are slaves by nature. What he says on this score falls far short of proof. If indeed there are any such [slaves by nature], I believe that they are those I have just discussed.

But since all men are born equal, slavery must be said to run contrary to nature, although in certain countries, it is founded on a reason derived from nature (*une raison naturelle*). A clear distinction must be drawn between such countries and those others where all the reasons drawn from nature run contrary to slavery. This is the case in Europe, where it has been so happily abolished.

In his life of Numa, Plutarch tells us that in the time of Saturn there was neither master nor slave. In our climate, Christianity has restored us to that age.

Chapter VIII
Uselessness of Slavery to Us

Natural slavery, then, ought to be limited to certain unusual parts of the world. In all others, it seems to me that however onerous the work demanded by society, it can all be done by free men.

What makes me think so is the fact that before Christianity abolished civil slavery in Europe, it was assumed that work in mines was so hard that it could be done only by slaves or [convicted] criminals. But today it is well known that there are miners[14] who live comfortably. By providing minor privileges, this occupation has been encouraged. By increasing pay for increased work, this work has been made so attractive that it is preferred by the miners to any other.

Provided that it is reason and not avarice that predominates, any labor, however onerous, may be brought to the level of the laborer's strength. By the advantages of machines invented or applied by man's artifice (*art*), substitutes can be found for the forced labor done elsewhere by slaves. The Turkish mines in the Bannat of Tameswaer, although richer than those of Hungary, produced less. This was because they could imagine no alternative to the arms of their slaves.

I do not know whether this chapter is dictated to me by my mind or by my heart. Perhaps there is no climate anywhere in the world where labor may not be performed by free men. Badly designed laws made men lazy; because they were lazy, men were enslaved.[15]

Chapter IX[16]

Nations in Which Liberty Is Generally Established

We are always told how good it could be for us to have slaves.

To arrive at an adequate judgment on this matter, it is not enough to consider whether in every nation it would be useful to that small part that is rich and voluptuous. No doubt slavery would be useful to those belonging to that group. But let us take another point of view. I do not believe that anyone of them would submit to a lottery determining which part of the nation would be free, and which, slave.[17] Although those in favor of restoring slavery would be most horrified to become slaves, would the most miserable persons in the society feel any differently? The demand for slavery is, therefore, the demand for luxury and voluptuousness; it has nothing to do with concern for public felicity. No doubt every individual would be content, indeed, to be master of the property, the honor, and the lives of others. Whose passions would not be awakened by such a prospect? In such matters, if there is any question whether individual desires are legitimate, it may be resolved by determining [whether they are compatible with] the desires of everyone else.[18]

[Chapters X–XVIII are omitted.]

XIX
Laws: Their Relation to Those Principles that Form the General Spirit, *Moeurs*, and *Manières* of a Nation

Chapter I
The Subject of This Book

My subject is very broad. In treating the host of ideas it suggests to me, I shall attend more to the order of things than to the things themselves. I shall have to make detours to the right and to the left; I must penetrate to the heart of the matter, and shed some light upon it.

[Chapter II is omitted.]

Chapter III
On Tyranny[1]

There are two sorts of tyranny: that which is real and consists of the violence of government; and another which is a tyranny of opinion and makes itself felt when those who govern institute things contrary to a nation's mode of thought.[2]

Dio Cassius writes that Augustus wished to have himself called Romulus, but changed his plans when he learned of the people's fear that he intended to make himself king. The first Romans had refused to have a king because they could not suffer his power; the Romans of that later time refused to have a king because they could not suffer his *manières*. For although Caesar, the triumvirs, and Augustus in reality were all kings, they maintained the external appearance of equality, and their private lives presented something of a contrast to the pomp of other kings of the period. Thus when the Romans altogether refused to have a king, this meant that they wished to maintain their own *manières* rather than taking on those of African and oriental peoples.

Dio Cassius[3] tells us that the Roman people was indignant toward Augustus because he had instituted laws of excessive severity. But as soon as he brought back the actor Pylades, who had been banished by certain factions, discontent vanished. Such a people felt tyranny more keenly when an actor was banished than when it was deprived of all its laws.

Chapter IV
What is Meant by the General Spirit

Men are ruled by many causes: climate, religion, laws, maxims of government, examples drawn from the past, *moeurs*, *manières*. Out of them is formed the general spirit of a nation.

To the extent that any one of these causes acquires greater force in a nation, the other causes are weakened. Nature and climate virtually dominate savages, *manières* govern the Chinese, laws are the tyrants in Japan, *moeurs* once set the tone of life in Sparta, as did their maxims of government and ancient *moeurs* for the Romans.

Chapter V

How Important It Is Not to Change the General Spirit of a Nation

If in this world, a nation could be found whose temperament were sociable, frank, relishing life, discerning in its tastes, and with a flair for communicating its ideas; if this nation were at the same time lively, agreeable, gay, sometimes imprudent, often indiscreet; if it combined with all this, courage, generosity, candor, and its own sense of honor, surely no one who sought to maintain such virtues would impose constraint by law upon such *manières*.[4] If the character of a people is for the most part good, its few defects become insignificant.

It might be possible to impose further limits upon the ladies of this nation, make laws to raise the level of their *moeurs*, while diminishing the extent of their luxury. But who could be certain that such measures would not destroy that good taste which is the source of the nation's wealth, or that politeness (*politesse*) which attracts so many foreign visitors to its shores.

The legislator ought to follow the spirit of the nation whenever to do so is not contrary to the principles of its government. For we do best what we do freely while following our natural genius.

Were pedantry to be imposed upon a nation, which is naturally gay, the state would gain nothing either at home or abroad. Let it then do frivolous things seriously, and serious things gaily.

Chapter VI

Not Everything Has to Be Changed

If only we could be left as we are, wrote a nobleman of a nation that much resembles the one just described.[5] Nature repairs everything. Upon us it has bestowed a vivacity that may offend by pushing us past the limits prescribed by respect; that same vivacity is corrected by the politeness it instills in us, inspiring a taste for the things of the world, and above all, for a civilized relationship with women.

If only we could be left as we are. Our tendency toward indiscretion, joined with our lack of malice, is such that there is no need for laws that would restrain our sociable temperament.

Chapter VII
The Athenians and the Spartans

The Athenians, this nobleman added, were a people not unlike us. They brought gaiety to their public business, a shrewd stroke of mockery was no less as welcome in a public assembly than in the theater. The Athenians brought the same vivacity to both public deliberation and execution. The character of the Spartans was grave, serious, dry, taciturn. If bored, an Athenian could no more be won over than a Spartan, if amused.

Chapter VIII
Sociability and Its Effects

The more peoples communicate, the more easily they change their *manières*. This is because each of them is something of a spectacle to the other, a situation in which individual differences are more easily discerned. The climate that inclines a nation to like communicating with others also inclines it to like change; what inclines a nation to like change also forms its taste.

When men spend much time in feminine company, their *moeurs* deteriorate, and their taste improves. The desire to please more than anyone else leads to elegance in dress; the desire to please others rather than oneself leads to the rise of fashions. Fashion is an important matter: simply by capitulating to this frivolous impulse, a nation may give a tremendous impetus to every aspect of its trade.[6]

Chapter IX
Vanity and Pride in Nations

As the spring of a government, vanity is as advantageous as pride is dangerous.[7] To be convinced of this, we need only to consider, on the one side, the innumerable benefits that result from vanity: luxury, industry, the arts, fashion, politeness, taste; and, on the other, the innumerable evils that result from the pride of certain nations: laziness, poverty, negligence in everything, the destruction of peoples brought by chance under their domination, and finally, their own ruin.[8] Laziness is produced by pride; work, by vanity.[9] The pride of a Spaniard leads him to shun work; the vanity of a Frenchman, to work harder than anyone else.

All lazy nations are grave, for those who do not work regard themselves as the superiors of those who do.

If we consider all nations known to us, it becomes clear that gravity, pride, and laziness go together.

. . .

In a number of places, people let their fingernails grow in order to prove that they do no work.

. . .

It need scarcely be said that different effects are produced by moral qualities when combined with others. Thus pride, when joined to the Romans' infinite ambition and notions of their own grandeur, produced the effects we know so well.

Chapter X
Character of the Spaniards and Chinese

The character peculiar to a nation combines virtues and vices, both good and bad qualities. Those combinations that produce the most desirable outcomes often occur where least expected; the same is true of the great evils produced by other combinations.

The Spaniards have always been famous for keeping their word. Justin[10] told of how carefully they guarded whatever was entrusted to them, for they often died rather than reveal such secrets. Today they still possess that reliability. All the nations that trade with the port of Cadiz entrust their wealth to the Spaniards and have never regretted it. But combined with their laziness, this admirable quality produces a combination with effects ruinous to the Spanish: all the commerce of their monarchy is carried on by the other nations of Europe, and this under their very eyes.

The character of the Chinese forms another combination, and one that contrasts with the character of the Spaniards. The life of the Chinese is so precarious[11] that it stimulates prodigious activity and an excessive desire for gain. No commercial nation can trust them.[12] Such notorious unreliability has been responsible for their continued monopoly over trade with Japan. No European trader has dared to attempt to trade with Japan through Chinese agents, however easy the access to Japan from the northern maritime provinces of China.

Chapter XI
A Reflection

Nothing said here should be understood as diminishing in any way the infinite distance separating virtues from vices. God forbid that such distinctions be obliterated! What I have sought to make my reader understand is only that all political vices are not moral vices, and that all moral vices are not political vices. This ought not be ignored by those who make laws contrary to the general spirit of their society.

Chapter XII
Manières and *Moeurs* in the Despotic State[13]

No maxim is of greater importance to despotism than that in such a state, *moeurs* and *manières* must never be changed: nothing would be better calculated to incite a revolution. In despotic states, there are, so to speak, no laws, but only *moeurs* and *manières*. Once these are overthrown, everything else is overthrown as well.

Laws are established, *moeurs* are inspired; *moeurs* are connected to the general spirit, laws to some one institution. For to overthrow the general spirit is as dangerous, or even more so, than to change any one institution.

In those countries where everyone, whether as superior or inferior, either exercises or suffers arbitrary power, there is less communication than in a country where liberty reigns in every rank of society. In a despotic society *manières* and *moeurs* change less. The most stable *manières* are those that are most like laws. Thus a ruler or legislator [in a despotism] must be more careful not to upset *moeurs* and *manières* than in any other kind of country.

Usually women are shut away, and exercise no influence whatever. In other countries, where women associate more with men, their desire to please and the desire to please them which they evoke in society, produce a continuous change in *manières*. The two sexes spoil each other, each of them loses its distinctive and essential quality; what once was absolute is made to depend upon personal inclination, and *manières* change every day.

Chapter XIII

Manières in China

But it is in China that *manières* are indestructible. In addition to the absolute separation of women from men, *manières* are taught in the schools in the same way as *moeurs*. A member of the literati may be recognized[14] by the flowing way he bows. Once such matters are settled by the precepts of grave savants, they become fixed moral principles, and never again change.

Chapter XIV

What Are the Natural Means of Changing the *Moeurs* and *Manières* of a Nation

We have said that laws are established by a legislator as his own, most precisely realized work; and that *moeurs* and *manières* are established by a nation as a whole. It follows that when *moeurs* and *manières* are to be changed, this ought not be done by law, for to do so would appear too tyrannical, but rather by introducing other *moeurs* and other *manières*.

Thus when a ruler wishes to effect great changes in his nation, he must reform by law what is established by law, and he must change by *manières* what is established by *manières*. The worst policy is to change by law what ought to be changed by *manières*.

It was tyrannical to ordain the law which required the inhabitants of Moscow to cut off their beards and shorten their clothes; it was tyrannical for Peter I to use violence to compel those entering the city to cut off their long cloaks at the knee. Means exist for preventing crimes, the establishment of penalties by law; means exist for changing *manières*, the power of example.

The ease and speed with which this nation achieved order, proved both that its ruler had too low an opinion of it, and that the people were not animals, as he had called them. There was no necessity for the violent means he employed; he could have achieved his end just as well by milder means.

He himself learned by experience how easy it was to effect these changes. Women had been sequestered, and were, to some extent, slaves. He invited them to his court, had them dress in the German style, sent them fine fabrics. Immediately the women relished this style of life which so flattered their taste, their vanity, and their passions; they caused the men to relish it as well.

What made the change easier was that before it began, the *moeurs* had been inconsistent with the climate. For these *moeurs* had been brought to that nation by a mixture of its peoples and by conquest. Peter I found it far easier than he had anticipated to introduce the *moeurs* and *manières* of Europe to a European nation. Climate is the most fundamental of all causes.

Peter had no need of laws to change the *moeurs* and *manières* of his nation; it would have sufficed to introduce new *moeurs* and *manières*.

Peoples generally are much attached to their customs, and are made unhappy when deprived of them by force. Thus customs ought not be changed [directly], but rather by actions the people themselves have been encouraged to take.

Any unnecessary punishment is tyrannical. Law is not a mere act of power; its jurisdiction does not extend to things, which, by their nature, are irrelevant to it.

Chapter XV

The Influence of Domestic upon Political Authority

No doubt this alteration in the *moeurs* of women will much influence the government of Moscow. All these matters are intimately related: the despotism of the ruler is by its nature inseparable from the servile condition of women; the liberty of women is inseparable from the spirit of monarchy.

Chapter XVI

How Some Legislators Have Failed to Distinguish
the Principles that Govern Men

Moeurs and *manières* are usages unmentioned by law, either because they could not be so established, or were not intended to be.

There is this distinction between laws and *moeurs*: laws are directed primarily at men's actions *qua* citizens; *moeurs*, at their actions *qua* men. There is this distinction between *moeurs* and *manières*: *moeurs* are more concerned with conduct considered from the inside; *manières*, with conduct considered from the outside.

Some states fail to make these distinctions.[15] Lycurgus drew up a code to regulate indiscriminately laws, *moeurs*, and *manières*, and this was also done by those who gave the Chinese their codes.

Nor is it surprising that those who drew up laws for the Spartans and Chinese fell into this confusion among law, *moeurs*, and *manières*. For their *moeurs* played the part of law; their *manières*, that of *moeurs*.

The primary purpose of those who gave the Chinese their codes was to ensure tranquillity. These legislators wished men to respect one another, that everyone be aware at all times of how much he owed his fellows, so that there could be no citizen who did not in certain regards depend upon someone else. Therefore they extended the rules of civility as far as possible.

Thus in Chinese villages, the ceremonies practiced by their inhabitants[16] among themselves do not differ from those of persons of high station. Such means serve to encourage gentleness, to maintain peace and good order among the people, and to remove all vices that stem from a harsh temper. Indeed, is it not the case that anyone seeking to emancipate himself from the rules of civility in fact wishes to be untroubled by his faults?

Civility is better, in this respect, than [mere] politeness. Politeness flatters the vices of others; civility keeps us from displaying our own; it is a barrier which men set up between themselves in order not to corrupt one another.

Lycurgus, who established harsh institutions, scarcely aimed at civility when he set out to mold his people's *manières*. Rather his purpose was to inspire a war-loving spirit. He wished to bring into being men whose relations to one another would be virtuous rather than courteous. For they would always be administering discipline, or being themselves disciplined; training others, or being trained; such men are at once simple and rigid.

Chapter XVII
The Distinctive Quality of Chinese Government

Those who gave the Chinese their codes went even further.[17] They failed to make any distinction among religion, law, *moeurs*, and *manières*; all were included in morality, all in virtue. The precepts involving these four divisions were included in what were called rites. In China, government excelled in making these rites observed to the last detail. Youth was devoted to learning them; the rest of life, to their practice. They were taught by the literati, and preached by the magistrates. And since these rites extended to all the petty actions of life, China was well governed whenever means were found for having them strictly observed.

Two things have contributed to the ease with which these rites came to be engraved in the minds and hearts of the Chinese. First, their extremely complicated mode of writing has had the effect of making them devote their minds[18] to these rites for most of their lives. For they had to learn to read from books, and all books were devoted to rites. Secondly, because the precepts taught by the rites contained nothing spiritual, but were only simple rules governing common practice, it was easier to convince and impress men's minds by them than by anything intellectual.

Those princes who governed by the use of corporal punishment, rather than by rites, were attempting to establish *moeurs*, which cannot be done in this way. Such punishment may be successful in isolating from society citizens who have abandoned their *moeurs* and violated the law. But if everyone abandons his *moeurs*, will punishment restore them? Although punishments may put a stop to many effects of such a general evil, the evil itself cannot be cured by punishment. And so when the Chinese government abandoned its principles, and morality disappeared, the state fell into anarchy, and revolutions occurred.

Chapter XVIII
What Follows from the Preceding Chapter

It follows from what has been said that conquest does not destroy the laws of China. Since Chinese *manières*, *moeurs*, laws, and religion amount to the same thing, these cannot be all changed simultaneously. Yet either the conqueror or the conquered must change. In China, it has always been the conqueror. For the *moeurs* of the conqueror are not identical with its *manières*; its *manières* with its laws; its laws, with its religion. Thus it has been easier for conquerors to adapt themselves piecemeal to the people they have vanquished than for the Chinese to adapt to its new rulers.

There is still another unfortunate consequence: it is almost impossible that Christianity could ever be established in China.[19] Vows of chastity, allowing women to worship in churches, the necessity for them to communicate with priests, the participation of women in the sacraments, confession, extreme unction, monogamy – all these provisions would overturn China's *moeurs* and *manières*, no less than its religion and laws.

By establishing charity, public worship, and the participation by all in the same sacraments, Christianity seems to demand that all men be united; the rites of the Chinese seem to require that all be separated.

And since such separation[20] has been shown to follow from the spirit of despotism, here is a reason for believing that monarchy, along with every other moderate form of government, is that most compatible[21] with the Christian religion.

Chapter XIX
How Religion, Laws, *Moeurs*, and *Manières*
Came to Be Identical in China

The Chinese received their codes from legislators who believed that the principal objective of government was to ensure the tranquillity of the empire. This could best be maintained, they thought, by establishing that relationship among men which depends upon the subordination of some to others. This belief led them to exert all their energies in the effort to inspire respect for the fathers of families. Chinese legislators established an infinite number of rites and ceremonies to honor fathers both when alive and after their death. To instill respect for deceased fathers could not but lead to the same attitude toward the living. Ceremonies for deceased fathers were related more closely to religion; those for the living, to laws, *moeurs*, and *manières*. But these both formed parts of the same code, which extended to almost every aspect of life.

Respect for fathers was necessarily tied to everything they stood for: [the authority of] the eldest, teachers, magistrates, the emperor. Such respect for the father presupposed a reciprocal love for his children; and therefore the same reciprocity of feeling on the part of the old toward the young, of magistrates toward those under their jurisdiction, of the emperor toward his subjects. Taken together, these [relationships] made up the rites, which constituted the general spirit of the nation.

The reader will not fail to perceive that relationship which apparently irrelevant things may have to the fundamental constitution of China. For that empire is founded on the idea of the government of a family. If paternal authority is diminished, or even if there is a curtailment of those ceremonies which express respect for it, respect for magistrates will be weakened, because these are regarded as fathers. Nor will magistrates manifest the same concern for the people, whom they should consider as their children. And that relationship of love between ruler and subjects will disappear little by little.[22] To curtail any one of these observances is to shake the state to its foundations. In and of itself, it matters little whether a daughter-in-law upon awakening every morning, fulfills some obligation or other to her mother-in-law. But these ritual practices continuously revive a feeling that must be imprinted in all hearts, and then [once imprinted] flows from them to form that spirit which governs the empire. It is in this sense that every one of these separate practices is necessary.

Chapter XX
How to Explain a Paradox about the Chinese

Nothing is more surprising about the Chinese than the fact that, although their lives are governed by rites in every detail, they are the most deceitful people on earth. This is especially true of them when they are engaged in commerce. For although that activity by its nature depends upon good faith, it has no such effect upon the Chinese. Every buyer should carry[23] his own scales. For every merchant owns three sets: one for buying, which registers a weight beneath the actual one; one for selling, which registers a weight above the actual one; and a third set for those who are on their guard. I believe that this contradiction may be explained.

The Chinese received their codes from men who had two ends in view: that the people be submissive and tranquil, and that it be industrious and skillful. Because of the nature of its climate and terrain, the life of the people was precarious. Only by ingenuity and hard work could they continue to live.

When everyone obeys and works hard, the state is in a fortunate situation. It is necessity, and perhaps the nature of the climate that has made all Chinese incredibly avid for gain. This quality their laws have never sought to combat. Rather they permitted nothing to be acquired by violence; while anything could be acquired by either fraud or hard work. Thus Chinese morality must not be compared to that of Europe. In China, everyone must pay strict attention to his own advantage: the swindler attends to what will profit him; his victim ought to do no less. In Sparta, theft was permitted; in China, fraud.

Chapter XXI
How Laws Ought to Be Related to *Moeurs* and *Manières*

Only exceptional institutions thus confuse things as disparate in nature as laws, *moeurs*, and *manières*. Yet although different, there are significant relationships among them.

When Solon was asked if the laws he had given to the Athenians were the best, he replied, "I have given them the best laws they could bear." That fine phrase ought to guide every legislator. When Divine Wisdom said to the Jews, "I have given you precepts that are not good," this meant their goodness was only relative. Here is the sponge to wipe away all the difficulties that can be raised about the Mosaic law.[24]

Chapter XXII
The Same Subject Continued

When a people's *moeurs* are good, its laws become simple. Plato[25] observed that Rhadamanthus, who governed over an extremely religious people, was very quick in deciding legal cases, for [to discover the truth] he had only to put everyone concerned on oath. But as Plato also wrote,[26] when a people is not religious, oaths can be used only when the person taking the oath has no interest in the case, as for example, a judge or witnesses.

Chapter XXIII
How Laws Follow *Moeurs*

During the time that the Romans' *moeurs* were pure, there was no law specifically prohibiting the embezzlement of public funds. When this crime began to be committed, it was regarded as so infamous, that to be condemned to restore[27] what had been taken was thought to be a very severe punishment: witness the sentence of L. Scipio.[28]

Chapter XXIV
The Same Subject Continued

Those laws [of inheritance] which make mothers the legal guardians of their children are most concerned with the care of the young; those laws which make the nearest of kin guardians are most concerned with the preservation of the estate. In the case of peoples with corrupted *moeurs*, it is best to make mothers guardians. In the case of peoples whose laws reflect confidence in the *moeurs* of their citizens, the position of guardian may be assigned to either the heir to the estate, or to the mother, or sometimes to both.

Upon reflection, it will be seen that the spirit of Roman law conformed to what has just been said. When the laws of the Twelve Tables were drawn up, Roman *moeurs* were admirable. The nearest relative of the child was made its guardian because it was thought that as a potential beneficiary of the inheritance he ought to bear the burden of serving as guardian. It did not occur to anyone that the child's life might be endangered by putting him in the hands of that person who would profit by his death. But when Roman *moeurs* changed, legislators changed their way of thinking accordingly. "If, when designating the successor to the heir," wrote Gaius[29] and Justinian,[30] "the testator fears that such an arrangement may endanger the young person who is to be placed under the guardian, another arrangement may be used.[31] By it the testator may allow the vulgar form of substitution to be discovered, but put the pupillary form of succession in a part of the will which may not be opened until after the passage of a stipulated time." Here is an example of fears and precautions unknown to the earliest Romans.

[Chapter XXV is omitted.]

Chapter XXVI
The Same Subject Continued[32]

The provisions for renouncing a spouse under the law[33] of Theodosius and Valentinian were taken from the earlier *moeurs*[34] and *manières* of the Romans. Among the valid grounds for such repudiation, the Romans included the behavior of a husband[35] who beat his wife in a way that disgraced her as a free-born woman. In the next versions of the same law,[36] this ground was not included: this was because the *moeurs* had changed on this point. Oriental usages had displaced European. According to history, the empress, wife of Justinian II, was threatened by her eunuch with the same punishment as that used on children at school. This could happen only after certain *moeurs* had become established or during an attempt to make them so.

We have seen how the laws follow the *moeurs*; let us see how the *moeurs* follow the laws.

Chapter XXVII

How a Nation's Laws May Contribute

to Its *Moeurs*, *Manières*, and Character

The customs of an enslaved people constitute a part of their slavery; those of a free people, a part of their liberty.

In Book XI,[37] I spoke of a free people; I stated the principles of its constitution. Let us now see what effects have necessarily followed from it, the character which emerged, and the *manières* that resulted from it.

I do not wish to deny that its climate has been responsible in large part for the laws, *moeurs*, and *manières* of this nation. But I maintain that its *moeurs* and *manières* must have a close connection to its laws.

In this state, there are two visible powers: the legislative and the executive.[38] And since every citizen has a will of his own and is able to assert his independence whenever he pleases, most of them prefer one power to the other. This is because the majority of men are seldom equitable or sensible enough to care equally for both these powers.

What is more, because the executive power controls all public employment, it can stimulate great expectations without ever arousing fears. Thus all those who receive favors from it are led to take its side; all those who have nothing to hope, attack it.

Since here all the passions have free rein, hatred, envy, jealousy, ambition for wealth and distinction – all these manifest themselves to the greatest possible extent. Were this not so, the state would be like a man so weakened by illness that he lacks passion because he lacks strength.

Between the two parties there is a hatred which continues because it is always impotent.

Since free men make up these parties, if one becomes too powerful for the other, the effect of liberty will be to humble the victor. For the citizens act like hands that help somebody who has fallen. They raise up the weaker side.

Since every individual is independent and much given to following his whims and fantasies, he frequently changes party. He abandons the one to which belong all his friends for the one to which belong all his enemies. In this nation, the laws of friendship and hatred are easily forgotten.[39]

The monarch is in the same position as private individuals. Contrary to the usual maxims prescribed by prudence, he is often obliged to place his confidence in those who have most abused it, and to dismiss those who have best served him. Thus he does out of necessity what other rulers do by choice.[40]

We always fear the loss of an advantage we appreciate, yet do not understand, and which, therefore, we fear may be taken from us by deceit. And what is feared always appears larger than it is in reality. When the people feels uncertain of its position, it believes itself endangered even when it is most secure.

Those who most vigorously oppose the executive power, cannot admit the self-interest that underlies their opposition. Hence they tend to magnify the fears of the people, which never can know for certain whether or not it is in danger. But even this uncertainty helps the people avoid the genuine perils to which it may later be exposed.

But because the legislative body enjoys the people's confidence, and is better informed, it may correct the people's bad impressions and calm its disorders.

Here is the great advantage of this type of government as compared to the ancient democracies where the people exercised power directly. For when stirred up by orators, the people always responded.

Thus when [in a representative government] citizens become terrified by fears not based upon anything definite, the worst that happens are ineffective uproars and insults. There may even be a good effect: the citizens become more attentive because all the springs that move the government become stretched to their capacity. But when the citizens' fears are caused by the [actual] overthrow of fundamental laws, they become sullen, sinister, and cruel and produce only catastrophes.

Soon a frightening calm follows during which all unite against the power that had violated the law.

If, at a time when there is no focus for [public] uneasiness, a foreign power should appear to menace the state and to endanger its prosperity or glory, petty interests would then yield to greater ones and everyone would join to support the executive power.

If a violation of fundamental laws has occasioned a dispute, and a foreign power should then appear, there would be a revolution. But this would change neither the form of the government nor its constitution. For revolutions that create liberty only confirm liberty.

A free nation may have a liberator; a conquered nation can have only another oppressor.

For anyone strong enough to overthrow the absolute ruler of a state can himself become its master.

If a state is to enjoy and preserve liberty, everyone must be able to say what he thinks. In a free state, therefore, a citizen may speak and write anything not expressly forbidden by the laws.

A nation such as this is always impassioned. Thus it is more easily moved by its passions than by reason, which never produces great effects on the minds of men. It is easy for those who govern this nation to lead it into enterprises contrary to its true interests.

Because its liberty is real, no other nation loves its liberty more than this one. To defend it, the nation stands ready to sacrifice its wealth, its comfort, its interests; it will support the burden of taxes so onerous that even the most absolute prince would never dare impose their like on his subjects.

But because the people know exactly why they must submit to such taxes, they pay them in the well-founded hope that their burden is only temporary. Thus their discomfort stems more from what they actually pay, than from their fear of being taxed even more. In certain other states, the opposite is true.

The basis of this nation's credit is sound, because it borrows from itself, and repays what it owes. It conceivably might attempt enterprises surpassing its own natural strength and bring to bear against its enemies immense sums of imaginary riches which the credit and nature of its government would then convert into reality.

To preserve its liberty, this nation borrows from its own subjects. Knowing that the national debt will be worth nothing in the event of defeat, its subjects thus acquire still another motive for exerting themselves in defense of their liberty.

Since this nation is set on an island, it will never attempt to become a conqueror.[41] For conquests if distant, would only weaken it. This is all the more true since its own soil is satisfactory. Thus it has no need to make war to enrich itself. And since no citizen is subject to any other, each cares more about his own liberty than about the glory of some few citizens, or that of any one person.

Military men are regarded there as members of a profession, which, although sometimes useful, is often dangerous, as men who burden the nation by the very services they render. Their qualities are less highly esteemed by this nation than those of a civilian.

Because of peace and liberty, this nation has grown prosperous. Freed from destructive prejudices, it has been led toward commerce. It possesses some of those raw materials used to make those articles whose value is much enhanced by the skill of artisans. Hence it can create manufacturing establishments that enable it to enjoy to the fullest extent such gifts of heaven.

This nation which is situated towards the north, produces a surplus of many commodities. On the other hand, it lacks many things denied it by its climate. Thus it must engage in large-scale commerce with the peoples of the south. By choosing those states with which it can trade advantageously, it enters into mutually advantageous treaties with them.[42]

In this nation, where there is, on the one hand, extreme opulence, and, on the other, excessive taxation, it is difficult to live on a small fortune without turning to industry. Many, therefore, under the pretext of traveling or bad health, exile themselves from their native land to go in search of wealth, even to those countries where slavery exists.

A commercial nation has an extraordinary number of small private interests. Thus it may injure or be injured in an infinite variety of ways. Such a nation is dominated by jealousy, and its annoyance at the prosperity of others exceeds any pleasure produced by its own well-being.

Its laws, otherwise mild and flexible, are so rigid in all matters involving commerce and transport that it might seem that this nation trades only with enemies.

When it establishes far-off colonies, it does so more to extend its trade than its domination over others.

Since men like to establish elsewhere those institutions they have at home, this nation has given its own form of government to the people of its colonies. Since such government carries prosperity with it, great peoples will arise out of those very forests where this nation has sent its colonists.

In the past, this nation conquered a neighbor,[43] which aroused jealousy by its favorable location, the excellence of its ports, and the nature of its resources. Although this neighbor has now been given its own laws, it still is in a state of such great dependence upon its conqueror that although its people are free, their state is itself enslaved.

Although the conquered state has an excellent civil government, it is crushed by international law. The laws imposed by the conqueror are such that the prosperity of the conquered nation can never be other than precarious, held on demand for its master.

Since the dominant nation inhabits a large island and carries on a considerable commerce, it has every facility for becoming a great sea power. And because the preservation of its liberty requires that there be no strongholds, fortresses, or land armies, it needs a navy to protect it from invasion. And this is superior to that of other powers, all of which must use their financial resources for war on land, and therefore do not have enough left for war at sea.

Dominance at sea has always produced natural pride in those peoples who have enjoyed it. Because they know that they can attack anywhere, they believe their power to be as boundless as the ocean.

This nation exerts great influence upon its neighbors' affairs because it does not use its power for conquest. Despite the instability of its government and its domestic unrest, its friendship is more sought after, and its hatred more feared than might be expected.

Thus it is the fate of the executive power to be almost always in trouble at home while respected abroad.

When this nation on several occasions became the center of negotiations among European states, it brought to them rather more probity and good faith than did the others. Because its ministers had to justify themselves frequently before a popular assembly, their negotiations could not be secret. On this point at least, they had to be a little more honorable.

Furthermore, since they are up to a point responsible for the consequences of any irregular conduct, they are safest when following the straight path.

The nobles once possessed excessive power over the rest of the nation. The monarch found means to put the nobles down while raising the status of the people. Servitude must have been at its worst between that moment when the nobles had been abased and the moment when the people began to sense their power.

Since this nation was once subject to an arbitrary power,[44] its style has on many occasions been preserved, with the result that a government based on freedom often has the appearance of an absolute government.

As far as religion is concerned, every citizen of this state has freedom of choice, and is therefore guided either by his own knowledge or by fantasies. Hence it follows that either everyone is sovereignly indifferent to religions of any kind, in which case all will be inclined to embrace the dominant religion, or else that all will be full of religious zeal, in which case sects will multiply.

Among the people of this nation, there are some, who, although not believers in any religion, nevertheless might object to being forced to change what would be their religion if they had one. To begin with, they perceive that their life and property are no more their own than is their mode of thought. Whoever can deprive them of one, can with better reason do the same to the other.

If, among all these different religions, an attempt were made to establish one of them by enslaving the population, this religion[45] would become hated. For we judge things by their associations and the secondary meanings we attach to them. Such circumstances would make it impossible to link this religion with the concept of liberty.

Although those who profess this religion are punished by law, the penalties are not harsh, for such penalties are unimaginable under freedom. Nevertheless, these laws are so repressive that they cause every evil that may be achieved in cold blood.

In a thousand different ways, the clergy has come to be held in such small esteem that all other citizens have gained proportionately. Thus, rather than separate itself from them, the clergy prefers to pay the same taxes as do the laity and, in this respect, to rank as members of the same estate. Yet, since the clergy has always aimed at gaining the respect of the people, its members distinguish themselves by their more retired life, reserved behavior, and greater purity of *moeurs*.

Because this clergy lacks the power to coerce, it can no more protect religion than it can be protected by religion; it seeks only to persuade. From the pens of its members flow excellent works designed to prove the revelation and providence of the Supreme Being.

Yet the wishes of the clergy's assemblies are evaded, and it is not allowed to correct its own abuses. By liberty carried to the point of delirium, this nation prefers to leave the reform of the church unfinished, rather than to allow it to reform itself.[46]

Since titles of nobility (*les dignités*) form part of the fundamental constitution, they are more rigidly fixed here than elsewhere. But seen from another aspect, in this country of liberty, the notables are closer to the people. Thus, while there is a greater distance among ranks, their members mix more.

When those who govern are themselves subject to a power that must be constantly reaffirmed and renewed, they care more about those who may be useful than about those who amuse them. Thus there are not many courtiers, flatterers, and sycophants; in short, fewer of all those types who profit from the emptiness characteristic of the minds of the great.[47]

Men are esteemed, not for frivolous talents and traits, but for real qualities. Of these, there are but two: wealth and personal merit.

Even luxury is solid, founded not on the refinement of vanity, but on real needs. No pleasures are sought beyond what nature can bestow.

Although the rich are favored with more money than they need, they look down on frivolity. Thus many have resources in excess of their opportunities for spending them. And thus they use their means in bizarre ways; this nation has more intelligence than taste.

Since its inhabitants are constantly kept busy by the pursuit of their interests, they possess none of that polish which derives from idleness. Really they have not the time for it.

The period when the Romans acquired polish (*politesse*) coincided with the establishment of absolute power. Absolute government produced idleness; idleness gave rise to polish.

The more people there are in a nation who must treat one another with care so as not to cause displeasure, the more politeness (*politesse*) will be in evidence. But what ought to distinguish us from barbarians is our politeness, not in *manières*, but in *moeurs*.

In a nation where every man, in some way, takes part in administering the state, women ought not to spend much time with men. For [in such a country] the women will be modest, or, rather, timid, and this is the appropriate form of virtue for them. As for the men, who lack all gallantry, they plunge into debauchery. This leaves them with complete freedom and leisure.

Since the laws are not made for the benefit of any one person over any other, everyone considers himself a monarch. In such a nation, men are more allies than fellow-citizens.

The climate has endowed a good many people with restless minds and far-ranging perspectives. And since this country assigns everyone a part in the government and political interests, politics is much discussed.[48] There are men who spend their lives in attempting to calculate events, which, considering the nature of things and the caprices of fortune, that is, of men, are not at all subject to such calculation.

In a free nation, it often matters little whether individuals reason well or badly, so long as they reason at all. For this is the source of that liberty which protects them against the effects of their reasoning.

Similarly, under despotic government, it is equally dangerous to reason well or badly. The very fact of reasoning is enough to offend the principle of government.

[In this country], there are a good many men who choose to please no one, and indulge themselves in whatever humor may strike them. Most of them with any intelligence (*de l'esprit*) use it to torment themselves. Filled with disdain and disgust for everything, they are not happy, despite all their reasons to be.

Since none of its citizens fears any other, this nation is proud. For the pride of monarchs is due to nothing else than their independence.

Free nations are arrogant; all others find it easier to be vain.

These men who are so proud live for the most part by themselves. But when they find themselves, as often happens, among peoples unknown to them, they become timid, and display on most occasions an odd mixture of pride and excessive scruple.

This nation's character appears most clearly in its intellectual works, which reveal reflective men who have done their thinking in solitude.

Life in society makes us aware of how ridiculous men can be; withdrawal from it makes us more sensitive to their vices. Satirical writing in this country cuts to the bone; there are many Juvenals, but not a single Horace.

In the most absolute monarchies, historians betray the truth because they lack the requisite freedom; in those states that are most free, historians betray the truth precisely because of their freedom. For its exercise always creates divisions, and everyone is as much enslaved by the prejudices dear to his faction as he would be under the rule of a despot.

Their poets more often possess rough originality and inventiveness than that delicacy imparted by good taste. Their work is more akin to the power of a Michelangelo than to the grace of a Raphael.

BOOK XXIII
How Laws Are Related to the Number of Inhabitants

[Chapters I–XXVIII omitted.]

Chapter XXIX
Charitable Institutions (*Des Hôpitaux*)[1]

A man is not poor because he has nothing, but because he does not work. The man who has no property but works is as well off as one who lives off his annual income of a hundred crowns. The man who owns nothing but practices a trade is not poorer than one who possesses ten acres of land that he has to work in order to stay alive. The artisan who teaches his children his skill has given them an inheritance which will multiply in proportion to their number. The same is not true of a man with ten acres, which he must divide up among his children.

In commercial countries, where many own only their skills, the state is often obliged to provide for the needs of the old, the sick, and orphans. A well-governed state finances such support from the useful arts and trades themselves, and puts some of the needy to work on whatever they are capable of, while teaching others how to work. Such instruction creates still another type of employment.[2]

The state does not fulfill its obligations merely by giving alms to a naked man on the street. Rather it owes all its citizens regular means of subsistence, proper clothes, and a mode of life that does not endanger their health.

Aurengzebe,[3] when asked why he built no charitable institutions, replied, "I shall make my empire so rich that none will be needed." What he should have said was, "I shall begin by making my empire rich, and then I shall build charitable institutions."

If a state is to be rich, it must have considerable industry. When there are so many kinds of commerce, there must always be one branch which suffers, putting its workers in a situation of temporary distress.

Whenever this occurs, the state must provide prompt relief, whether this be done to prevent the people from suffering, or to forestall rebellion. It is in such a situation that charitable institutions, or their equivalent, are needed, to prevent such suffering.

But when a nation is poor, the poverty of individuals is due to the misery of the society as a whole, and constitutes, so to speak, that general misery. All the charitable institutions in the world are powerless to cure such private poverty. On the contrary, the spirit of laziness they inspire adds to the general poverty, and consequently to that of individuals.

Henry VIII,[4] who wished to reform the Church of England, destroyed monasticism. He did so because the monks made up an idle nation of their own, which encouraged idleness among others by providing hospitality to any number of idle persons, noble and bourgeois, who spent their lives running from one monastery to another.[5] He also did away with the almshouses, which provided subsistence for the lower class of the people (*le bas peuple*) as the monasteries had done for noblemen. Since these changes were made, the spirit of commerce and industry has been established in England.

In Rome, almshouses are responsible for making everyone comfortable except those who work, those who are industrious, those who practice useful trades, those who own land, those engaged in commerce.

I have stated that rich nations need charitable institutions because fortune exposes them to a thousand accidents. But temporary aid is much better than institutions established for all time. When the trouble is of the moment only, its relief ought to be of the same nature, applicable to particular accidents.[6]

BOOK XXIV

How Laws Are Related to Every Country's Established Religion (Considered Intrinsically and in Terms of Its Practices)

Chapter I

Religions in General

We can judge among shadows and determine their relative size; we can judge among abysses and determine their relative depth. In the same way, we can investigate false religions and discover which of them do most to promote the good of society, those, which, although they do not lead men to the felicities of the life to come, can most contribute to human happiness in this world.[1]

Thus my examination of the various religions is purely in terms of the good they produce in civil society, although I shall allude both to that religion rooted in heaven, and to many others rooted in this earth.

In this work, I am not a theologian, but a political writer. Hence I may make statements which are altogether correct only when considered from a human point of view. They have not been considered in terms of any connection to more sublime truths.

As for the only true religion, anyone who is at all fair will see that I have never attempted to subordinate its interests to those of politics. My intention, to the contrary, has been to unite both interests, and to make this possible by understanding them.

The Christian religion ordains that men should love one another. No doubt it also wishes the best political and civil laws for all peoples, because after Christianity itself, such laws are the highest good men can give and receive.

Chapter II
Bayle's Paradox

Mr. Bayle[2] has attempted to prove that it is better to be an atheist than to worship idols; in other words, that it is less dangerous to have no religion than to have a false one. "I should rather have it said of me," he wrote, "that I do not exist, than that I am a bad man." This is nothing more than a sophism because it centers on an assertion of no use whatever to the human race, the assertion that a certain human being exists. What matters most in terms of utility, is the belief in the existence of God. From the idea that God does not exist follows that of our independence, or, if not that, the idea of our disobedience. To assert that because religion does not always succeed in restraining us, it provides no motives for restraint is as absurd as to make the same argument about civil laws, which also do not invariably restrain. Whoever writes a long treatise to make a case against religion abuses reason when he gives a detailed enumeration of all the harm it has done without ever considering the good things to its credit. I could produce a parade of horrors, if I set out to recount all the evils ever produced by civil laws, by monarchies and republics [and yet these are the best forms of government]. Even when it serves no purpose for subjects to have a religion, this is not the case when it comes to rulers who foam in their rage against the only reins that restrain those who fear no man-made laws.[3]

A ruler who loves and fears religion is a lion who yields to the hand that strokes him, or to the voice that calms him; a ruler who fears and hates religion is like those wild animals which bite at the chain that keeps them from attacking passersby; a ruler unrestrained by any religion, is a terrible animal who feels free only when he can dismember and devour [at will].

The question at issue is not whether it is better that a person or people have no religion than be abused by one they practice. Rather it must be asked, which is the lesser evil? That religion occasionally produce abuses? Or that it altogether cease to exist?

In order to diminish the horror aroused by atheism, [authors like Bayle] have been unfair to idolatry. For it is not true that when the ancients raised altars to some vices, this meant that they loved them. On the contrary, this meant that they did so because of their hatred for these vices. When the Spartans erected a temple to fear, this did not mean that such a warlike nation was requesting fear to seize the hearts of its soldiers in combat. Men pray to some divinities not to inspire wrongdoing, and to other gods to shield them from wrongdoing.

Chapter III
Moderate Government Is More Compatible with Christianity; Despotic Government, with Mohammedanism

The Christian religion is far removed from pure despotism. That gentleness so recommended in the Gospels cannot be reconciled with the despotic rage in which such rulers punish their subjects and display their cruelty.

Since Christianity forbids polygamy, rulers are not so confined [to their harems], not so separated from their subjects, and hence, are more humane. They are more inclined to limit themselves by law, more capable of realizing that they cannot do everything they wish.

Mohammedan rulers usually punish by the penalty of death, and are themselves punished in the same way. But Christian rulers because of their religion, are less fearful and, hence, less cruel. The Christian ruler relies on his subjects, and they on him. How admirable that Christianity, which is ostensibly concerned only with felicity in the next life, in addition confers happiness on earth!

It is Christianity that has prevented despotism from being established in Ethiopia, despite the scale of the empire and the defects of its climate. Thus the Christian religion has carried into the middle of Africa the *moeurs* of Europe as well as its laws.

In Ethiopia, the heir to the throne is given a principality, where he presents to other subjects an example of love and obedience. Nearby,[4] Mohammedanism is responsible for keeping in confinement the sons of the king of Sennar. At his death, his council had his sons' throats cut, in the interests of the next ruler.

We ought not to lose sight of the fact that in Greece and Rome, kings and chiefs were always being massacred, any more than we allow ourselves to forget the destruction of entire peoples and cities by Tamburlaine and Genghis Khan, who devastated Asia. In this way can be seen what we owe to Christianity, which has given us both public law (*droit politique*) in our governments, and international law (*droit des gens*) in time of war. For this, humanity (*la nature humaine*) can never be too grateful.

Because of international law, the victor concedes to conquered peoples among us [in Europe] such great benefits as their life, liberty, property, and always their religion – always provided that the victor is not blinded [by his success].

We may say that today disunity is no greater among the peoples of Europe than it was under the Roman Empire after it had become a military despotism. Then there was disunity between peoples and armies, and among the armies themselves. On the one hand, armies made war against one another; on the other, they pillaged the cities, and divided or confiscated the lands.

Chapter IV

The Effects of Christianity and Mohammedanism

The characters of Christianity and Mohammedanism are such that we ought, without further consideration, embrace the first and reject the second. For it is much easier to prove that a religion improves men's *moeurs* than to demonstrate its truth.

It is a misfortune for humanity (*la nature humaine*) when religion is imposed by a conqueror. Mohammedanism, which speaks only by the sword, continues to act upon men in that destructive spirit by which it was founded.

. . .

Chapter V

Catholicism Is More Compatible with Monarchy;
Protestantism, with Republics

When a religion is conceived and takes form in a state, usually it adopts the scheme of government of that state. For both those who embrace this religion and those who sponsor it have no other conception of order than that of the state in which they were born.

When the Christian religion was unfortunately divided two centuries ago into Catholicism and Protestantism, it was the peoples of the north who became Protestants, while those of the south remained Catholics.[5]

This was due to the fact that the peoples of the north have and always will have a spirit of independence and liberty lacking in those of the south. Thus a religion with no visible leader is better suited to the independence produced by their climate than a religion whose leader is visible.

In the very countries where Protestantism became established, the changes that were made followed the scheme of government in each state. Since Luther's support came from great princes, he was in no position to make them relish an ecclesiastical authority unaccompanied by any sign of visible hierarchy. Since Calvin's support came from peoples living in republics, or from the obscure bourgeoisie of monarchies, he could not establish hierarchies or distinctions. Each of these two religions could believe itself the more perfect: Calvinism judged itself closer to the words of Jesus Christ; Lutheranism, to the actual practice of the Apostles.

[Chapters VI–XIII are omitted.]

Chapter XIV

How the Force of Religion May Be Applied to Civil Laws

Both religion and the laws of civil society (*les lois civiles*) ought to tend for the most part to make men good citizens. Hence, if either of them fails in this aim, the other ought to compensate for it. The less repressive the religion the more repressive ought to be the laws of society.[6]

Thus, in Japan, where the dominant religion has almost no dogmas and promises neither paradise nor hell, the laws must compensate for their absence. Not only are laws severe there, but their execution is extraordinarily prompt.

When a religion teaches the dogma that all human actions are predetermined, penalties imposed by law ought to be more severe, and enforcement (*la police*) more vigilant. For without these measures, men would behave with complete abandon. But if the dogma taught by religion is that of free will, the situation is altogether different.

Idleness in the soul produced the Mohammedan dogma of predestination; this led to [a further] idleness in the soul. Since it has been proclaimed that something is the decree of God, men must await it quietly. In such a case, the laws ought to awaken those lulled to sleep by religion.

Whenever religion condemns things which ought to be permitted by the laws of society (*les lois civiles*), there is a danger that these laws may permit what religion ought to condemn. Either of these cases indicates an absence of harmony and proportion in thought, which cannot but have an effect upon both religion and the laws.

Thus it was a sin and even a capital crime among the Tartars[7] of Genghis Khan to put a knife into fire, to lean against a whip, to beat a horse with its bridle, to break one bone with another. Yet the same people did not believe it sinful to break their word, to seize another person's property, to injure, or even to kill a man. In a word, laws which cause men to regard as necessary what is really insignificant produce the corresponding disadvantage of causing men to regard as insignificant what is really necessary.

. . .

When salvation is made to depend upon something determined purely by accident, a religion throws away the most powerful spring of human action. In India, it is believed that the waters of the Ganges have the power to sanctify.[8] Those who die on its banks are thought to be exempt from punishment in the next life, and to merit residence in that part of it which is full of delights. Because of this teaching, urns containing the ashes of the dead are sent from the most remote regions to be thrown into this river. What difference does it make whether a man lives virtuously or not, if his remains are to be thrown into the Ganges?

The idea of a place of reward [in the next life] necessarily carries with it that of a place where punishment is administered. If men are allowed to hope for rewards without fearing punishment, the laws of society will lose all force. All those who believe in the certain rewards of the life to come, will escape the legislator, for they will look upon death with too much contempt. How can a man be held in check by the laws when he believes that the greatest punishment a magistrate can inflict will last only a moment, to be followed by [eternal] happiness.

Chapter XV
How the Laws of Society Sometimes Correct False Religions

Respect for ancient practices, simplicity, superstition have sometimes established indecent mysteries or ceremonies. Examples are not difficult to find. Aristotle[9] tells us that in such cases, the law permitted fathers of families to go alone to the temple so as to celebrate the mysteries for their wives and children. This was an admirable law of society, for it protected the *moeurs* against religion.

. . .

Chapter XVI

How Religious Laws Correct the Disadvantages
of the Political Constitution

Considered from another point of view, religion can support a
state when the laws themselves lack the power to do so.

Thus when a state is frequently agitated by civil wars, religion
can do much by establishing one region which remains peaceful at
all times. This was the case in Greece, where the Eleans, as priests
of Apollo, enjoyed eternal peace. The city of Miyako in Japan is
left in peace because it is sacred,[10] and this rule is enforced by
religion. As a result, this empire, which appears to be unique in the
world in not depending, nor wishing to depend upon strangers,
always has a domestic commerce that cannot be ruined by war.

In states where wars are not made as the result of general deliberation, or where the laws provide no means for either terminating
or preventing them, religion establishes times of peace or truce so
that the people may do those things necessary for subsistence such
as sowing their crops.

Every year all hostility among Arab tribes ceases for four
months;[11] the least disturbance would be judged impiety. In the
period when every lord in France could make war or peace, religion set truces to be observed in set seasons.

[Chapters XVII–XVIII are omitted.]

Chapter XIX

It Is Not So Much the Truth or Falsity of a Dogma
that Makes It Useful or Pernicious to Men in Society
as the Use or Abuse that Is Made of It

The truest and most holy of dogmas may produce the worst consequences when not connected to the principles of society. On the
other hand, those dogmas which are most false, when they bear
the proper relation to the principles of society, may produce the
most admirable results.

The religion of Confucius denies the immortality of the soul, as
did the sect of Zeno. Yet it must be said that from their defective
principles, both sects derived conclusions, which although incorrect, have been admirable for their societies.

Taoism and Buddhism[12] share a belief in the immortality of the soul. Yet from this holiest of doctrines, they have drawn dreadful conclusions.

When misunderstood, belief in the immortality of the soul almost everywhere and in every age has led women, slaves, subjects, and friends to promise to kill themselves so that they might go and serve in the next world whomever they had respected and loved while alive in this one. It was so in the West Indies, in Denmark,[13] and remains the practice in Japan,[14] Madagascar,[15] and many other places.

These customs (*coutumes*) derive not so much from the doctrine that the soul is immortal as from belief in the resurrection of the body. From this it has been deduced that after death, the same individual will have the same needs, the same sentiments and passions. From this point of view, the doctrine of the immortality of the soul has a prodigious effect on mankind. This is because the notion that death is simply a change of residence is at once easier to grasp and more likely to flatter our hearts than the notion of a new mode of life.

It is not enough for a religion to establish a doctrine; it must direct it as well. This is what Christianity has done so admirably with the teachings we have discussed. It makes us hope for a condition in which we believe, not one that we experience or know. Every one of its teachings, even that of the resurrection of the body, leads us to spiritual ideas.

BOOK XXV
How Laws Are Related to Established Religions and Their Provisions for Maintaining Orthodoxy

[Chapters I–VIII omitted.]

Chapter IX
Religious Toleration

My subject here is politics, not theology. But even for theologians there is a great difference between tolerating a religion and approving it.

When a state's laws permit the practice of many religions, these must be made by law to tolerate one another. It is a [well-established] principle that every repressed religion will itself become repressive. For if allowed by some chance to emerge from persecution, it will immediately attack the religion that has repressed it, not as a religion, but as a tyranny.

Thus it is useful for the laws to provide both that the several religions not disturb the state, and also that they maintain peace among themselves. A citizen does not satisfy his legal obligations simply by refraining from disrupting his state. He also has the obligation not to disturb his fellow-citizens.

[Chapter X is omitted.]

Chapter XI
Change of [a State's Established] Religion

Any ruler attempting to destroy or change the established religion of his state, exposes himself to great dangers. If his government is despotic, he runs a greater risk of revolution than from any conceivable act of tyranny, which in such states is no novelty. The revolution would be caused by the fact that a state cannot change

238

its religion, *moeurs*, and *manières* instantaneously, and certainly not as rapidly as a ruler can ordain the establishment of a new religion.

Furthermore, the former religion has links to the constitution of the state, while the new one does not; the former religion is in accordance with the climate, while frequently the new one is opposed to it. Nor is this all: the citizens will become disgusted with their laws, they will scorn the established government, and substitute suspicion of both religions for their [former] secure belief in one of them. In short, such a change, at least for some time, will make the people of a state into bad citizens and bad believers.

Chapter XII
Laws that Punish Religious Belief

Laws should not be used to punish religious belief. It is true that such penal laws inspire fear. But because religion has penal laws of its own, which have the same effect, the first source of fear is outweighed by the second. [Caught] between these two types of fear, men's souls turn into something horrible.

Religion has at its command overwhelming threats and promises of reward. Once we become aware of them, all the efforts of magistrates to make us renounce them will be futile. For it seems to us that we are left nothing when deprived of our religion, and lack nothing when allowed to practice it.

Religion cannot be successfully attacked by filling men's souls with fear, for it is at just this time that religion matters most to them. It is better to subvert a religion by the promise of personal favor and material comforts, by the hope of better fortune; not by what arouses men, but by what leads them to forget; not by what makes them indignant, but by lulling religious feeling into somnolence. Then other passions dominate men, and religion becomes inactive. As a general rule, when changing the state's established religion, inducements are more effective than punishments.

The human mind shows its character even in the choice [by a society] of penal sanctions. What was most revolting about the persecutions [of Christian converts] by the Japanese was the cruel tortures they used,[1] not the duration of the punishments meted out. These were more exhausting than fierce, and more difficult to recover from because they appeared less severe.

In short, history teaches that penal laws [punishing the practice of religion] have never had anything but a destructive effect.

Chapter XIII

A Most Humble Remonstrance to the Inquisitors of Spain and Portugal

The burning of an eighteen-year-old Jewess[2] during the last auto-da-fé in Lisbon occasioned the following little piece, perhaps the most futile known to me. When it is attempted to prove matters so clearly true, failure is certain.

The author declares that although a Jew, he respects the Christian religion. Indeed, he cares for it enough to deprive those rulers who are not Christians of their most plausible pretexts for persecuting that faith.

"You complain," he tells his inquisitors, "about the emperor of Japan burning every one of his Christian subjects to death over a slow fire. But he will reply to you: 'We treat you who do not believe what we do, as you yourselves treat those who do not believe what you do. You really lament only your weakness, which prevents you from exterminating us, while permitting us to exterminate you.'

"But it must be said that you are much more cruel than this emperor. We are put to death by you because although believing only what you do, we do not believe everything that you believe. We follow a religion you yourselves recognize as once dear to God, which we think still is, while you think it is not. Because this is your judgment, you punish by fire and sword those who have committed the eminently pardonable error of believing that God[3] still loves what He once loved.

"If you are cruel to us, you are even more so to our children. You have them burned because they follow the inspirations given them by those whom the natural law and the laws of all peoples teach them to regard as gods.

"You deprive yourselves of the advantage given you over the way in which the Mohammedans established their religion. When they boast of the number of their believers, you answer that they have been gained by force, that their religion has been spread by the sword. Why, then, do you establish your own by fire?

"When you wish us to adopt your religion, our objection is

based upon a source, from which you are proud to have descended. You then reply to us that although your religion is more recent, it is divine. This you argue is true because your religion grew through persecution by the pagans and the blood shed by your martyrs. But today you assume the role of Diocletian while forcing upon us what was your relationship to him.

"We implore you, not in the name of the mighty God we serve, as do you, but in that of Christ. You tell us that he took on the human condition as an example for you to follow. We implore you to treat us as He himself would have done, were He still on earth. You wish us to be Christians, but you do not wish yourselves to be.

"But if you do not wish to be Christians, at least be men. Treat us as you would if guided only by the feeble light of justice given us by nature, as you would if you had no religion to guide you and no revelation to enlighten you.

"If Heaven has loved you enough to enable you to recognize the truth, you have been favored by a great gift. But is it right for those who have received their father's heritage to hate those who have not?

"If you possess this truth, do not hide it from us by the form in which you present it. The characteristic of truth is its capacity to win over hearts and minds; it has no relation to that impotence you concede when you attempt to compel belief by torture.

"If you were reasonable, you would not put us to death because we are unwilling to deceive you. If your Christ is the Son of God, we hope that He will reward us for not having wished to profane his mysteries. We believe that the God both you and we serve will not punish us for having endured death for a religion He gave us long ago, for our belief that He has never taken it away from us.

"You live in a century when natural reason (*la lumière naturelle*) is more potent (*vive*) than ever before. Philosophy has enlightened the minds of men; the morality taught by your Gospel has never been better known. Nor has there ever been a time when the rights owed one man by another have been so acknowledged, when the force exerted by one conscience over the next has been so great. You must overcome your old prejudices, which, unless you guard against them, will turn out to be nothing more than your passions. Otherwise it will have to be conceded that you are incorrigible, capable of profiting neither from reason nor instruction; that any nation which gives authority to men like you is unfortunate indeed.

"Shall we quite simply tell you what we think? You regard us more as your enemies than as the enemies of your religion. If you really loved your religion, you would not allow it to become corrupted by so gross an error.

"We must warn you that if in the future anyone ever claims that Europe was civilized in our time, you will be cited as the best proof of its barbarism. Your reputation will cause posterity to regard our century as disgraceful and to hate everyone who lived at our time."

End of Selections from *The Spirit of the Laws*

There are many riches in the subsequent books of *The Spirit of the Laws*, which continues on in the original for three hundred more pages. But I have exhausted the space available to me. The end of my introduction discusses briefly the closing chapters. *The Spirit of the Laws* concludes as it began in the preface, with a felicitous reference to Vergil's *Aeneid*: "Italy! Italy! I finish my treatise on fiefs where most authors begin." The passage from the *Aeneid* (III, 680–691) describes the arrival of the Trojans after their long journey:

> And now Aurora reddens as the stars
> take flight. We sight the dim and distant hills,
> the low coastline of Italy. Achates
> is first to cry out, Italy; with joy
> the rest shout Italy . . . .
>
> The wished-for winds have quickened now; nearby
> a harbor opens up. . . . .[1]

Notes

Editorial Preface

1   The best complete edition of Montesquieu to date is that by André Masson, *Oeuvres complètes de Montesquieu* (3 vols; Paris: Nagel, 1950–55). It reprints the best eighteenth-century edition with corrections by Montesquieu and has the most complete collection of his correspondence, as well as a chronological arrangement of Montesquieu's notebooks, and many valuable articles. The most available edition is that of Roger Caillois, *Montesquieu: Oeuvres Complètes* (2 vols; Paris: Bibliothèque de la Pléiade, 1949–51). In 1939, the Bibliothèque Nationale acquired from Montesquieu's family the only surviving manuscript of *De l'Esprit des lois*. As yet there is no critical variorum edition that collates the 1758 edition with the manuscript. The edition that comes closest to doing so is *De l'Esprit des lois*, ed. Jean Brethe de la Gressaye (4 vols; Paris: Les Belles Lettres, 1950–61). A new critical edition of all Montesquieu's works, planned by a distinguished international committee headed by Jean Ehrard, will be published by the Voltaire Foundation.

The best critical editions of the *Lettres Persanes* are those by H. Barckhausen (Paris, 1897), Antoine Adam (Geneva and Lille, 1954), and Paul Vernière (Paris, 1960); of the *Considérations*, by H. Barckhausen (Paris, 1900) and Gozague Truc (Paris, 1954). All references to *The Spirit of the Laws* will cite the book in capital roman numerals and the chapter in arabic numerals (for example, I, 1 for Book I, chapter 1.)

For many years, the only English translation of *De l'Esprit des lois* was the eighteenth-century version of Thomas Nugent, last reprinted by Franz Neumann (New York: Haffner, 1949), which omits the notable ninth chapter of Book XV, here translated for the first time. Apart from its textual inadequacies (it was not based on the corrected edition Montesquieu himself prepared for this *Oeuvres complètes*), the Nugent version is unsatisfactory. He failed to translate Montesquieu's technical terms consistently; he often distorted Montesquieu's meaning by instead using the nearest British institutional or legal equivalent. Finally, because of changes in English usage, Nugent's language is often either obscure or archaic.

2   Melvin Richter, *The Political Theory of Montesquieu* (Cambridge and New York: Cambridge University Press, 1977).

3   See my comments on the *Dictionnaire* in Melvin Richter, "Montesquieu, the Politics of Language, and the Language of Politics," *History of Political Thought* X (1989), 71–88.

Introduction

I. Montesquieu's Mind and Influence

1   F. T. H. Fletcher, *Montesquieu and English Politics* (London, 1939), p. 121.

2   John Millar, *A Historical View of the English Government* (4th ed; 4 vols; London, 1818), II, 429–30.

3   Hamilton, Madison, and Jay, *The Federalist*, IX.

4   Ibid., XLVII.

5   A distinguished editorial committee headed by Jean Ehrard is at work on a new critical edition to be published by the Voltaire Foundation

6   The sections in this volume from *De l'Esprit des loix* have been completely retranslated by me.

7   "An Essay on the Causes That May Affect Men's Minds and Characters," trans. with an introduction by Melvin Richter, *Political Theory* 4 (1976), 132–62.

8   Auguste Comte, *Cours de philosophie positive* (6 vols.; Paris, 1839), V, 243. Emile Durkheim, *Montesquieu et Rousseau: Précurseurs de la Sociologies* (Paris, 1953), p. 26. Ernst Cassirer, *The Philosophy of the Enlightenment*, trans. Fritz Koelln and James Pettegrove (Princeton, 1951), p. 212; Franz Neumann, ed., *Montesquieu, The Spirit of the Laws*, trans. Thomas Nugent (New York, 1949), pp. xl–xli; Sir Frederick Pollock, *An Introduction to the Science of Politics* (Boston, 1960), pp. 86–87; Friedrich Meinecke, *Historism*, trans. J. E. Anderson (New York, 1972), pp. 90–143; G. W. F. Hegel, *The Philosophy of Right*, trans. T. M. Knox (Oxford, 1942), p. 16; John Maynard Keynes, Preface, French ed. *General Theory of Employment, Interest, and Money*, cited by N. E. Devletogou, "Montesquieu and the Wealth of Nations" (Athens, 1963), p. 11; Neumann, op. cit., p. lix; Jean Ehrard, ed., *Montesquieu, De l'Esprit des lois* (Paris, 1969), Raymond Aron, *Main Currents in Sociological Thought* (2 vols.; New York, 1965) I, 55–56; W. G. Runciman, *Social Science and Political Theory* (Cambridge, 1963), p. 24.

9   *Spirit of the Laws*, X, 3.

10   Caillois, I, 1127; Masson, II, 348.

11   This was removed from the manuscript of *The Spirit of the Laws* (I, f: 63); It would have ended III, 9.

12   Franco Venturi, *Utopia and Reform in the Enlightenment* (Cambridge, 1971), pp. 120–21.

II. Montesquieu's Life and Milieu

13   Thomas L. Pangle, "Montesquieu," in David Miller, ed., *The Blackwell Encyclopedia of Political Thought* (Oxford, 1987), and *Montesquieu's Philosophy of Liberalism* (Chicago, 1973).

14 A Marxist version is to be found in Louis Althusser, *La politique et l'histoire* (Paris, 1959); a non-Marxist version in Franklin L. Ford, *Robe and Sword* (Cambridge, Mass., 1953), especially ch. XII. Ford's view was, however, shaped by Albert Mathiez, "La place de Montesquieu dans l'histoire des doctrines politiques du XVIIIe siècle, "*Annales historiques de la Révolution francaise*, VII (1930), 97–112.

15 There is no easy or universally accepted way to convey the meaning of this distinction. In general, the nobility of the sword claimed to be descended from medieval warriors, or even from the Frankish conquerors of Gaul. The nobility of the robe derived their titles from judicial or administrative office. Judicial offices could be purchased, sold, or inherited. For an extended treatment, see Ford, op. cit., ch. II.

16 Montesquieu, *Spirit of the Laws*, VIII, 6.

17 *Pensées*, 1297 (86); Caillois, I, 997; Masson, II, 358. There are two numbering systems for Montesquieu's *Pensées*. Their original editor, Barckhausen, arranged them topically. This order is preserved by Caillois. However, the Masson edition 17. presents the *Pensées* in order of the manuscript notebooks in which they were written. It also contains an important contribution by Shackleton, the identification of the handwriting of Montesquieu's secretaries, along with their periods of employment. On the basis of this, Desgraves was able to date the *Pensées* and arrange them chronologically. This is significant because it enables us to know just when Montesquieu formulated his ideas. Masson contains a concordance with the Barckhausen arrangement and includes many *Pensées* omitted by Barckhausen or crossed out by Montesquieu.

18 Robert Shackleton, *Montesquieu: A Critical Biography* (Oxford, 1961), p. 396.

III. Montesquieu on Comparative and Natural Law

19 An excellent account of Hotman's thought and significance is to be found in the introduction to Francois Hotman, *Francogallia*, Latin text ed. Ralph Giesey; trans. J. H. M. Salmon (Cambridge, 1972).

20 Masson, II, 443, 556; Caillois, II, 1038.

21 Since my statements here are in no sense intended as more than a summary of commonplaces, I shall cite only a few fairly recent sources in English: Leo Strauss, "Natural Law," *International Encyclopedia of the Social Sciences* (New York, 1968), XI, 80–85; Richard Wollheim, "Natural Law," *Encyclopedia of Philosophy* (New York, 1968), V, 450–54; A. P. d'Entrèves, *Natural Law* (New York, 1965); Richard Tuck, *Natural Rights* (Cambridge, 1979).

22 Perhaps the most useful brief account of these thinkers is Robert Derathé, *Jean-Jacques Rousseau et la science politique de son temps* (Paris, 1950), ch. 11. See also his discussion of legal terms, pp. 380–97. An important recent discussion is Richard Tuck, *Natural Rights*.

23 Grotius, *De Iure Belli Ac Pacis* (2 vols.; Oxford, 1925) I, 10; II, 38–39. Vol. II is the English translation. Pages refer to the translation.

24 Ibid., I, x, 5; II, 40.

25 Ibid., "Prolegomena," 58; II, 30.

26 Among the closest analyses of this book are in Shackleton, *Montesquieu*, M. H. Waddicor, *Montesquieu and the Philosophy of Natural Law* (The Hague, 1970), Jean Ehrard, *l'Idée de Nature en France dans la première moitié du XVIIIe siècle* (2 vols.; Paris, 1963); David Lowenthal, "Book I of Montesquieu's *The Spirit of the Laws*," *American Political Science Review* 53 (1959), 485–98.

27 Rousseau, *Contrat Social*, I, ii.

28 Rousseau, *Manuscrit de Genève*, I, Ch. V, and *Emile*, V.
29 Waddicor, op. cit., pp. 16–21.
30 Ehrard, *l'Idée de Nature*, II, 725. Ehrard is unexcelled in his treatment of French eighteenth-century theories of human nature and a concept basic to Montesquieu, *la nature de choses* (the nature of things); see his II, chs. X–XI.
31 *Spirit of the Laws*, XXVI, 1.

IV. The *Persian Letters* (1721)

32 Caillois, *Montesquieu*, 'Préface,' I, 5.
33 *Persian Letters*, LXXXIII.
34 Ibid.
35 "*Defense de l'Esprit des lois, Seconde partie.*" Masson, I, 456; Caillois, II, 1137.
36 Margaret T. Hodgen, *Early Anthropology in the Sixteenth and Seventeenth Centuries* (Philadelphia, 1964), ch. V. For a discussion of comparison in political and social theory, see Melvin Richter, "Comparative Political Analysis in Montesquieu and Tocqueville," *Comparative Politics* I (1969), 129–60.
37 The best survey is in Shackleton, *Montesquieu*, pp. 46–67.
38 *Persian Letters*, CXXIX.
39 Ibid., LXXX.
40 The most complete treatment in English of these aristocratic critics is by Lionel Rothkrug, *Opposition to Louis XIV* (Princeton, 1965).
41 This has been established by Alessandro Crisafulli, "Montesquieu's Story of the Troglodytes: Its Background, Meaning, and Significance," *Publications of the Modern Language Association of America* LVIII (1943), 372–92.
42 Cited from Shaftesbury's *Characteristics* by Crisafulli, op. cit.
43 For an interpretation of the myth of the Troglodytes, see Melvin Richter, *Political Theory of Montesquieu*, 39–45.
44 See Melvin Richter, "Despotism," *Dictionary of the History of Ideas* (5 vols.; New York, 1974), II, 1–18.
45 Fénelon, *Ecrits et lettres politiques*, ed. Charles Urbain (Paris, 1920), p. 181.
46 Comte Henri de Boulanvilliers, *Essais sur la noblesse de France* (Amsterdam, 1732), p. vii. Cited by Ford, op. cit., p. 27.
47 *Persian Letters*, IX.
48 Ibid., CLXI.

V. *Considerations on the Causes of the Romans' Greatness and Decline* (1734)

49 Hugh Trevor-Roper, "The Historical Philosophy of the Enlightenment," *Studies of Voltaire and of the Eighteenth Century*, ed. Theodore Besterman (Geneva, 1963), 1667–87; Frank Manuel, *Shapes of Philosophical History* (Stanford, 1965); and Meinecke, *Historism*.
50 *Considerations*, XVIII.
51 Ibid.
52 *Considerations*, IX. The opening paragraph is taken from Machiavelli, *Discourses*, I.
53 *Spirit of the Laws*, V, 7; XX–XXIII, esp. XX, 1, 2. See Albert O. Hirschman, *The Passions and the Interests* (Princeton, 1977), 69–81.
54 See Henry Vyverberg, *Historical Pessimism in the French Enlightenment* (Cambridge, Mass., 1958). This places Montesquieu's view of history within its context, as does Peter Gay, *The Enlightenment* (2 vols.; New York, 1969), II, ch. 2.

VI. *The Spirit of the Laws* (1748)

55 William F. Church, "The Decline of the French Jurists as Political Theorists, 1660–1789," *French Historical Studies* (1967), 32.

56 Cited by Brethe, op. cit., I, 230.

57 *Spirit of the Laws*, I, 1.

58 Ibid., X, 3.

59 Ibid., I, 3.

60 Montesquieu, "An Essay on the Causes That May Affect Men's Minds and Characters," trans. and annotated by Melvin Richter, *Political Theory* 4 (1976), 139–62.

61 Caesare Beccaria, *On Crimes and Punishments*, trans. Henry Paolucci (Indianapolis, 1963), p. 9.

62 Durkheim, *Montesquieu et Rousseau*, (Paris, 1953), pp. 90–91.

63 Wolin, *Politics and Vision* (Boston, 1960), pp. 359, 392.

64 Franz Neumann, op. cit., pp. lxiii–lxiv.

65 Caillois, I, 1139; Masson, II, p. 343.

66 *Persian Letters*, LXXXIII.

67 Caillois, I, 109; Masson, III, 160.

68 Pangle, op. cit., pp. 33–34; C. Oudin *Le Spinozisme de Montesquieu* (Paris, 1911); Lowenthal, "Book I of Montesquieu's *The Spirit of the Laws*."

69 *"Defense de l'Esprit des lois,* Réponse à première objection." Caillois, II, 1123; Masson, I, 436.

70 Peter Gay, *The Party of Humanity* (New York, 1964); Carl Becker, *The Heavenly City of the Eighteenth-Century Philosophers* (New Haven, 1932).

71 John Plamenatz, *Man and Society* (2 vols.; New York, 1963), II, 263.

72 This is from a sentence in the manuscript omitted from the printed text.

73 *Spirit of the Laws*, I, 2.

74 Ibid., XXX, 1.

75 Cassirer, loc. cit.

76 *Spirit of the Laws*, Montesquieu's Introduction.

77 Ibid., II, 4.

78 In the important new study by Gerd van den Heuvel, *Der Freiheitsbegriff der Französischen Revolution* (Göttingen, 1988), see the entries for *despotisme* in the index.

79 *Spirit of the Laws*, III, 10, which summarizes the cited passage from *Considerations*, XXII.

80 Ibid., III, 10.

81 Ibid., XX, 6.

82 Ibid., VIII, 3.

83 I owe this formulation, as I do much of what follows in this section, to an exemplary book, which, although brief, shed new light on a subject that seemed exhausted: W. B. Gwyn, *The Meaning of the Separation of Powers* (New Orleans, 1965). M. J. C. Vile, *Constitutionalism and the Separation of Powers* (Oxford, 1967), ch. I, provides an informative summary of the history of constitutionalism.

84 For a more detailed analysis, see my *Political Theory of Montesquieu*, 85–89.

85 *Spirit of the Laws*, XI, 6.

86 Ibid.

87 Ibid.

88 Gwyn, op. cit., pp. 110–11.

89 *Spirit of the Laws*, XI, 6.

90 See the definitions provided in French Terms Used in the Translation.

91 *Spirit of the Laws*, XIX, 27.

92 Ibid.

93 Ibid., XI, 3.

94 Ibid., XI, 4.

95 Ibid., XI, 3.

96   Ibid., XII, 7–10.
97   Ibid., XII, 19.
98   Ibid., VI, 9, 12.
99   Ibid., XI, 4.
100   Ibid., XV, 1.
101   Ibid., XV, 2.
102   Ibid., XV, 5.
103   Ibid., XIX, 4.
104   Ibid., XIX, 16.
105   Ibid., XIV, 6.
106   Ibid., XXIV, 14, 16.
107   Ibid., XIX, 22.
108   Ibid., XIX, 16.
109   Alexis de Tocqueville, *De la Démocratie en Amérique*, I, Chapter XVII.
110   *Spirit of the Laws*, XIV, 13.
111   Ibid., XXIX, 1.
112   Ibid., XXX, 10.
113   Ibid., XI, 6.
114   R. R. Palmer, *The Age of Democratic Revolution* (2 vols.; Princeton, 1959, 1964), I, pp. 57–58.
115   *Considerations*, XVIII.
116   *Spirit of the Laws*, V, 7.
117   Ibid., XXIX, 18.
118   Ibid., XXIII, 19.
119   Ibid., XV, 17.
120   Ibid., XV, 3; and Preface.
121   Jean Ehrard, *Montesquieu, De l'Esprit des lois*, pp. 36–37.
122   Ibid. Ehrard provides an excellent critical discussion.

The *Persian Letters* [Myth of the Troglodytes]

1   *Mullah*, or *mollah* (Montesquieu used *mollak*) in Mohammedan countries is a term for a learned man, a teacher, a doctor of the law. Montesquieu is here suggesting a comparison between learned Moslem and Christian scholars. He seems to be suggesting that the natural justice Usbek believes proper to men is to be preferred, if not to revealed truths, at least to the subtlety of learned casuists.
2   Montesquieu here echoes the stoicism of Cicero's *De Officiis*, from which the last three phrases are taken.
3   The apparent sources are Herodotus, IV, 183 and Pomponius Mela, *De Orbis Situ*, I. Both placed the Troglodytes to the south of Libya, rather than in Arabia.
4   Vernière has argued that this utopia is strongly influenced by the Bétique of Fénelon's *Télémaque*. Cf. Vernière's edition of the *Lettres persanes*, pp. 31n.–32n.
5   The primitivism of this sketch was to have important consequences in the eighteenth century, as was also true of Montesquieu's identification of communal ownership with the virtuous qualities of simple nature.
6   On the subject of virtue, see the "Sequel to the Story of the Troglodytes." It is significant both that Montesquieu returned to the theme, and that he never saw fit to publish it. The "Sequel" was put into Montesquieu's *Pensées*, Masson, II, 463–5; Caillois, I, 377–9.
7   "I thought of continuing the story of the Troglodytes, and here is the idea I had." This sequel was recopied into Montesquieu's *Pensées* by one of his later

secretaries from an earlier manuscript that has not survived. Dr. Shackleton believes that the sequel was written relatively early in Montesquieu's career (personal communication to editor. Montesquieu never printed it.

Considerations on the Causes of the Romans' Greatness and Decline

Chapter III. How the Romans Could Expand

1 This chapter is based principally on the history of Appian, and perhaps on that of Sallust.

2 In chapter I, Montesquieu had stated the issue clearly in terms of what might be called the relationship between human nature and the logic of a historical situation:

> One of two things had to happen: either Rome would change its type of government, or else it would remain a small and poor monarchy.

> Modern history furnishes us with an example of what then occurred at Rome. This is altogether remarkable. For men have always had the same passions. There is a difference in the occasions that produce great changes (*révolutions*), but the causes are always the same.

> Just as Henry VII of England increased the power of the commons in order to reduce that of the notables, Servius Tullius before extended the privileges of the people in order to cut back the power of the senate. But in both cases, the people was made more insolent and overthrew the monarchy.

3 These primary resources consisted both of the original lots resulting from divisions of the land, and of subsequent divisions made of conquered lands.

4 "This is the census discussed by Dionysius of Halicarnassus in Book IX, art. 25, and which appears to me to be identical with that reported by him at the end of Book VI. It was taken sixteen years after the expulsion of the kings" (Montesquieu's note).

5 "Ctesicles in Athenaeus, Book VI" (Montesquieu's note).

6 "These were citizens of the city, properly called Spartans. Lycurgus gave them two thousand shares; he gave thirty thousand to the remaining inhabitants. See Plutarch, *Life of Lycurgus*" (Montesquieu's note).

7 "See Plutarch, *Lives of Agis and Cleomenes*" (Montesquieu's note).

8 "See Plutarch, Ibid." (Montesquieu's note).

9 Livy, "First Decade," Book VII, ch. xxv. This was some time after the capture of Rome, under the consulate of L. Furius Camillus and of Ap. Claudius Crassus" (Montesquieu's note).

10 "Appian, *The Civil War*, Book I, ch. XI" (Montesquieu's note).

Chapter VI. The Means Used by the Romans to Subjugate All Other Peoples

1 This chapter is based primarily on the *History* of Polybius. See also Machiavelli's *Discourses*, II, 1 and *Prince*, V.

2 "An example of this is their war against the Dalmatians. See Polybius" (Montesquieu's note). The reference is to the *History*, XXXII, XIX.

3 "See especially their treaty with the Jews, in the first book of *Maccabees*, ch. 8" (Montesquieu's note).

4   "Ariarathes made a sacrifice to the gods, Polybius writes, to thank them for
    the alliance he had obtained" (Montesquieu's note). The reference is to the
    History, XXXIV, XV.
5   "See Polybius on the cities of Greece" (Montesquieu's note). The reference is
    to the *History*, XXII, XXVI.
6   "Son of Philopator" (Montesquieu's note).
7   "This was the case with Antiochus" (Montesquieu's note).
8   "This prohibition was applied to Antiochus even before he made war. It later
    was extended to all other kings as well" (Montesquieu's note).
9   "Appian, *The War with Mithridates*, ch. XIII" (Montesquieu's note).
10 "A fragment of Dionysius, taken from the *Extract of Embassies* (Montes-
    quieu's note). The reference is to XVII, III.
11 "Livy, Book VII" (Montesquieu's note). This is an error and should read VIII,
    XV.
12 After James II had been dethroned and replaced by William of Orange, Louis
    XIV of France supported James. Catholic Ireland then revolted in behalf of
    James. Like many Frenchmen of his time, Montesquieu believed that it would
    have been good policy to have separated Ireland from England by a French
    military intervention limited to making James supreme in Ireland.
13 "As happened to Ariarathes and Holophernes in Cappadocia. Arrian, *Syrian
    Wars*, ch. 47" (Montesquieu's note).
14 "In order to be able to ruin Syria in their capacity as its regents, they declared
    themselves in favor of Antiochus's son, who was still a child, and against De-
    metrius, whom they held as a hostage. He implored them to be just to him,
    saying that Rome was his mother, the senators his fathers" (Montesquieu's
    note).
15 "This was their consistent practice, as can be seen from history" (Montes-
    quieu's note).
16 See how they conducted themselves during the Macedonian War.
17 Thus the Romans distinguished the state, *civitas* or *res publica* (French, *la cité*)
    from the city, *oppidum* (French, *la ville*).
18 In this case, the Romans had the better argument. The phrase occurs in a pre-
    cise formula of surrender. But the Aetolians did not understand that they were
    surrendering unconditionally.
19 "They treated in the same way the Samnites, Lusitanians, and the peoples of
    Corsica. On these last, see a fragment of Dio, Book I" (Montesquieu's note).
    The reference is to Dio Cassius.
20 "They treated Viriathus in the same way. After making him return their de-
    serters, they demanded that he give up his arms, a request to which neither he
    nor his men could consent. Fragment of Dio" (Montesquieu's note).
21 "The presents sent by the senate to the kings were but bagatelles, such as an
    ivory chair or baton, or some magistrate's robe" (Montesquieu's note).
22 "Florus, Book III, ch. 9" (Montesquieu's note). The reference is to his *Epit-
    ome of Roman History*.
23 "As much as they could, they concealed their power and riches from the Ro-
    mans. On this, see a fragment of Dio, Book I" (Montesquieu's note). This is
    fragment LXVI and deals with Perseus.
24 "They did not dare to expose their colonies there. They preferred to create an
    eternal jealousy between the Carthaginians and Masinissa, and to make use of
    the aid provided by both to subdue Macedonia and Greece" (Montesquieu's
    note).
25 "This is reported by Dionysius of Halicarnassus, Book VI, ch. 95, Oxford edi-
    tion" (Montesquieu's note).

26   Montesquieu is discussing this issue because of his preoccupation with centrali-
      zation and uniformity, and their relationship to monarchy and despotism (see
      Spirit of the Laws, XI, 9). He is concerned to defend the effectiveness of the
      Roman Republic, organized as it was at this time, on the basis of a general
      obedience to Rome, but without any set of laws applicable to all countries
      subject to the Romans. Montesquieu, in speaking of the barbarians, was invok-
      ing the cases of the Merovingian and Carolingian Empires. He argued (*Spirit of
      the Laws*, XXX–XXXI) that the laws of feudal Europe were Germanic in ori-
      gin, and had been brought in by the barbarian invaders.

Chapter VIII. The Internal Divisions that Always Existed at Rome

1   The title of this book apparently was suggested by some chapters in Florus.
      Livy is the most important source, although there is some reliance on
      Polybius.
2   "The patricians even had something of a sacred quality. Only they could take
      the auspices. See the harangue of Appius Claudius in Livy, Book VI" (Montes-
      quieu's note).
3   "For example, only they could have triumphs, since only they could be con-
      suls and command armies" (Montesquieu's note).
4   Montesquieu referred to the hatred of absolute monarchy. The reference is to
      Spirit of the Laws, XI, 13.
5   The curule magistracies were those of the consuls, the dictator, praetors, cen-
      sors, and curule aediles.
6   "Zonaras, Book II" (Montesquieu's note).
7   "Origin of the tribunes of the people" (Montesquieu's note).
8   "The people, who loved glory, were men who had passed their lives in making
      war. They could not refuse their votes to a great man, under whom they had
      fought. They obtained the right to elect plebeians, and they elected patricians.
      They were forced to tie their own hands when they established the provision
      that one of the consuls would always have to be plebeian. Thus the plebeian
      families that first won office were thereafter returned continually to it. When
      the people elevated to honors a nobody (*homme de néant*) such as Varro or
      Marius, this was a sort of victory over themselves" (Montesquieu's note).
9   "In order to defend themselves, the patricians were in the habit of establishing
      a dictator, a practice that worked admirably well for them. But the plebeians,
      once they had succeeded in making themselves eligible for the consulate, could
      also be elected as dictators — something that disconcerted the patricians. See in
      Book VIII of Livy how Publilius Philo humbled them during his dictatorship;
      he made three laws most prejudicial to them" (Montesquieu's note).
10   "The patricians retained only several sacerdotal offices, and the right to create
      a magistrate called the *interrex*" (Montesquieu's note).
11   "Like Saturninus and Glaucia" (Montesquieu's note).
12   "It can be seen how they degraded those who, after the battle of Cannae, had
      believed that Italy ought to be abandoned; those who had surrendered to Han-
      nibal; those who, by an evasive interpretation, had violated their pledges to
      him" (Montesquieu's note). The reference is to Livy, XXIV, xviii.
13   This relationship between mores (*moeurs*) and laws (*lois*) was crucial to Mon-
      tesquieu's theory, and nowhere more than in his analysis of Rome. "Rome was
      a vessel held by two anchors during the storm, religion and mores (*moeurs*)."
      (*Spirit of the Laws*, VIII, 13.)
14   "This was called *aerarium aliquem facere, aut in Caeritum tabulas referre*.
      Such a person was expelled from his century and deprived of his right to vote"
      (Montesquieu's note).

15   "Livy, Book XXIX" (Montesquieu's note). The reference is to ch. 37.
16   "Valerius Maximus, Book II" (Montesquieu's note). The reference is to ch. IX, art. 5.
17   "The dignity of being a senator was not a magistracy" (Montesquieu's note).
18   "Book I" (Montesquieu's note). The reference is to chs. XLII, XLIII.
19   "Book IV, art. xv et seq." (Montesquieu's note).
20   "Called *turba forensis* (rabble of the forum)" (Montesquieu's note). This is Livy's phrase in IX, XLVI.
21   "See Livy, Book IX, ch. XLVI" (Montesquieu's note). The Latin is *Maximus*.
22   "Nor even more power" (Montesquieu's note).
23   Montesquieu meant Parliament. His two most sustained analyses are in *Spirit of the Laws*, XI, 6 and XIX, 27.
24   Montesquieu here repeats the view that conflict can produce politically beneficial effects. Cf. Machiavelli, *Discourses*, I, 4.

Chapter IX.   Two Causes of Rome's Downfall

1   Appian is the principal source for this chapter. Montesquieu also used Florus, I.
2   "Except for pressing cases, the freedmen and those called *capite censi*, because they had very little property and were taxed only on a per capita basis, were at first not enrolled in the army. Servius Tullius had put them into the sixth class, and soldiers were taken only from the first five. But when Marius was leaving on the campaign against Jugurtha, he enrolled everyone without distinction. '*Milites scribere, non more majorum, neque classibus; sed uti cujusque libido erat, capite censos plerosque.* (Marius raised soldiers, neither in the old way, nor according to their class, but from those who wished to go with him, and these for the most part, were from the *capite censi*).' Sallust, *The Jugurthine War*, LXXXVI. Note that in the division by tribes, those in the four tribes of the city, were almost the same as those who were in the sixth class when divided according to centuries" (Montesquieu's note).
3   "If a democracy conquers a people in order to govern it as a subject, then it endangers its own liberty because of the excessive power it must confide to the magistrates it sends to the conquered state." (*Spirit of the Laws*, X, 11.)
4   "Latin rights, Italian rights" (Montesquieu's note).
5   "The Aequi said in their assemblies, 'Those who have been able to choose have preferred their laws to the rights of the Roman state. These have been unavoidable penalties for those peoples who could not defend themselves against them.' Livy, Book IX, ch. XLV" (Montesquieu's note).
6   "The Asculans, the Marisi, the Vestini, the Marrucini, the Grentani, the Hirpini, the Pompeiians, the Venusini, the Japyges, the Lucanians, the Samnites, and others. Appian, *The Civil War*, Book I, XXXIX" (Montesquieu's note). The Asculans and the Japyges are not mentioned in the Loeb edition of Appian's *Roman History*.
7   "The Tuscans, the Umbrians, the Latins. That led some peoples to submit; and, since they also were made citizens, others joined in laying down their arms. Finally, there remained only the Samnites, who were exterminated" (Montesquieu's note).
8   "Imagine such a monstrous head made up of the peoples of Italy; by the vote of each of its citizens, it guided all the rest of the world" (Montesquieu's note).
9   "See the letters of Cicero to Atticus, Book IV, letter XVIII" (Montesquieu's note).
10   Florus, Appian, Bossuet are among those espousing the view here attacked by

Montesquieu, who took a position resembling that of Machiavelli, *Discourses*, I, IV.

11 For the origins of this comparison, cf. Aristotle, *Politics*, I, V; and Cicero, *De Republica*, II, XLII. We owe this text to the fact that it was reproduced by St. Augustine, *City of God*, 2.21.

12 *Bonheur* is the French word translated by "happiness." It was a very significant word indeed in the eighteenth century, as its presence in the American Declaration of Independence indicates. Cf. Robert Mauzi, *l'Idée du Bonheur au XVIIIe siècle* (2d ed.; Paris, 1965) and Ehrard, *l'Idée de Nature*, II, ch. IX, "Nature et Bonheur."

13 The phrase "Asiatic despotism" has since Montesquieu's time gained a certain currency. In the original edition, "Asiatic" was lacking, but apparently Montesquieu decided to avoid trouble with the royal censorship by inserting it, and thus avoiding the suggestion that his ideas might apply to his own government. Cf. my article, "Despotism," op. cit.

14 Montesquieu held the view that a republic by the logic of its nature had to be small. Cf. *Spirit of the Laws*, VIII, 16 and 2, 3, 12. This point was the subject of much discussion by the Americans, especially at the time when the constitution was being discussed. Cf. *The Federalist*, IX, where Hamilton attempted to refute by a detailed analysis of Montesquieu, the allegation made by the opponents of the constitution that it violated Montesquieu's principles. Hamilton cited Montesquieu on the advantages of a confederation of republics (*Spirit of the Laws*, IX, 1–3). Cf. Jefferson's comments (for the most part hostile on this point) in *Pensées choisis de Montesquieu tirées du 'Common-place Book' of Thomas Jefferson*, ed. Gilbert Chinard (Paris, 1925), pp. 16, 16n., 44n.

15 The canton of Berne in Switzerland. Berne in 1712 scored a decisive victory over the Catholic cantons; its great economic prosperity lasted until the middle of the eighteenth century.

Chapter XVIII. The New Maxims Adopted by the Romans

1 The principal source of this chapter is Ammianus Marcellinus. This chapter covers for the imperial period the equivalent of the material on the early Romans discussed in ch. II of the *Considerations*.

2 "At first everything was given to the soldiers; then, to the enemy" (Montesquieu's note).

3 "Ammianus Marcellinus, Book XXV" (Montesquieu's note). The reference is to XXV, VI.

4 "Ammianus Marcellinus, Book XXVI" (Montesquieu's note). The reference is to XXVI, V.

5 " 'Do you wish riches?' said an emperor to his complaining army. 'There is the country of the Persians; let us go seek riches there. Believe me, nothing remains of all those treasures once possessed by the Roman Republic; and this evil is due to those who taught rulers to buy peace from the barbarians. Our finances are exhausted, our cities destroyed, our provinces ruined. An emperor who knows no other goods than those of the soul is unashamed to admit an honest poverty.' Ammianus Marcellinus, Book XXIV" (Montesquieu's note). The reference is to XXIV, III, where Ammianus attributes these words to the emperor Julian.

6 "This is an observation of Vegetius; and it appears from Livy, that if the number of auxiliaries was in excess, this was by very little" (Montesquieu's note). The references are to Vegetius, *Epitoma rei militaris*, III, 1; and Livy, XXI, LV.

7 Since this paragraph is among the most important in the *Considerations*, and indeed in all Montesquieu's work, it may be worth pointing out the difficulties

confronting any translator of Montesquieu's final sentence. The French reads: "En un mot, l'allure principale entraine avec elle tous les accidents particuliers." *Allure* means a usual and general pattern or trend. Another key use of it comes in *Spirit of the Laws* (XXX, 4): "La monarchie avait son allure par des ressorts qu'il fallait toujours remonter." (The monarchy's way of proceeding depended upon springs that it continually had to rewind.)

8   Montesquieu explained how this could be so in ch. X, "The Corruption of the Romans," and his explanation is based on two moral causes: "In addition to the fact that religion is always the best support of men's mores (*moeurs*), the Romans were unusual in that they combined religious sentiment with their love of their native land (*patrie*). This city, founded under the best auspices; this Romulus, their king and their god; this capitol, eternal like the city; and this city, eternal like its founder – these, in earlier times, had made on the spirit of the Romans an impression it would have been desirable to preserve." Although Rome became corrupt in many regards, "the strength of its original establishment had been such that it preserved its heroic valor, with all its application to war in the midst of riches, laxity, and voluptuousness – something which has happened in no other country in the world." Another explanation is based on the professions: "Roman citizens regarded commerce and the manual arts as the occupations of slaves – they did not practice them at all. . . . But in general, they knew only the art of war, which was the only route to magistracies and to honors. Thus the martial virtues remained after all the others were lost."

9   "They did not wish to subject themselves to the work expected from the Roman soldiers. See Ammianus Marcellinus, Book XVIII, who treats as an extraordinary event the time when, to please Julian, who wished to put certain fortified places in a state of preparedness, they did what he wished" (Montesquieu's note). The reference is to Book XVIII, II.

10   "This was scarcely surprising in this mixture of nations which had been migrant, which knew no native land (*patrie*), and from which whole bodies of troops often joined the foe that had conquered them against their own nation. See in Procopius what the Goths were like under Vittigis" (Montesquieu's note). The reference is to *The Gothic War*, I, XXV.

11   "See all of the fifth book of *The Government of God*; see also in the *Embassy* written by Priscus, the speech of a Roman established among the Huns about his happiness in that country" (Montesquieu's note).

12   "See again Salvian, Book V, and the laws of the *Code* and of the *Digest* on this" (Montesquieu's note). The references are to Justinian's *Code*, XI, XLVII and *Digest*, XXXIII, VII.

The Spirit of the Laws
Title Page

1   The text followed here is that of the posthumous edition of 1757 (*De l'Esprit des Loix*), which is the same as that of 1758 in the *Collected Works*, or *Oeuvres de Monsieur de Montesquieu*, revue, corrigée, and considérablement augmentée par l'auteur; A. Amsterdam, and A. Leipsick. Chez Arkstée and Merkus. M. DCC. LVIII. This edition has been reproduced in the best available set of Montesquieu's work, put together under the supervision of André Masson, with notes and articles by leading Montesquieu scholars. This edition is indispensable because it prints Montesquieu's correspondence; dates most of Montesquieu's writings, including his unpublished notes and reflections (including the *Spicilège* and *Pensées*); provides excerpts from the only extant manuscript of *Spirit of the Laws*; and has articles by Robert Shackleton on

that manuscript and on the handwriting of Montesquieu's secretaries. This edition will be referred to as Masson [*Oeuvres complètes de Montesquieu*. Publiées . . . sous la direction de M. André Masson (3 vols.; Paris: 1950–55)].

The two most available editions are those of the Pléiade edition by Roger Caillois, *Oeuvres complètes de Montesquieu* (2 vols.; Paris: 1949–51); and the edition by Daniel Oster (Paris: 1964). Both editions omit Montesquieu's correspondence and print his *Pensées*, not dated and chronologically as does Masson, but by subject matter. Their annotation is minimal. Because Caillois is in print and generally available, I shall cite it.

Despite the existence of a manuscript of *Spirit of the Laws*, there has never been a complete annotated variorum edition of it. The closest thing to such an edition is that by Jean Brethe de la Gressaye [Montesquieu, *De L'Esprit des Loix*. Texte etabli et présenté par Jean Brethe de la Gressaye. (4 vols.; Paris: 1950)]. Unlike Masson, who simply reprinted the 1758 edition, Brethe has provided the most detailed annotation and critical commentary yet available. I have leaned heavily on his work. One disadvantage of it, however, is the fact that it was done before the appearance of Masson. Thus Brethe, although often referring to Montesquieu's notebooks, does not date their entries. Although he sometimes provides excerpts from the manuscript when it contains materials not included in the printed text, he does not provide as many as does Masson. Nor does Brethe always give other excerpts preserved in Montesquieu's library and reprinted by Masson. These are materials omitted from *Spirit of the Laws*. We do not as yet possess an edition that would enable us to trace the development of Montesquieu's thought during the twenty years that he took to write *Spirit of the Laws*.

2   The meaning of Montesquieu's epigraph is disputed. One interpretation is that Montesquieu is claiming originality for his work, which is based on no previous model. Another reading of the epigraph interprets it as meaning that this work in praise of political liberty has been written in a country where there was none.

Montesquieu's Introduction

1   This was written in response to criticism leveled against Montesquieu on moral and religious grounds. He was accused of arguing that neither moral nor Christian virtues are required by a monarchy. Eventually the entire work was condemned by the Faculty of Theology at the Sorbonne; Rome placed it on the Index. Montesquieu had replied to his critics in a sharply argued '*Defense of The Spirit of the Laws*,' two "Clarifications" published in subsequent editions of the book itself, and a response to charges made by the Faculty of Theology at the Sorbonne. It was in the posthumous edition of 1757 that this notice was first printed in its final form and placed ahead of the Preface with which Montesquieu had begun his original edition in 1748.

2   *Patrie*. See the list of French terms.

3   Although there appears to be a logical gap between "love of one's native land" and "love of equality," Montesquieu's special use of these terms was his way of taking the position that the only true *patrie* is that in which all citizens possess equal rights. See *Patrie*.

Preface

1   Brethe de la Gressaye (hereafter cited as Brethe) has provided a telling comment and citations:

"Montesquieu here states his subject: the explanation of positive laws by seeking their causes. This is his originality. He did not write a treatise on natural law to show what laws ought to be, as had so many writers of the seventeenth and eighteenth centuries. Nor did he write a treatise on jurisprudence, that is, an exposition of French law as then practiced, as was done by so many of his contemporaries. (I, 230) He also cites a passage from the manuscript that is omitted in the book.

> This book is not a treatise on jurisprudence, but rather one kind of method for studying jurisprudence. It is not the sum total of laws that I am seeking, but what animates them (*leur âme*)."

[Bibliothèque Nationale Manuscript (hereafter cited as MS), V, f. 332], also in Caillois, II, 1025, and Masson, II, 625–6.

> "I have not written to teach what the laws are, but rather to show how they ought to be taught. And I have not treated the laws themselves, but their spirit (*l'esprit des lois*)."

Cited in Brethe, I, 230.

2   The nature of things is a concept that is crucial to Montesquieu's thought. See Introduction, VII.

3   *Ludibria ventis* (Montesquieu's note). "Plaything of the winds." This is a reference to Vergil, *Aeneid*, VI, 75. It is significant that both of Montesquieu's citations in this preface came from the same section. Aeneas, having escaped from burning Troy with some countrymen, has come through numerous adventures. As the result of having taken divine counsel, Aeneas has come to see the Sibyl at Cumae in Italy. This is the entry to the underworld, which Aeneas wishes to enter in order to consult with his dead father. From him Aeneas hopes to learn what wars remain to be fought by the Trojans before they can settle. Their destined new home will, of course, turn out to be Rome.

The Sibyl is a goddess inspired by divine madness. To her was attributed the power to foretell the future and to prophesy what the gods will. Montesquieu's reference here is to the Cumean Sibyl's practice of placing her prophecies on leaves in the precise order in which events would occur. In an earlier revelation, Phoebus Apollo had warned Aeneas against permitting the Sibyl to make her prophecies on leaves, for these could easily become *ludibria ventis*, playthings of the winds. (*Aeneid*, II, 443–457).

In this final paragraph, Montesquieu twice refers to Cumae. Authors who do not find it easy to terminate their works, may understand why Montesquieu thought it appropriate to preface the work of twenty years by analogy to entering hell, or at least the other world; they may be consoled, as he was, by the thought that Aeneas did return.

4   *Bis patriae cedidere manus* (Montesquieu's note). Vergil, *Aeneid*, VI, 33. "Twice his paternal hands fell."

Montesquieu by this reference to Vergil, was invoking the legend that the shrine to Apollo at Cumae had been established and decorated by Daedalus. It was he, who after constructing a labyrinth for Minos on Crete, was himself imprisoned in it with his son, Icarus. Daedalus then constructed wax wings, with which both he and his son managed to escape. But when Icarus flew too close to the sun, his wings melted and he fell to his death. To give thanks for his own escape and to mourn his son's death, Daedalus dedicated a temple to Apollo at Cumae, where he had landed. On the gates of this shrine, Daedalus, a fabulous craftsman, depicted the key episodes in his own life.

When Daedalus came to the episode of his escape from the labyrinth, he twice attempted to render the figure of Icarus, his son. But overcome by his grief, Daedalus on both occasions was unable to do so, and his tools dropped from his hands.

By invoking this scene, Montesquieu alluded to the difficulties of intellectual creation, which not infrequently include temporary paralysis. His readers,
who could be counted on to know Vergil, must have relished this invocation
of the mysteries and setbacks of Montesquieu's lifework. But these only prepare the way for what is to follow, that is, the completed text of *Spirit of the
Laws*. Montesquieu did not conceal his great expectations.

5   *Ed io anche son pittore* (Montesquieu's note). This is a famous phrase. Correggio greatly admired Raphael. Struck with awe when visiting Raphael's paint-
ing, he nevertheless realized that his own work had established him as a creative artist.

Book I. Laws in General

1   " 'The law,' says Plutarch, 'is the queen who rules over all, mortals and immor-
tals alike.' See his treatise, 'To an Uneducated Ruler' " (Montesquieu's note).
Plutarch rightly attributes this saying to Pindar. In the Greek text, the law is
called "king" rather than "queen." Plutarch, *Moralia*, trans. Harold North, X,
57.

2   Montesquieu attributes this position to Spinoza. Despite Montesquieu's attack
here and elsewhere, he was accused by Catholic critics of having followed
Spinoza's alleged pantheism and atheism. Montesquieu specifically confronted
these accusations in his *Défense de l'Esprit des Lois*. The best assessment is
that by Paul Vernière, *Spinoza et la pensée française avant la révolution* (2
vols.; Paris, 1954), II, 447–66, ff. 457–8.

3   Like most of ch. 1, this idea is thought by most authorities to have been borrowed from Samuel Clarke, two of whose books were translated into French
in 1705 and 1706. Hume, while concurring in this judgment, thought that
Clarke himself had derived his rationalist position from the Christian Cartesian, Nicolas Malebranche. See Hume, *An Enquiry Concerning the Principles
of Morals* (London, 1751), pp. 54–5.

4   Although Hobbes is not mentioned by name, he is Montesquieu's target.
Hobbes is discussed in ch. 2. See n. 7.

5   Brethe notes correctly that Montesquieu takes this position as a way of justifying natural law. The state of man prior to society was a concept familiar to the
secular natural lawyers. This notion was analytical and did not refer to an actual stage of history when men lived in isolation. Montesquieu had mocked
this theory in *Persian Letters*, XCIV. There he ridiculed efforts to discover the
origins of human society, which he thought to be natural to man.

6   "As can be seen from the savage found in the forests of Hanover and taken
over to England during the reign of George I" (Montesquieu's note).

7   Although Montesquieu claims to be citing Hobbes verbatim, I have not been
able to find any text that corresponds exactly to this translation. I have not
been able to consult the French translation of Hobbes' *De Cive*, owned by
Montesquieu. But Hobbes did say approximately what is here attributed to
him in at least three places; Preface, *De Cive*, ed. Sterling P. Lamprecht (New
York, 1949), p. 11; n. to I, 2, ibid., p. 24n.; *Leviathan*, ed. M. Oakeshott (Oxford, 1947), I, 13, p. 82. Montesquieu often relied on his memory for his
notes. The passage he cites reads in the original: "We see even in well-governed
states, where there are laws and punishments for offenders, yet particular men
travel not without their sword by their sides, for their defences, neither sleep
they without shutting not only their doors against their fellow subjects, but
also their trunks and coffers for fear of domestics" (Preface, *De Cive*).

8   Montesquieu makes no allusion here to the notion of the social contract as an
explanation of how men proceed from the state of nature to that of civil soci-

ety. He was familiar with the notion of contract, but chose not to use it. Thus he differs from Locke on this point, as he does from Hobbes and Rousseau.

9 Some confusion may arise from the fact that in French, *droit* means both "right" and "law." Here Montesquieu himself more often used the term to mean "law." Montesquieu's own most comprehensive classification of laws occurs in XXVI, 1:

Men are governed by different kinds of laws: by natural law; by divine law, which is that of religion; by ecclesiastical law, otherwise called canon law, which is concerned with the supervision of religion; by the law of nations, which may be considered as the civil law of the universe, in that every people is considered a citizen of it; by public law in general (*le droit politique général*), which is directed by that human wisdom which has founded all societies; by municipal public law (*le droit politique particulier*), which concerns each society; by the law of conquest, which comes into being because one people has wished, has been able, or has been morally obliged (*a du*) to use violence against another people; by the civil law of every society, by which a citizen can defend his property and life against any other citizen; and, finally by domestic law, which derives from the fact that a society is divided into different families, each of which needs to be ruled.

Thus there are different orders of laws. The sublimity of human reason consists in its ability to determine which order of law is most relevant to that matter with which a legislator is concerned, as well as in its ability to avoid throwing confusion into those principles that ought to govern men [end of citation].

A precise account of what these legal distinctions meant to Montesquieu and the secular natural law theorists of his time is to be found in Derathé, *Jean-Jacques Rousseau*, pp. 386–97.

10 Montesquieu derived his knowledge of the Iroquois from the accounts of missionaries. These details are probably drawn from Father Charlevoix, *Histoire et déscription générale de la nouvelle France* (1744) or Father Lafitau, *Les moeurs des sauvages américaines comparées aux moeurs des premiers temps* (1724).

11 For Gravina, see Glossary of Proper Names.

12 No doubt Montesquieu was thinking of Sir Robert Filmer and Bishop Bossuet. See Glossary of Proper Names.

13 Montesquieu here restates the concept of natural law as identical with human reason. It is not clear what is the relationship between this older view (see Introduction) and what Montesquieu presents as his own contribution to the study of law in the rest of this chapter.

14 For the meaning of *moeurs* and *manières*, see list of French terms.

Book II. Laws that Derive Directly from the Nature of the Government

1 Montesquieu here broke with Aristotle's scheme of classification in the *Politics*, III, VII and VIII. Instead of distinguishing between right and perverted forms of rule by one, the few or many, or by social class, Montesquieu's classification was tantamount to taking a position in contemporary disputes about the fundamental nature of the French monarchy. For two of his three types involved one-man rule, while rule by the few and the many were both republican in his view. Thus Montesquieu put himself on the side of the *parlementaires* who held the *thèse nobiliare*. Voltaire, who championed the *thèse royale*, wrote in his *Commentaire sur l'Esprit des Lois* (1777) that monarchy and despotism are "two brothers who resemble each other in so many ways

that one is often taken for the other." For further details, see the Introduction to this volume. To understand Montesquieu's typology, it is necessary to know what historical cases he had in mind. Democracy he found in Periclean Athens and the Roman Republic; aristocracy in Venice and Genoa; monarchy was in France when kings adhered to its constitution and other European states of Montesquieu's time (England was on the whole a monarchy, although in V, 19, Montesquieu called England a republic in the guise of a monarchy). Despotism Montesquieu identified with the governments of Asia: Persia, Turkey, China (Montesquieu did not accept the more favorable view then more current among the *philosophes*), and the Moscow of Peter the Great.

2 "*Déclamations* 17 and 18" (Montesquieu's note).

3 "See *Considerations on the Causes of the Romans' Greatness and Decline*, ch. IX, Paris, 1755" (Montesquieu's note).

4 "Pages 691 and 692, edition of Wechelius, 1596" (Montesquieu's note). The reference is to the *Polity of the Lacedaemonians*.

5 "Book I" (Montesquieu's note).

6 "Book IV, art. 15, and what follows" (Montesquieu's note).

7 "See in the *Considerations on the Causes of the Romans' Greatness and Decline*, ch. IX, how this spirit of Servius Tullius was preserved in the republic" (Montesquieu's note).

8 "Dionysius of Halicarnassus, *Eulogy of Isocrates*, p. 97, tome 2, edition of Wechelius. Pollux, Book VIII, ch. X, art. 130" (Montesquieu's note).

9 "See Demosthenes's oration 'De Falsa Legatione,' and that against Timarchus" (Montesquieu's note).

10 "This provision was so significant that two tickets were drawn by lot for each position: The first awarded the office to an individual; the second named his successor if the original choice was rejected" (Montesquieu's note).

11 "Books I and II of the *Laws*" (Montesquieu's note). Cicero began his *De Legibus* about 52 B.C. Only three books of it have been preserved.

12 "They were called *leges tabulares*. Each citizen received two tablets, the first marked with an 'A,' for *antiquo*; the second marked with an 'U' and a 'R,' *uti rogas*" (Montesquieu's note). The first meant "no"; the second, "yes."

13 "Athenian citizens voted by raising their hands" (Montesquieu's note).

14 "As at Venice" (Montesquieu's note).

15 "The thirty tyrants of Athens, in order to manage the Aréopagites, ordered them to vote in public. Lysias, 'Oratio contra Agoratos,' 8" (Montesquieu's note). Lysias, *Orations*, trans. W. R. H. Lamb (London, 1930).

16 "See Dionysius of Halicarnassus, books 4 and 9" (Montesquieu's note).

17 "See Mr. Addison's *Travels to Italy*, p. 16" (Montesquieu's note). The actual title was *Remarks on Several Parts of Italy*. The author was Joseph Addison.

18 "At first they were named by the consuls" (Montesquieu's note).

19 "This is what ruined the Roman republic. See *Considerations on the Causes of the Romans' Greatness and Decline*, ch. IX, Paris, 1755" (Montesquieu's note).

20 "Tournefort's *Voyages*" (Montesquieu's note). The actual title was *Relation d'un voyage au Levant* (2 vols.; 1717).

21 "At Lucca the magistrates hold office for only two months" (Montesquieu's note).

22 "Diodorus, Book XVIII, p. 601, Rhodoman's edition" (Montesquieu's note).

23 This formula both resembles and diverges from Harrington's formulation: "But a *Monarchy* divested of her *Nobility*, hath no refuge under Heaven, but an *Army*. . . . But without a *Nobility* or an *Army* (as hath been shew'd) there can be no *Monarchy*. Wherefore what is there in Nature, that can arise out of

these ashes; but a *Popular Government*, or a new *Monarchy* to be erected by
the victorious *Army?" James Harrington's Oceana*, ed. S. B. Liljegren (Heidel-
berg, 1924), p. 50. Montesquieu follows up Harrington's argument about the
essential identity of interest between the nobility and the monarch (V, 11),
and applies it to the question of civil war, as does Harrington, Cf. fn. 24
on V, 11.

24   *The Dictionary of the French Academy* (3d ed.; 1740) gives several definitions
     of *seigneur*: "master, possessor of a land (*un Pays*), a State (*un Etat*), a tract of
     ground (*une Terre*)"; also signifies "master, possessor of a tract of ground (*une
     Terre*), which has fiefs dependent upon it"; and "in England, the upper cham-
     ber is called *La Chambre des Seigneurs*." Nugent, the eighteenth-century trans-
     lator of Montesquieu, renders *seigneurs* as "lords" or "nobility." He thus ig-
     nores the distinction Montesquieu makes between *seigneurs* and *noblesse*, and
     blurs the point that Montesquieu is making, i.e., that the abolition of feudal
     rights gave additional power to the monarchy. Harrington went into great de-
     tail on this range of questions, and his comparisons with the French are
     worthy of note, although any formulation involving "the gentry," as does Har-
     rington's will call forth widespread disagreement among those who know the
     period best. Harrington remarked: "But . . . if neither the People, nor Divines
     and Lawyers can be the *Aristocracy* of a Nation, there remains only the *Nobil-
     ity*, in which style, to avoid further repetition, I shall understand the *Gentry*
     also; as the *French* do by the word *Noblesse*." *Oceana*, ed. Liljegren, p. 118. A
     detailed analysis of the Nobility follows, pp. 119–127.
25   Montesquieu's point is that liberty in England is not maintained by intermedi-
     ary powers, such as a semi-independent nobility, but by the balance of powers
     discussed in XI. David Hume agreed in his letter to Montesquieu of 10 April
     1749 (Masson, III, 1217).
26   John Law's enterprise was granted the management of the mint, the coin issue
     for nine years, and the collection of taxes on the condition that he undertake
     the payment of the national debt. In 1720 Law left France after the collapse
     of his enterprise, due to its overissue of paper money and the hostility of the
     government and public.
27   "Ferdinand, King of Aragon, made himself grand-master of the orders, and
     that alone changed the constitution" (Montesquieu's note). Montesquieu's ref-
     erence is to Ferdinand's domestic policy of smashing the powerful nobility.
     The great military orders, founded at the time of the Christian struggle to ex-
     pel the Moors, had come to be dominated by the nobility. By making himself
     master of all military orders, Ferdinand gained control over their administra-
     tion and revenues. He thus added to his power and wealth, while striking a
     blow at the nobility's.
28   Montesquieu is here affirming the position taken by the French *parlements*, es-
     pecially those of Paris and Bordeaux. The *parlements* claimed both judicial
     functions as courts, and constitutional functions as guardians of the funda-
     mental laws of the realm. In the view of the *parlements*, laws did not go into ef-
     fect until the *parlement* of a province had registered them. The crown claimed
     that the *parlements* were bound to register royal decrees; the *parlements*
     claimed the right to examine laws in terms of their conformity with the prin-
     ciples of law and justice, and with the interests of the king and his subjects. If
     they found fault on any of these grounds, the *parlements* would refuse to reg-
     ister the laws and address remonstrances to the king. From the fourteenth cen-
     tury on, the French monarchy favored instead the use of an administrative
     council subject to the king, and hence contrary to feudal practice. Such a *con-
     seil du roi* simply recorded the king's decrees.

29 " 'Oriental kings always have viziers,' says M. Chardin" (Montesquieu's note).
30 The MS names the pope: Clement X (Altieri), who reigned from 1670–76 and was eighty at the time of his election. Montesquieu's version of his reign has been disputed.

Book III. The Principles of the Three Governments

1 "This is a very important distinction, from which I shall draw many consequences. It is the key to an infinite number of laws" (Montesquieu's note).
2 "Cromwell" (Montesquieu's note).
3 Cf. *Considerations*, XI.
4 Cf. *Considerations*, XII, XIV, XV.
5 Such transformations of the vocabulary of politics have been noted in modern totalitarian states. But the phenomenon is not new, any more than is Montesquieu's rhetoric. Cf. Plato, *Republic*, VIII, 560e, where he analyzes the democratic man in terms of verbal disorder. Thucydides, *History of the War between Athens and Sparta*, III, 82 performs a similar analysis in terms of the effects of the first popular revolution to occur in Greece, that on Corcyra. See also *Considerations*, XIII.
6 "Plutarch, *Life of Pericles*; Plato, *Critias*" (Montesquieu's note).
7 "There were 21,000 citizens, 10,000 foreigners, and 400,000 slaves. See Athenaeus, Book VI" (Montesquieu's note).
8 "She had 20,000 citizens. See Demosthenes, *Against Aristogiton*" (Montesquieu's note).
9 "They passed a law that punished by death anyone who proposed transferring to military purposes money appropriated for the theaters" (Montesquieu's note).
10 "This war lasted three years" (Montesquieu's note).
11 "Under this form of government, public crimes may be punished, because they affect the interest of all [the nobles] ; private crimes will go unpunished because it is to the interest of all [the nobles] not to punish them" (Montesquieu's note).
12 "I refer here to that political virtue, which is also a moral virtue in that it is directed toward the public good; I make little reference to the moral virtues of individuals, and do not refer at all to that virtue which relates to revealed truths. This will emerge clearly in Book V, ch. II" (Montesquieu's note).
13 "This is to be understood in the sense specified by the preceding note" (Montesquieu's note).
14 " 'Persons of low degree ought not to be employed; they are apt to be too austere and too difficult,' is what he writes" (Montesquieu's note).
15 "This term, 'a good man' (*homme de bien*), is to be understood here in a political sense only" (Montesquieu's note).
16 "See note 15" (Montesquieu's note).
17 "See Perry, p. 447" (Montesquieu's note). The reference is to the French translation of John Perry, *The State of Russia under the Present Czar* (London, 1716).
18 "As often happens in a military aristocracy" (Montesquieu's note).
19 A judge in a Mohammedan court, in which decisions are based upon the canon law of Islam.
20 "Ricault, *The Ottoman Empire*" (Montesquieu's note). The reference is to the French translation of Sir Paul Rycaut, *The History of the Present State of the Ottoman Empire* (London, 1668), Book I, ch. II. See Glossary of Proper Names.
21 A pasha (bacha, bassaw) was a Turkish person of high rank. Although viziers

were called by this title, Montesquieu apparently refers to the governor of a province.

22 "See the history of this revolution by Father Ducerceau" (Montesquieu's note). Montesquieu's source was Jean Antoine du Cerceau (1670–1730), *Histoire de la dernière révolution de Perse* (Paris, 1728). Mir-Oweis, or Mir-Weis, an Afghan chief, revolted in 1719 against the sophi Hussein, who was dethroned by Mir-Oweis's son in 1722.

23 "His government was military, which is one species of despotic government" (Montesquieu's note). The source is Suetonius.

24 The MS contained a final comment that was not included in the final draft. It has great interest because of Montesquieu's admiration for Machiavelli, who much affected his thought. Montesquieu obviously had the *Prince* in mind when he wrote: "But it was mad for Machiavelli to have recommended to princes as the way to maintain their preeminence, those principles necessary only to despotic government. In a monarchy, such principles are useless, dangerous, and even impracticable. This error was due to the fact that Machiavelli did not know too well the nature of monarchy and its distinguishing characteristics. And this is unworthy of a mind as great as his." (I, f°, 63)

25 This passage demonstrates the extent to which despotism and freedom are inextricably linked in Montesquieu's exposition. If there is any question of what politics or the political meant to Montesquieu, this passage should clarify much. Note that the chapter is based on a dichotomy that puts into a single category both republics and monarchies as governments where power is not absolute, but moderated or checked. On the other hand, despotism is characterized by absolute, that is, unchecked power.

26 "See Chardin" (Montesquieu's note).

27 "Ibid." (Montesquieu's note).

28 Cf. *Considerations*, XIII, which used the same example. As Brethe remarks, this is one of the few passages where Montesquieu refers explicitly to natural law (*droit naturel*).

Book IV. The Laws Governing Education in a State Ought to Be Relative to Its Principle of Government

1 This subject is discussed in detail by Plato, not only in the *Republic*, VI–VII, but in his *Laws*, VII; somewhat closer to Montesquieu are Books VII and VIII of Aristotle's *Politics*. Both Plato and Aristotle take it as axiomatic that the polis must regulate education; both do not shrink from doing so by legislation. Montesquieu, although insisting that education ought to be relative to the principle of each type of state, does not stress censorship and coercion by law as do the Greeks. He passed over the dangerous question of whether education should be in the hands of the church or the state, although what he said suggests that he preferred education by the state in republics at least. In the manuscript (f°, 304) there are draft titles that stress *moeurs* and institutions rather than education.

2 The term *l'honnête homme* is still used here in the special sense given it in the seventeenth century, as Brethe notes: a "person brought up in good society, with excellent manners, refined according to polite standards, well-to-do, knowing how to express himself elegantly, who relished the pleasures of conversation . . . in 1748 at the time that *The Spirit of the Laws* was published, this conception came under a spirited attack by Touissant, *Les Moeurs* (1748) . . . who wrote: 'All the men of honor (*tous les honnêtes gens ensemble*) are not worth a single virtuous man.' " Cf. Brethe, I, 258.

3 "See d'Aubigné's *History*" (Montesquieu's note). The reference is to the *l'Histoire universelle* of Theodore Agrippa d'Aubigné.

4 "I am speaking of what is, not of what ought to be. Honor is a prejudice, which religion sometimes seeks to remove, and at other times, to regulate" (Montesquieu's note).
5 "*Politics*, Book I" (Montesquieu's note).

Book V. The Laws Provided by the Legislator Ought to Be Relative to the Principle of Government

1 Brethe notes that Montesquieu should have called this chapter "What is Meant by Virtue in a Popular State."
2 What Montesquieu refers to is an episode in Alcibiades' life when he sought refuge in Sparta. Montesquieu maintains that while at Sparta, Alcibiades startled his hosts by his adherence to their rules of stern frugality. For when in Athens, he had been notorious for his prodigality and other excesses. Montesquieu's view of Alcibiades was attacked by Voltaire.
3 "Solon established four classes. The first was made up of those with an income of 500 minas either in grain or liquid fruits; the second, of those with an income of 300 minas, who could maintain a horse; the third, those with an income of only 200 minas; and the fourth, which was made up of all those who worked with their hands. Plutarch, *Life of Solon*" (Montesquieu's note).
4 "Solon excludes from public office all those belonging to the fourth class" (Montesquieu's note).
5 "They insisted upon larger pieces of the conquered lands. Plutarch, *Moralia, Lives of the Ancient Kings and Commanders*" (Montesquieu's note).
6 "In them, women's dowries ought to be very much limited" (Montesquieu's note).
7 *Polity of the Lacedaemonians* (Montesquieu's note). The reference is to ch. viii. Despite the quotation marks, the citation is not exact. Xenophon's meaning is accurately reported.
8 "Roman history demonstrates how this power was used to the advantage of the republic. To refer only to the time of its greatest corruption: Aulus Fulvius had already set out to join Catalina when his father called him back and put him to death. Sallust, *De Bello Catil.* Many other citizens behaved in the same way. Dio, Book XXXVII" (Montesquieu's note). The references are to ch. xxxix of Sallust and to Dio Cassius's *History of Rome*.
9 "In our own time, the Venetians, who in many respects have conducted themselves very wisely, once took this way of resolving a dispute about precedence in a church between a noble Venetian and a gentleman from a province on the mainland: They decided that outside Venice a noble Venetian enjoys no advantage over any other citizen" (Montesquieu's note). The distinction being made rests upon the fact that while the city of Venice was built upon islands, it also had provinces on the mainland (*terre firme* or *terra firma*).
10 "These provisions were inserted by the decemvirs into the last two tables. See Dionysius of Halicarnassus, Book X" (Montesquieu's note).
11 The tribunes of the Roman people were charged with the defense of the lives and property of the plebians. The tribunes asserted the right of veto against any act of the magistrates, against elections, laws, *senatus consulta*, or advice of the senate to the magistrates (otherwise binding).
12 "As in some aristocracies of our own time. Nothing weakens the state more than this" (Montesquieu's note). Montesquieu referred to Italian aristocracies.
13 "See in Book XIV of Strabo how the Rhodians conducted themselves in this respect" (Montesquieu's note). The reference is to Strabo's *Geography*, page 13, note 1.
14 "Amelot de la Houssaye, *Of the Government of Venice*, part III. The Claudian law forbade senators to have at sea any ship holding more than forty hogs-

heads. Livy, Book XXI" (Montesquieu's note). [Amelot de la Houssaye, *History of the Government of Venice* (Paris, 1676).] Montesquieu was wrong about his assertion that the nobles had never been permitted to engage in commerce. He had not read any works in Italian on the subject. Houssaye's account does not support Montesquieu's analysis.

15 "Into it, informers threw their letters of accusation" (Montesquieu's note).

16 "See Livy, Book XLIX. A censor could not be troubled even by another censor. Each of them made his own entry in the census without consulting his colleagues. When any other procedure was followed, the censorship was, as it were, overthrown" (Montesquieu's note). The censors were Roman magistrates with great authority. Charged with maintaining the official list of citizens or census, they could strike off the names of those who had given false statements or been guilty of acting against law or public morality.

17 "At Athens the *Logista*, who held all the magistrates accountable for their conduct, did not themselves have to make any accounting" (Montesquieu's note).

18 "This is allowed only to the common people. See the third law in the code, *De comm. et mercatoribus*, which is full of good sense" (Montesquieu's note). Montesquieu shared the prejudices of his class against trade. In his time, throughout most of France, a noble would lose his rank if he engaged in commerce. Louis XIV, however, by edict permitted nobles to engage in wholesale trade and in maritime commerce.

19 "*Testament politique*" (Montesquieu's note). Richelieu was denouncing the *parlements*. The *Dictionary of the French Academy* (1740) defines *compagnie* in this sense as: "A body (*corps*) or an assembly of persons established to perform certain functions. Particularly that of serving as a body (*corps*) of magistrates." The text appears in the edition of Louis André (Paris, 1947), p. 246.

20 See II, 4 where Montesquieu so defined the nature of monarchy as to make into an essential quality its recognition of intermediate groups such as the *parlements* here discussed.

21 " '*Barbaris cunctatio servilis; statim exequi regium videtur.*' Tacitus, *Annals*, Book V" (Montesquieu's note). The citation is incorrect. It occurs in VI, 32. What it means is: "To barbarians, hesitancy is the vice of a slave; immediate action, the quality of a king. . . ."

22 The extent to which Montesquieu and his milieu were permeated with corporatist and hierarchical ideas is difficult for a twentieth-century mind to grasp. The first meaning of *ordre* given in the French Academy's *Dictionary* (1740) is: "Arrangement, disposition of things according to their rank." Examples given include, "the order of Providence," "order of nature," and "order of grace." The special meaning of the term as used in this passage by Montesquieu is given as: "The bodies (*les corps*) which compose a state. At Rome there were, the Order of Senators, the Order of Knights, the Plebian Order. In France the Estates are composed of three Orders, the Ecclesiastical Order, the Order of the Nobility, and the Third Estate (*En France, les Etats sont composez de trois Ordres. . . .*)."

23 "Cicero, *Laws*" (Montesquieu's note). Although Montesquieu's rendering gives an accurate version of Cicero's passage, the translation is not as literal as the quotation marks would appear to indicate. The translation by Clinton Walker Keyes in the Loeb Library edition of *De Republica and De Legibus* (Cambridge, Mass. and London, 1961), III, x, 485, reads: " 'The tribunes of the plebs have too much power,' you say. Who can deny it? [Montesquieu's translation begins] But the power of the people themselves is much more cruel, much more violent; and yet this power is sometimes milder in practice because

there is a leader to control it than if there were none. For a leader is conscious that he is acting at his own risk, whereas the impulse of the people has no consciousness of any risk to itself."

24 "See the first note of Book II, ch. 4" (Montesquieu's note). There is only one note in the chapter cited, and that does not appear to be in point. Brethe conjectures that Montesquieu altered this chapter while it was being printed. What Montesquieu seems to be referring to is his argument that without a king, there can be no nobility; without a nobility, there can be no king. In short, the French crown was wrong to perceive the nobility as its enemy. Even when the nobility revolted, it did not do so to overthrow the crown, but to defend its rights. Harrington had made a very similar comment on this same issue: "For whereas a *Nobility* striketh not at the *Throne* without which they cannot subsist, but at some King that they do not like; *Popular* power striketh through the *King* at the *Throne*, as that which is incompatible with it." *Oceana*, ed. Liljegren, p. 48. Just before this passage Harrington had referred to the French experience: ". . . the *King*, where he hath had a *Nobility*, and could bring them to his party, hath thrown the *people*, as in France and Spain." Ibid.

25 "*Mémoires* of Cardinal de Retz and other histories" (Montesquieu's note).

26 "*Testament politique*" (Montesquieu's note). See the discussion in the André edition, p. 321 et seq.

27 "*Lettres édifiantes*, receuil XI, p. 315" (Montesquieu's note). This was a published collection of letters written by Jesuits (Paris, 1715). Shackleton, op. cit., pp. 235–6 discusses the stages by which this passage evolved. The original description is of an Indian village in Illinois.

28 "Continuation of Pufendorf, *Univ. Hist.*, in the article on Sweden, ch. x" (Montesquieu's note).

29 "According to Chardin, there is no council of state in Persia" (Montesquieu's note). The term *Conseil d'Etat* carries both a general meaning and a reference to an institution, first of the French monarchy, and then of modern governments since Napoleon I.

30 In short, a despotism ought to turn its frontier areas into devastated zones equivalent to deserts.

31 Montesquieu is here referring to the reforms of Peter the Great.

32 "Ricaut, *Histoire de l'Etat Présent de l'Empire Ottoman* (edition of 1678), p. 196" (Montesquieu's note). See entry for Rycaut in Glossary of Proper Names.

33 "For the Turkish law of inheritance, see *Lacédémone ancienne et moderne* and Ricaut, *De l'Empire Ottoman*" (Montesquieu's note). *Lacédémone* . . . (Paris, 1676) was written by La Guilletière (Guillet Saint-Georges). It was a travel book in which the author compared the *moeurs* of the ancient Spartans to those of the peoples who lived under Turkish domination in the territory that once had been Sparta.

34 "*Receuil des voyages qui sont servi à l'établissement et aux progrès de la compagnie des Indes,* [*orientales, formée dans les Provinces-Unies des Pays-Bas*] (5 vols.; Amsterdam, 1710), t. I. The law of Pegu is less cruel; if there happens to be children, the king succeeds to only two-thirds. Ibid., t. III, p. 1" (Montesquieu's note). Bantam was a kingdom on the island of Java, which was conquered by the Dutch at the end of the seventeenth century; Pegu was a part of India beyond the Ganges, which was part of the Burman Empire in the eighteenth century. This is Montesquieu's first reference to a work upon which he relied too heavily. For this collection was an unreliable source compiled by Dutch merchants who were much more superficial and inaccurate observers than the Jesuit missionaries. Voltaire had good reason to question the authen-

ticity of Montesquieu's data (Voltaire, *Commentaire*, #25).

35 On this point, Montesquieu differed from the ancient Greeks who described oriental despotisms as founded upon accepted laws of succession and a sort of tacit consent. Thus despotisms were thought by the Greeks to be long-lived. Cf. Richter, "Despotism" op. cit.

36 "See its different constitutions, especially that of 1722" (Montesquieu's note).

37 "See Justin" (Montesquieu's note). According to Justin, Artaxerxes, king of Persia, had 115 sons, of whom 50 conspired against him and were put to death.

38 "See the Book [XIV] dealing with the relationship between laws and climate" (Montesquieu's note). Montesquieu here makes one of his few indications of how one part of *Spirit of the Laws* is linked to another. The relevant discussion is in XIV, 2.

39 "La Guilletière, *Lacédémone ancienne et nouvelle*, p. 463" (Montesquieu's note).

40 Montesquieu is addressing himself to the point that under the Roman Law and that of the Old Regime in France, bankrupt debtors could cede all the assets of their estate to creditors and thus escape imprisonment, even though such assets fell short of their total indebtedness. He thus argues that bankruptcy laws ought to vary from one form of government to another.

41 "The same is true of agreements made with creditors in bankruptcy proceedings where the debtor is considered in good faith" (Montesquieu's note). The distinction is between simple commercial failures and fraudulent bankruptcies.

42 "No such provision existed in law until the edict of Julian, *De cessione bonorum*. This allowed debtors to escape prison and the ignominious division of their assets" (Montesquieu's note).

43 "It seems to me that when Athens was a republic, it overindulged the taste for confiscations" (Montesquieu's note).

44 " '*Ut esse Phebi dulcius lumen solet Jamjam cadentis...*' " (Montesquieu's note). The citation is from Seneca, *Troades*, 1140–41: "As Phoebus' light is wont to appear more glorious at the moment of his setting." *Seneca's Tragedies*, and trans. Frank Justus Miller (2 vols.; London and Cambridge, Mass., 1960), I, 219.

45 " '*Ne imperium ad optimes nobilium transferretur, senatum militia vetuit Gallenius, etiam adire exercitum.*' Aurelius Victor, *De Viris Illustribus*" (Montesquieu's note). "In order to prevent a transfer of power to the elite of the nobility, Gallien refused to allow senators to perform military service, or even to approach the army." This work is no longer attributed to Aurelius Victor.

46 Montesquieu means England. This characterization of England as a republic is an important key to Montesquieu's subsequent discussions of English government as embodying liberty.

47 On this passage Hume wrote to Montesquieu, "This remark ... may perhaps be confirmed by a well-known example from the time of our civil wars. The Long Parliament passed an ordinance renouncing, 'self-denying,' by which its members excluded themselves from any command in their own army. The immediate result of this ordinance was the separation of the army from Parliament, and the total loss of all our liberties." I have translated this from the French. (Letter from Hume to Montesquieu, London, 10 April 1749, Masson, III, 1217.)

48 " 'Augustus took away the right to bear arms from senators, proconsuls, and governors.' Dio Cassius, Book XXXIII" (Montesquieu's note).

49 "Constantine. See Zosimus, Book II" (Montesquieu's note).

50 "Ammianus Marcellinus, Book XVI. '*More veterum, et bella recturo*' " (Mon-

tesquieu's note). The passage cited means: "according to ancient usage the control of civil and military affairs." *Ammianus Marcellinus*, ed. and trans. John C. Rolfe (3 vols.; London and Cambridge, Mass., 1937), II, Book XXVI, ch. 12, p. 631.

51 Venality of office was a practice of long-standing under the Old Regime. Many government positions were sold like any other commodity, and offices thus acquired could be passed down to heirs. Montesquieu seems to ignore the single most important reason for this practice – the monarchy's fiscal difficulties. Of course venality of office greatly added to the expense of administration, while making it highly inefficient. Montesquieu himself inherited a high judicial office, which he sold after holding it for twelve years. Voltaire wrote: "Let us lament that Montesquieu has defamed his work by such paradoxes. But we can forgive him: his uncle purchased the office of *President* [*à Mortier*] . . . , and left it to him. After all we find the man. No one of us is without his weak point." (*Commentaire*, #27) On the other hand, Hume thought that venality of office had greatly added to the independence of French judges from administrative or royal pressure. (Letter from Hume to Montesquieu, London, 10 April 1749, Masson, III, 1218–9.)

52 "Fragments from the Embassies of Constantine Porphyrogenitus" (Montesquieu's note). Suidas is the name of a lexicon (not an author, as was once believed), which was compiled about the end of the tenth century and contains many fragments of works now lost.

53 "*Republic*, Book VIII" (Montesquieu's note). The passage occurs at 551c. As usual, Montesquieu, despite his use of direct quotation, does not give a literal translation of Plato. Once again his condensation of Plato does not distort the text. However, Plato is criticizing oligarchy, not describing a republic founded on virtue, as Montesquieu claims immediately following the citation.

54 "Note the laziness of Spain, where all public offices are given away" (Montesquieu's note).

Book VIII. Corruption of Principle in the Three Governments

1 The MS (II, 43) gives an informative elaboration: "Tyranny is not so much a particular type of a state as the corruption of every type of state, and this corruption almost always begins with the corruption of its principles."

2 The translation is from Xenophon's "Banquet," or "Symposium," IV, 30–2, and except for its beginning, is almost literal. In addition to Xenophon, Montesquieu relied heavily on Plato's *Republic*, VIII, 562d–564a and Cicero's *Laws*, I, chs. XLIII–XLIV, which Cicero took from Plato.

3 "See Plutarch's Lives of *Timoleon* and *Dio*" (Montesquieu's note).

4 "It was that of the Six Hundred, mentioned by Diodorus" (Montesquieu's note).

5 "After expelling the tyrants, they made citizens of foreigners and mercenary troops. This caused civil wars. Aristotle, *Politics*, Book V, ch iii. Since the people were responsible for the defeat of the Athenians, the republic was changed. Ibid., ch. iv. The form of this republic was again changed as the result of the passion of two young magistrates. One of them had stolen a young boy from the other, who seduced the wife of the first. Ibid., Book VII, ch. iv" (Montesquieu's note). Of Montesquieu's three references only one is correct.

6 "Aristotle, *Politics*, Book V, ch. iv" (Montesquieu's note). The passage cited occurs in V, iii.

7 "Ibid." (Montesquieu's note). Also in V, iii.

8 "Aristocracy becomes transformed into oligarchy" (Montesquieu's note).

9 "Venice is among those republics which has known best how to compensate

for the disadvantages of hereditary aristocracy" (Montesquieu's note).

10 "Justin attributes the extinction of Athenian virtue to the death of Epaminodas. Deprived of the rival they sought to emulate, they wasted their money on
celebrations, *frequentius coenam quam castra visentes*. It was at this time that
the Macedonians emerged from obscurity. Book VI" (Montesquieu's note).
Justin comments on the death in battle of Epaminodas and its adverse effects
upon the Athenians. The Latin cited by Montesquieu means: "frequenting the
festival rather than seeing to the military camp." The texts I have consulted
read *scenam* (theater) rather than *coenam* (festival).

11 The version given in the MS (II, f. 56) is both more complex and precise: "the
prerogatives of intermediary bodies, the privileges of cities, the functions of
tribunals."

12 "Compilation of writings made under the Ming dynasty, recorded by Father
Du Halde" (Montesquieu's note). Père Jean Baptiste Du Halde, *Description
geographique, historique, chronologique, politique, et physique de l'Empire de
la Chine et de la Tartarie chinoise* (4 vols.; Paris, 1735), II, 648. The Ch'in
dynasty (246–207 B.C.) was largely the work of the "first emperor," Shih
Huang Ti, one of the great unifiers and centralizers in Chinese history also
notable for his public works, burning of books, and ruthlessness, all of which
Montesquieu particularly disliked. The Sui dynasty (589–618 A.D.) reunified
China after three and a half centuries of disunion; it was succeeded by the
T'ang dynasty (618–906 A.D.), which made China into the largest, strongest,
and most civilized empire on earth. Montesquieu did not refer to any of these
consequences of centralization. Montesquieu's citation is exact and is taken
from the French translation by the Jesuit, Father Du Halde, of a work by Su
Tze, who lived during the Sung dynasty (960–1279 A.D.).

13 Just as the reference to China was an indirect attack upon the centralizing
policy of the French monarchy, so this passage, as Brethe notes, is an allusion
to the Court of Versailles and to Louis XIV, and his famous remark, "The
State, it is I."

14 "During the reign of Tiberius, statues were erected to informers, who also
received triumphal ornaments. These two types of honors were thus debased
to the point where those who really merited them came to disdain them. Fragment of Dio, Book LVIII, taken from the *Extract of Virtues and Vices*, by
Constantine Porphyrogenitus. See in Tacitus how Nero, under the pretext of
discovering and punishing a conspiracy, bestowed the ornaments designating
triumph upon Petronius Turpilianus, Nerva, and Tigellinus. *Annals*, Book XIV.
See also how the generals refused to make war because they scorned whatever
honors might result from it. *Pervulgatis triumphi insignibus*. Tacitus, *Annals*,
Book XIII" (Montesquieu's note). The first reference is in *Dio's Roman
History*, trans. John Jackson (4 vols.; London and Cambridge, Mass., 1962),
IV, 331. The Latin phrase means: "now that triumphal emblems had been
debased." Tacitus referred to the Roman commanders in Germany, who now
that triumphal emblems had been devalued, expected greater distinction from
the maintenance of peace than from making war. *The Annals*, op. cit., XIII,
LIII, (IV, 93).

15 "In this state, the ruler knew well what was the principle of his government"
(Montesquieu's note). Medusa was a legendary monster, the sight of which was
said to turn the viewer into stone.

16 "Herodian" (Montesquieu's note). For Commodus, see Glossary of Proper
Names.

17 At this point the original manuscript sent to the printer contained an eulogy
of Louis XV, then king of France. But Montesquieu deleted it at the last

minute, perhaps because he feared that it would appear too sycophantic.

18 Montesquieu here displays the underlying 'Europocentrism' which he shared with thinkers as cosmopolitan as Voltaire. Cf. Voltaire *Commentaire sur l'Esprit des lois* in *Oeuvres complètes de Voltaire* (Paris, 1785), t. 29, 408, 13n.

19 Montesquieu referred to the War of the Austrian Succession (1740–48), which had just ended. The Hungarian nobility received concessions in return for its support of Maria-Theresa. Montesquieu does not mention the immunity from taxation granted the Hungarians.

20 "Aristotle, *Politics*, Book II, ch. X" (Montesquieu's note). The reference is incorrect; the passage occurs in II, vii, 1272b.

21 "They always united immediately against foreign enemies, and this was called 'Syncretism ' Plutarch, *Moralia*, p. 88" (Montesquieu's note).

22 "*Republic*, Book IX" (Montesquieu's note).

23 "Plutarch, *Moralia*, treatise on "Whether an Old Man Should Engage in Public Affairs" (Montesquieu's note). Plutarch, *Moralia*, X, 127.

24 "*Republic*, Book V" (Montesquieu's note). This passage is a highly approximate paraphrase; the passages referred to occur at 452c, d, and e.

25 "The art of gymnastics was divided into two parts, the dance and wrestling. In Crete, the Curetes performed armed dances; in Sparta, those of Castor and Pollux; in Athens, the armed dances of Pallas, which were altogether appropriate for those not yet old enough to fight. 'Wrestling is the image of war,' Plato wrote, *Laws*, Book VII. He praised the ancients for having established but two dances, the pacific and the Pyrrhic. See how the second of these was applied to the art of war. Plato, ibid." (Montesquieu's note). The two references to the *Laws* are to be found at 795a–6, and at 814e–5.

26 ". . . *aut libidinosae Ledaes Lacedaemonos palaestras.* Martial, *Epigrams*, Book IV, ep. 55" (Montesquieu's note). "Those shameless Spartan gymnasia dear to Leda." Leda was said to have produced two eggs from her union with Zeus in the form of a swan. From one egg came Castor and Clytemnestra; from the other, Pollux and Helen. As is indicated by Montesquieu's note immediately prior to this one, the dances of the Spartans were considered to have originated with Castor and Pollux.

27 "Plutarch, *Moralia*, 'The Roman Questions' " (Montesquieu's note).

28 "Ibid." (Montesquieu's note).

29 "Ibid., '*Table-Talk*,' Book II" (Montesquieu's note).

30 *Politics*, II, viii.

31 "About a hundred years later" (Montesquieu's note).

32 Polybius, *History*, VI, CX.

33 Livy, XXXIII, XLVI.

34 The censor was a Roman magistrate who possessed great authority because he controlled public morals and supervised the leasing of public areas and buildings. There were always two censors; the office reached its zenith of power under the republic.

35 "See Dio, Book 38; Plutarch, *Life of Cicero*; Cicero to Atticus, Book IV, letters X and XV; Asconius on Cicero's *De Divinatione*" (Montesquieu's note).

36 "As when a petty sovereign maintains himself between two great states as the result of their mutual jealousy; but he can only do so precariously" (Montesquieu's note).

37 Montesquieu derived these ideas from Pufendorf's *History*. Cf. *Pensées*, Masson, II, 231.

38 " 'It is the club (*baton*) that governs China,' writes Father Du Halde" (Montesquieu's note). Du Halde, op. cit., II, 134.

39 "See among others, the account of Lange" (Montesquieu's note). Laurent Lange's book was *Relation du voyage du Laurent Lange à la Chine*, and appeared in a collection owned by Montesquieu, *Recueil des voyages au nord* (Amsterdam, 1715). For Lange, see Glossary of Proper Names.

40 The reference is to Lord George Anson or, more exactly, to the account by his chaplain, Richard Walter, who wrote *Voyage Round the World in 1740–44* (London, 1748).

41 "Of the family of Sourniama, *Edifying Letters*, eighteenth collection" (Montesquieu's note).

42 "See in Father Du Halde, how the missionaries availed themselves of Canhi's authority to silence the mandarins, who always insisted that their country's laws forbad the establishment of any foreign religion within the empire" (Montesquieu's note). The reference is to Du Halde, op. cit., III, 104–11. Montesquieu uses Canhi for K'ang Hsi (1662–1752), one of the great Manchu emperors. The last phrase in this paragraph is obscure. It may mean that the populations of Asia would be less tolerant of Catholicism than their rulers, whose notion of their omnipotence could be played upon by missionaries.

43 "See Book XXIII, ch. 14" (Montesquieu's note). The reference is to *The Spirit of the Laws*.

44 "See the memorial of a certain Tsongtou, 'That the Land be Tilled,' *Edifying Letters*, twenty-first collection" (Montesquieu's note). Tsongtou was viceroy of Yunnan and Kweichou. Letter of Father Contancen, 19 October 1730.

45 Montesquieu's view of China marks an important change from the generally high estimate of that country, its government, and culture that had prevailed in Europe since the Jesuits had first published their accounts. China had been particularly esteemed by deists and freethinkers. Montesquieu, on the contrary, added China to his list of oriental despotisms. In part, this change may have been prompted by his detestation of the Jesuits who so praised China because they hoped to persuade the papacy to allow the Chinese to go on in their ancestral cults while becoming converts to Catholicism. At one point there seemed to be a good possibility of converting the emperor and his court, if the ancestral cult were not regarded as incompatible with Christianity. But the papacy, prompted by the Jesuits' rivals, the Dominicans, issued a bull that caused the Jesuits to be banished from the court. Montesquieu may also have been annoyed by the praise accorded to the Manchu emperor K'ang Hsi (1662–1732). The Jesuits, who recouped some of their losses under him, praised his achievements in a way that suggested that his was a benevolent despotism. This suggestion ran contrary to Montesquieu's strongest beliefs, and he was no more willing to consent to such a view of K'ang Hsi than he was to any similarly high estimate of K'ang Hsi's contemporary, Louis XIV (1654–1722). China is also a decisive case for Montesquieu in XIX.

Book IX. The Relation of Laws to the Power of Defense

1 After having classified three types of government with regard to internal structures, Montesquieu in Book IX turned his attention to the external relations of states.

2 "It is formed by about fifty republics each differing from the other. *State of the United Provinces*, by M. Janisson" (Montesquieu's note). Montesquieu is here referring to the Republic of the United Provinces, the basis for which was the Union of Utrecht created in 1579 by the Protestant provinces. The union is considered to be the first important experiement in modern federalism. Voltaire, in his *Commentaire*, noted that Montesquieu had taken each of the independent cities to be a republic.

3 "Civil liberty, goods, wives, children, temples and even sepulchers" (Montesquieu's note).

4 The reference is to Louis XIV.

5 This ought to be compared to the eulogy of the French in XIX, V.

Book XI. Laws that Comprise Political Liberty: Their Relation to the Constitution

1 "'I have' says Cicero, 'copied the edict of Scaevola, which permits the Greeks to resolve their differences according to their own laws; with the result that they consider themselves to be a free people'" (Montesquieu's note).

2 "The Russians would not submit to Czar Peter's order that their beards be cut" (Montequieu's note).

3 "The Cappadocians refused the status of a republican state offered them by the Romans" (Montesquieu's note).

4 Montesquieu uses "nature" in his own stipulated and technical sense. Only monarchy is by its nature free. When government by a single person is not free, then it is a despotism. See the opening sentence of II, 4. Book XI is concerned with the nature of governments: that is, do they have fundamental laws that limit the sovereign, whether one, a few, or many? Book XII is concerned with the principle of governments. If subjects are in constant fear, then they live under a despotism. The principle that power must check power is central to Montesquieu's argument in Book XI. Shackleton suggests that Montesquieu's thoughts were influenced by Bolingbroke, whose article in the *Craftsman* of 13 June 1730 stated that, "The love of power is natural. It is insatiable. . . . Our monarchy is in the middle point from whence a deviation leads on the one hand to tyranny and on the other to anarchy." (Robert Shackleton, *Montesquieu, Bolingbroke and the Separation of Powers. French Studies* (3) 1949), p. 35. Madison (*The Federalist LI*) abstracted a psychological meaning from Montesquieu's doctrine. He argued that the means of resisting an attack on the powers given to an office by the constitution should be tied to the ambitions of the office holders. Thus Madison combined the formula, "Ambition must be made to check ambition," with Montesquieu's formula, "Power must check power."

5 "The natural aim of a state that has no foreign enemies or believes it has secured itself against them by barriers" (Montesquieu's note).

6 "The peculiar disadvantage of the *liberum veto*" (Montesquieu's note). The Polish Diet operated on the rule of unanimity. The *liberum veto* was the power on the part of any member to block legislation.

7 The MS (II, f° 163) gives an earlier and more developed title: "The Principles of Political Liberty, as Found in the Constitution of England."

8 Montesquieu does not here define the executive power as that of carrying out the laws.

9 The separation of the executive and legislative powers from the judicial is not found in Locke, who seems on most other points to be Montesquieu's model in this chapter. Thus Montesquieu is here applying his notion that quasi-autonomous intermediate bodies such as the French *parlements* (which had to register laws before they became effective) are essential to liberty.

10 Montesquieu here defines the executive power for the first time as that of carrying out public resolutions.

11 "At Venice" (Montesquieu's note).

12 This sociological point was turned against Montesquieu by Bentham who saw no purpose in maintaining the separation of governmental powers, if all of them were staffed by men of the same social class.

13 "As at Athens" (Montesquieu's note).

14 Montesquieu seems to have believed that in England the role of the jury was far greater than in fact it was. He was misinformed about the status of professional judges, who played a much more important part than he realized. Cf. Brethe, II, 332–5.

15 Brethe notes correctly that Montesquieu, by subordinating the executive to the legislative power, here demonstrates that he did not believe in the absolute separation and independence of all three powers.

16 Montesquieu here repeats his previous argument (XI, 3) that citizens may be secured against invasions of their liberties by judges, if and only if, judges reduce their role to the strict application of the text of the law to particular cases.

17 Montesquieu was referring to the fact that peers of the Realm could be tried for felonies and treason only by other peers, i.e., in the House of Peers, or the House of Lords. As for English juries, at the time Montesquieu wrote they were made up exclusively of landowners. Persons from other social classes were not tried by members of their own class.

18 Montesquieu here referred to the writ of habeas corpus, an English liberty which had no equivalent in French law. The French king could imprison subjects without trial.

19 Under English constitutional procedures, Parliament could grant to the prime minister the right for one year to suspend the writ of habeas corpus in cases where a defendant was charged with treason.

20 In the MS (II, f° 181) this passage was applied as an argument against giving the legislative branch the right of impeachment.

21 Montesquieu here approves representative government, but the concept is imperfectly integrated into his typology of governments. He does not do much with the concept of representative democracy. He views direct democracy as the usual type.

22 Montesquieu was not a democrat. He did not mince words when he discussed what he called the basest class of the people. He accepted the view of his English friends that the votes of the unpropertied could easily be purchased. Hence it was right to exclude them from the suffrage. But he said nothing in *Spirit of the Laws* about the extraordinary corruption of English politics in his time, despite the exclusion of the unpropertied from the sufrage. What survives of Montesquieu's "Notes on England" as well as his correspondence is enough to show that he well knew and was even disturbed by the bribery and selling of votes that characterized English politics in the age of Walpole.

23 Note that at this point Montesquieu adds the notion of checks and balances to that of the separation of powers. And since he assigns each house of Parliament to a class (The House of Lords to the notables; the House of Commons to what was legally the people), Montesquieu is also making use of the theory of the mixed constitution.

24 As Brethe remarks, Montesquieu here gives another meaning to his earlier statement in this chapter that the judicial power is invisible and of no force because it is exercised through juries rather than through permanent institutions. Now Montesquieu declares that the power to judge is in a sense nothing. But this sense is that of political forces. The judicial power exerts no force comparable to those of the legislative and executive powers.

25 Montesquieu's formulation appears unsatisfactory when we consider the fact that members of the English executive or ministry were drawn from the House of Commons without any of the fatal consequences to liberty predicted by Montesquieu on the basis of the separation of powers. On the other hand, during the revolution the French Convention did exhibit many of the malignant

effects attributed by Montesquieu to the combination of legislative and executive functions.

26 The ephors were the five Spartan magistrates, who, combining executive, judicial, and disciplinary powers, dominated the state, including the two kings. The *cosmoi* were Cretan magistrates resembling the Spartan ephors. For discussions and criticisms, see Aristotle, *Politics*, II, 10; and Polybius, *History*, VI, 45–7.

27 Montesquieu here condemned the power of impeachment by the legislature when applied to the chief of state. His view was disregarded by the authors of the American Constitution. Montesquieu had in mind the trial and execution of Charles I by Parliament. He thought that the best constitutional solution was that he encountered in eighteenth-century England. The king was not responsible personally to Parliament, but his ministers were.

28 "These were magistrates elected annually by the people. See Stephen of Byzantium" (Montesquieu's note). The amimones were magistrates elected for life in the republic of Cnidos.

29 "The Roman magistrates could be held accountable after the expiration of their terms of office. See Dionysius of Halicarnasus, Book IX, the case of the tribune Genutius" (Montesquieu's note).

30 Montesquieu here refers to the impeachment procedure in English constitutional practice of his time. He has already excepted the king from its practice.

31 "*De minoribus rebus principes consultant, de majoribus omnes; ita tamen ut ea quoque quorum penes plebem arbitrium est apud principes pertractentur*" (Montesquieu's note). "On small matters the chiefs consult; on larger questions, the community; but with this limitation, that even the subjects, the decision of which rests with the people, are first handled by the chiefs." Tacitus, *Germania*, 11, trans. Maurice Hutton in *Tacitus* (London, 1963), p. 279. The full title of the *Germania*, or *Germany*, is: "Concerning the geography, the manners and customs, and the tribes of Germany."

32 Herodotus (IV, 144) reported that the Chaledonians could have built their city on the site of Byzantium but did not, despite the inherent superiority of the place. Thus Montesquieu reproaches Harrington for not appreciating the liberty existing in his own country and constructing instead the utopia of Oceana.

Book XIV. The Relation between Laws and the Nature of Climate

1 In this third part, Books XIV through XIX, Montesquieu treats the relations between laws and the nature of the climate, the nature of terrain, and the general spirit, the *moeurs*, and *manières* of a nation. The division of the work into six parts was omitted in the 1748 edition by the printer, Jean Vernet; it was restored in 1750 by Montesquieu, but abandoned in the 1757 and 1758 editions (it is not clear whether this was Montesquieu's decision or that of his executors). This chapter should be compared to Montesquieu's, "An Essay on the Causes that May Affect Men's Minds and Characters," *Political Theory*, 4 (1976), pp. 132–62.

2 "This even affects the appearance: in cold weather, people appear thinner" (Montesquieu's note).

3 "We know that it shortens iron" (Montesquieu's note).

4 "That for the Spanish succession" (Montesquieu's note). The War of the Spanish Succession began in 1701 and lasted until 1714.

5 In this chapter Montesquieu argues that an astute legislator can modify the deleterious effects of climate upon the disposition of a population.

6 "Panamanack. See Kircher" (Montesquieu's note). Athanasius Kircher, *Chine*

illustrée, 1667. The surname given to Brahma, as reported by Kircher was Paramanand.

7   "La Loubère, *A Traveler's Views of Siam*, p. 446" (Montesquieu's note).

8   "Buddha wished to reduce the heart to pure nothingness. 'We have eyes and ears; but perfection is to be found neither in seein nor hearing; we have a mouth, hands, etc., but perfection demands that these members be inactive.' This is taken from the dialogue of a Chinese philosopher, quoted by Father du Halde, t. III" (Montesquieu's note). Montesquieu used Foe for Buddha. This is Father du Halde's transcription of the Chinese name for Buddha. Buddha provided not laws, but a religion.

9   By "législateurs de la Chine," Montesquieu again refers to such figures as Confucius who created a religion and a way of life without promulgating positive laws.

10 "Ricaut, *Of the Ottoman Empire*, p. 204" (Montesquieu's note). Rycaut [1] 6, *Histoire de l'empire ottoman*, 1709.

11 "Suicide is contrary to the natural law and revealed religion." (Montesquieu's note). This note was added in the 1757 edition, fulfilling Montesquieu's pledge in his "Replies and Explanations Given to the Faculty of Theology."

12 "It could easily be complicated by scurvy, which, especially in some countries, renders a man odd and unbearable to himself. *Voyage of François Pyrard*, part II, chapter XXI" (Montesquieu's note). See Glossary of Proper Names.

13 "I take this word to mean the design to overthrow established power, especially that of democracy. This is the meaning given the word by the Greeks and Romans" (Montesquieu's note).

14 *The Dictionary of the French Academy* (1740) defines *une lime sourde* as "a file made specifically to file down or to cut iron without making much noise."

Book XV. How the Laws of Civil Slavery Are Related to the Nature of the Climate

1   "Justinian, *Institutes*, Book I" (Montesquieu's note). This chapter begins on the ironical note that Montesquieu so often strikes in this chapter when he is not manifesting moral outrage. As was noted by Jean Ehrard, Montesquieu in treating slavery, is confronted by a fundamental contradiction in the "nature of things." On the one hand, it is an almost universal social relationship, and as such must be explained by such "natural" causes as climate; on the other hand, Montesquieu finds slavery so abhorrent that he describes it in Book XI, 6, as "contrary to nature." Montesquieu in the same sentence states that in certain countries slavery is founded on a reason derived from nature, i.e., climate. Montesquieu never satisfactorily resolves this tension. Even when he is being most consistently deterministic, he nevertheless resorts to arguments from natural law. See my Introduction on this point.

2   Brethe notes that it was not the *Institutes*, but its commentators who so argued.

3   "With the exception of those that eat their prisoners" (Montesquieu's note). Again, an ironical note when Montesquieu is confronted with a contradiction. His exception is a reference to a similar passage dealing with the same problem in Book I, 3: "All countries have a law of nations. Even the Iroquois, who eat their prisoners have one. . . . The only trouble is . . . that its principles are false."

4   Montesquieu misrepresented the Roman law on this point. A freeman was not allowed to sell himself into slavery; liberty was inalienable. But a magistrate called the praetor could enslave a freeman who had engaged in a particular sort of fraud. This occurred when a freeman had himself sold as a slave by an

accomplice, with whom he shared the proceeds. Then the pretended slave would reveal himself to be a freeman and claim his liberty. The praetor could enslave him and award his ownership to the purchaser.

It may be, as Brethe suggests, that Montesquieu's real target was not so much the Roman jurists, as those modern theorists who defended slavery by deriving it from voluntary servitude, the equity of which they defended. For the respective treatments of this argument by Hobbes, Grotius, Pufendorf, and Locke, see Richter, "Despotism," op. cit. The special usage of "despotism," both in this sense of voluntary servitude, and that of the righful enslavement of captives in war, apparently began with Bodin. Montesquieu was no better disposed to this concept of despotism than to that he himself formulated. Rousseau attacked such defenses of slavery in Book I of the *Social Contract*.

5   *Peculium* was the private property allowed to a slave under the Roman Law.

6   "I mean slavery in the strict sense, as it existed among the Romans, and as it now has been established in our colonies" (Montesquieu's note). This formulation may be taken from Locke.

7   The French civil law, followed an enactment by Diocletian that permitted the voiding of a contract to sell real estate on certain conditions: if the seller suffered extraordinary damage, that is, if he received less than half of what the real estate was worth. Montesquieu argued that since such a principle was applied to the loss of real property, it had to be applied in cases of an even greater damage, that of losing one's liberty.

8   This was the position of both Grotius and Pufendorf.

9   "*Bibliothèque anglaise*, t. XIII, second part, XX, art. 3" (Montesquieu's note). The accuracy of this anecdote is dubious. Montesquieu cites it not from the original, but from a review of an English book that summarized the account of Lopez de Gama. Yet there were Spaniards who argued that the Indians could not be considered to be human because of their customs and religion. Cf. Lewis Hanke, *Aristotle and the American Indians* (Bloomington, Ill. 1959).

10   "See *History of the Conquest of Mexico* by Solis, and that of Peru by Garcilasso de la Vega" (Montesquieu's note). Although Montesquieu did not report inaccurately here the attitudes of some Spanish soldiers and theologians, he failed to do credit to those other Spaniards within the church who opposed, as did Montesquieu, the view that the Indians could be enslaved in order to convert them to Christianity. And the papacy specifically repudiated the position here attacked by Montesquieu.

11   "Father Labat, *New Voyage to the Isles of America*, vol. IV, p. 114, in-12" (Montesquieu's note).

12   The deliberate irony of this chapter was not perceived by the editor of *Spirit of the Laws*. He wrote: "The above arguments from a striking instance of the prejudice under which even a liberal mind can labor." (New York, 1949, p.239n).

13   "*Politics*, Book I, ch. 1" (Montesquieu's note).

14   "It is instructive to know the situation in the mines of the Hartz in Lower Saxony and those in Hungary" (Montesquieu's note). Montesquieu visited these while on his travels. His notes have been preserved.

15   Few passages in Montesquieu display more openly the conflict between his belief in natural law and his new mode of explanation based on the analysis of all the elements that make up the "nature of things."

16   This chapter appeared for the first time in the posthumous edition of 1757. It therefore does not figure in the Nugent translation, an omission noted and remedied, as far as I know, for the first time here.

17   This argument anticipates that condition of determining justice John Rawls

has called "the veil of ignorance."

18 Like "the veil of ignorance " this argument is an anticipation of Kant, which it also resembles in its derivation from rational natural law arguments.

Book XIX. Laws: Their Relation to Those Principles that Form the General Spirit, *Moeurs,* and *Manières* of a Nation

1 This chapter is based in large part upon *The Works of Tacitus,* trans. with commentary by Thomas Gordon. This was translated into French in 1742 as *Discours historiques, critique , et politiques sur Tacite.*

2 Compare Montesquieu's definition of tyranny in his note to XIV, 13.

3 "Book LIV, p. 532" (Montesquieu's note). The reference is to Dio's *History.* Compare *Considerations,* ch. XIII.

4 Montesquieu is referring to France.

5 Montesquieu is perhaps the nobleman in question.

6 "See *The Fable of the Bees*" (Montesquieu's note). The reference is to the work of Bernard Mandeville. See the discussion of Mandeville in my Introduction.

7 Montesquieu here contrasts France to Spain.

8 Montesquieu is again alluding to Mandeville's thesis that the vices of vanity and luxury are more profitable to society than are the virtues of humility and simplicity.

9 "The people who follow the khan of Malacamber, those of Carnataca and Coromandel, are proud and indolent; they consume little because they are wretchedly poor; whereas the subjects of the mogol and the people of Hindustan work and enjoy the conveniences of life, like the Europeans. *Collection of the Voyage for the Establishment of the India Company.* Volume I, p. 54" (Montesquieu's note). The reference is to the peoples who inhabited the southwest coast of the Hindustan peninsula near the present sites of Madras and Pondicherry.

10 "Book XLIII" (Montesquieu's note). The reference is to Marcus Junianus Justinus, *Historaie Phillippicae* ch. II.

11 "By the nature of the climate and the soil" (Montesquieu's note).

12 "Father du Halde, volume II" (Montesquieu's note). The reference is to p. 171, ibid.

13 For the definitions of *moeurs* and *manières,* see the list of French terms and XIX, 6.

14 "Says Father du Halde" (Montesquieu's note).

15 "Moses used the same code for both laws and religion. The first Romans confused their ancient customs with laws." (Montesquieu's note).

16 "See Father du Halde" (Montesquieu's note).

17 "See the classics from which Father du Halde has provided us with choice extracts" (Montesquieu's note).

18 "It is this which established emulation, eliminated laziness, and cultivated high esteem for knowledge" (Montesquieu's note).

19 "See the reasons given by the Chinese magistrates in their decrees proscribing the Christian religion. *Edifying Letters;* collection XVII" (Montesquieu's note). The reference is to Poncet, *Lettres édifiantes,* op. cit.

20 "See Book IV, chapter 3, and Book XIX, chapter 12" (Montesquieu's note). These are cross-references to *Spirit of the Laws.*

21 "See below, Book XXIV" (Montesquieu's note). The reference is to ch. 3.

22 Montesquieu seems to have forgotten his previous judgment that China is a despotism, whose principle is fear. Cf. VIII, 21. In the same place Montes-

quieu attempts to explain how China might once have been less despotic during its earlier dynasties. He rules out honor as the principle.

23 "Lange's *Journal* in 1721 and 1722; volume VIII, *Of Voyages to the North*, page 363" (Montesquieu's note). The reference is to Lange, *Recueil des Voyages* op. cit.

24 This passage has been cited as an example of Montesquieu's relativism. It represented a characteristic and very influential position that made him the principal source of pro-Jewish arguments in French eighteenth-century thought. This passage came as a response to a controversy about the merits of the ancient Greeks and Jews respectively. Montesquieu here was asserting that both cultures had merits relative to their situations. The Jews had been given the best laws compatible with their situation as an oriental people. Cf. Arthur Hertzberg, *The French Enlightenment and the Jews*. New York, 1968), p. 274 and ch. 9 generally. See XXV, 13, and on the other side, In "Essay on the Causes," op. cit., 153—4.

25 "*The Laws*, Book XII" (Montesquieu's note).

26 Ibid.

27 "In simplum" (Montesquieu's note).

28 "Titus Livy, Book XXXVIII" (Montesquieu's note). The reference is to Titus Livy, *History of Rome*, Book XXX, VIII sec. 55.

29 "*Institutes*, Book II, tit. VI, 52; Ozel's compilation at Leyden, 1658" (Montesquieu's note). The reference is to *Caii jurisconsulti antiquissimi institutiones cum notis perpetuis Jacobi Oiselii*, Lugduni Batavorum.

30 "*Institutes*, Book II, de pupil. substit. section 3" (Montesquieu's note).

31 "The vulgar arrangement is the following: If such a one does not accept the inheritance, I substitute for him, etc.; the pupillary arrangement provides: If such a one dies before attaining puberty, I substitute for him, etc." (Montesquieu's note).

32 In the MS (IV, f° 158), this chapter bore the title: "How laws follow *manières*: reasons for repudiation among the Romans."

33 "Leg. VIII, *cod*. de repudiis" (Montesquieu's note).

34 "And from the law of the Twelve Tables. See Cicero, *Second Philippic*" (Montesquieu's note).

35 "*Si verberibus, quae ingenuis aliena sunt, afficientem probaverit*" (Montesquieu's note). The reference is to the provision that allowed a freeborn woman to repudiate her husband for beating her in a way that disgraced her.

36 "In the revised version 117, ch. XIV" (Montesquieu's note).

37 "Ch. VI" (Montesquieu's note). Here Montesquieu deals with the effects of England's political constitution, or laws, upon its *moeurs*. Along with XI, 6, and XIV, 13, this chapter presentes an extensive analysis of England by Montesquieu's distinctive categories. But why did he choose here to take England as his preferred example of how laws may affect *moeurs*? Brethe has found some revelatory reflections by Montesquieu: "The English nation has scarcely any unique *manières* or *moeurs*. In addition, its respect for religion is limited to that felt by an enlightened population. [But] it has a prodigious attachment to those laws that are unique to it. Thus there is no limit to the force exerted by these laws when either they run counter to the climate or are supported by it." [*Pensées*, 1903; 854.] Compare the view given in Book XIV, 13.

38 In XI, 6, Montesquieu had said that the judicial power was in a sense invisible and played no political part.

39 Here Montesquieu deals with an aspect of faction that attracted Madison's attention in the *Federalist*, X: how to avoid a type of political conflict that

becomes irreconcilable because of the confrontation of two groups, each always including the same individuals. Montesquieu, however, here refers to the individualism of English society.

40 The reference is probably to France in Montesquieu's time.

41 Montesquieu here alludes only to conquest on the European continent.

42 Although his language is somewhat grandiloquent, Montesquieu here indicates his awareness of how significant were those English industries based on the manufacture of products derived from raw materials produced elsewhere.

43 Ireland.

44 Under the Tudors.

45 Montesquieu was here being vague in order to avoid the censorship of the church in France. He was no doubt referring to the religious policy of James II.

46 The Church of England could not reform itself; only Parliament could do so.

47 Montesquieu is making an invidious reference to the French royal court.

48 See XIV, 13.

Book XXIII. How Laws Are Related to the Number of Inhabitants

1 Montesquieu used the word *l'hôpital* in the sense that hospital used to have in English: "a charitable institution for the refuge, maintenance, or education of needy, aged, infirm, or young persons; as Christ's Hospital, London." (*Webster's New International Dictionary*, 2d ed. I have used the term "charitable institution."

2 Montesquieu seems to anticipate something like a system of social security for modern commercial nations. Although economic development is his primary remedy for the abolition of suffering, nevertheless he argues that there will always be need for government provision to those incapable of aiding themselves.

3 "See Chardin, *Travels through Persia*, volume VIII" (Montesquieu's note). The reference is to Jean Chardin, *Voyage en Perse et autres lieux de l'Orient*. Aurengzebe (reigned 1659–1707) was the grand mogol of the empire founded in India by Babur.

4 "See *History of the Reformation in England* by Burnet" (Montesquieu's note). The reference is to Gilbert Burnet, *History of the Reformation in England* (1679–1715).

5 This passage was censured by the Faculty of Theology at Paris, which interpreted it to mean that monks should support themselves by their own work. This the Faculty identified with the heretical doctrine of Wycliffe condemned by the Council of Constance. Montesquieu argued that he had not excluded charity as a means of supporting monks. But Montesquieu went on to claim the right for the state to limit the number of monks whenever it could be demonstrated that they produced effects damaging to the well-being of the population as a whole. However, Montesquieu promised to change the wording of his sentence to read "Henry VIII destroyed monasticism, because he regarded monks as an idle nation." However, Montesquieu did not make the change in his final edition.

6 By his distinction between rich and poor, commercial and agrarian nations, Montesquieu introduces ambiguity and ambivalence into his theory. His attack on the charitable institutions of the church in some ways anticipates the harsh doctrine of nineteenth-century charity reformers. Yet his doctrine has humane elements that run contrary to their teaching. It is almost as though he is saying that to abolish the church's charitable institutions is a necessary step for agrarian societies that need to become commercial. But once they have done so, they ought to provide for the needs of those suffering.

Book XXIV. How Laws Are Related to Every Country's Established Religion

1 Montesquieu argues that he is here concerned solely with the secular utility of religion.

2 *"Thoughts on the comet, etc."* (Montesquieu's note). The reference is to Pierre Bayle, *Pensées sur la Comète* (Cologne, 1682).

3 Montesquieu has already commented that the only check on despots is religion (II, 4).

4 *"A travelers's View of Ethiopia,* by Mr. Poncet, physician, in the fourth collection of *Edifying Letters"* (Montesquieu's note). The reference is to Charles Jacques Poncet, *Voyage en Ethiopie, fait dans les années 1698, 1699 et 1700,* first published in the *Lettres édifiantes.* Sennar was a Mohammedan kingdom in the Sudan.

5 Montesquieu is here applying the theory of climates first set forth in Book XIV.

6 Montesquieu here applies his theory of the causes of conduct operative in the general spirit. This is a theory that points out that men may be restrained by any one of a number of causes.

7 "See the account of Brother Jean Duplan Carpin, sent to Tartary by Pope Innocent IV in 1246" (Montesquieu's note).

8 *"Edifying letters,* fifteenth collection" (Montesquieu's note).

9 *"Politics,* Book VII, ch. 17" (Montesquieu's note).

10 *"Collection of the Voyages that Contributed to the Establishment of the East India Company,* Vol. IV, part I, p. 127" (Montesquieu's note). Miyako means "capital city" and refers to Kyoto at this time.

11 "See Prideaux, *Life of Mahomet"* (Montesquieu's note).

12 "A Chinese philosopher argues thus against the doctrine of Buddha; 'It is said, in a book of that sect, that the body is our domicile and the soul is the immortal guest which lodges within; but if the bodies of our parents are merely shelters, it is natural to regard them with the same contempt as we would have for an earthen hut. Is it not this wish to tear from the heart the virtue of love for our parents? This leads to the neglect of the body to the extent of refusing it the compassion and affection so necessary to its preservation. Thus the disciples of Buddha destroy themselves by the thousands.' Work of a Chinese philosopher in the collection of Father du Halde, volume III, p. 52" (Montesquieu's note).

13 "See Thomas Bartolin, *Antiquities of the Danes"* (Montesquieu's note).

14 "'An Account of Japan,' in the *Collection of Voyages that Contributed to the Establishment of the East India Company"* (Montesquieu's note).

15 "Forbin's *Memoirs"* (Montesquieu's note).

Book XXV. How Laws Are Related to Established Religions and Their Provisions for Maintaining Orthodoxy

1 "See the *Collection of Voyages that Contributed to the Establishment of the East India Company,* volume V, part I, p. 192" (Montesquieu's note). The reference is to *Recueil de Voyages qui ont servi à l'établissement de la Compagnie des Indes.*

2 Montesquieu here returns to the irony he used in attacking slavery.

3 "The source of blindness of the Jews is their failure to realize that the design of the Gospel is to be discovered in the order of God's decrees; and thus it is a consequence of his immutability" (Montesquieu's note).

End of Selections from *The Spirit of the Law*

1   *The Aeneid of Vergil*, trans. Allen Mandelbaum (Berkeley, 1971).

Glossary of proper names

ADDISON, JOSEPH – (1672–1719); English essayist, perhaps best known for his collaboration with Richard Steele on the *Spectator* and *Tatler*.

ALCIBIADES – (c.450–404 B.C.); Athenian statesman, brought up by his guardian, Pericles, and became the pupil of Socrates. His political and military careers figure prominently in the history of Athens.

AMMIANUS MARCELLINUS – (c.330–400 A.D.); historian whose work covers the reigns from Trajan to Valerius. His *History* is among the best sources for the period, although only eighteen books remain of the original thirty-one.

ANASTASIUS I – (c.430–518 A.D.); Byzantine emperor from 491 to 518.

ANSON, GEORGE – (1697–1762); English admiral who circumnavigated the globe in a campaign against the Spanish, the account of which, *Voyage Round the World in 1740–44*, was written by his chaplain, Richard Walter.

APPIAN – (2nd century); Greek historian. His principal work is the *Roman History*, in twenty-four books, arranged ethnographically according to the peoples conquered by the Romans.

ARISTOTLE – (384–322 B.C.); great Greek philosopher and student of Plato. His work includes the *Politics*.

ARRIAN – (c.96–180); Greek historian and philosopher.

ASCONIUS PEDIANUS – (9 B.C.–76 A.D.); writer whose work includes a commentary on Cicero's orations.

ATHENAEUS – (3rd century); Greek grammarian who lived first at Alexandria and then at Rome. His only extant work is *The Learned Banquet*.

AUBIGNE, THEODORE AGRIPPA D' – (1552–1630); major French poet, he was also renowned as a Huguenot captain and historian. His *l'Histoire Universelle* deals with the period from 1553 to 1602.

AURELIUS VICTOR SEXTUS – (4th century); African who served as a Roman governor and wrote a history of the Caesars.

BODIN, JEAN – (1520–96); writer whose *Six Books of the Republic* was the most important French work of the century in political theory, and served as a model for Montesquieu.

BOSSUET, JACQUES BENIGNE – (1627–1704); French bishop, historian, and orator. His principal works include *Funeral Orations* and *Discourse on Universal History*.

BOULAINVILLIERS, HENRI, COMTE DE – (1658–1722); French political writer and historian. Member of the Entresol and friend of Montesquieu. Critic of Louis XIV; champion of French nobility, whose rights he based on those of the Frankish conquerors of the Gauls.

BURNET, GILBERT – (1643–1715); Anglican prelate and author of the *History of the Reformation in England*.

CERCEAU, JEAN ANTOINE DU – (1670–1730); author of *Histoire de la dernière révolution de perse* (Paris, 1728).

CHARDIN, JEAN – (1643–1713); French Huguenot who traveled in both the Middle East and Far East before settling in England, where he was knighted. Montesquieu took much of his material for the *Persian Letters* and for his account of despotism from the ten volumes of Chardin's *Voyages en perse et autres lieux de l'Orient*.

CICERO, MARCUS TULLIUS – (106–43 B.C.); Roman statesman and writer whose works include *De Republica* and *De Legibus*.

CLARKE, SAMUEL – (1675–1729); English theologian, philosopher, and exponent of Newtonian physics.

COMMODUS, LUCIUS AELIUS AURELIUS – (161–192); the elder son of Marcus Aurelius, he was emperor from 180 to 192. He was an arbitrary ruler who seems to have been driven mad by the intoxication of power, and was put to death by his advisors.

CONSTATINE VII (PORPHYOGENITUS) – (905–959); Byzantine emperor from 913 to 959.

DEMETRIUS OF PHALERUM – (c.350 B.C.–?); escaped death as a pro-Macedonian and was made absolute governor at Athens by Cassander.

DEMOSTHENES – (384–322 B.C.); famous Athenian orator, who used his eloquence in both judicial and political proceedings.

DIO CASSIUS – (150–235); Roman administrator and historian. Author of a *History of Rome*.

DIODORUS SICULUS – (1st century B.C.); historian who wrote a *World History* in forty books from the earliest times to Caesar's Gallic War.

DIONYSIUS OF HALICARNASSUS – (30–8 B.C.); historian who taught in Rome. He wrote *Antiquitates Romanae* in twenty books.

DU HALDE, JEAN-BAPTISTE – (1674–1743); Jesuit who compiled the *Lettres édifiantes écrits des missions étrangères*, and was the author of *Description geographique, historique, chronologique, politique, et physique de l'empire de la chine et de la tartaire chinoise*, 1735.

EPAMINONDAS – (c.418–362 B.C.); Theban statesman and general whose character was much admired by ancient writers.

FENELON, FRANÇOIS DE SALIGNAC DE LA MOTHE – (1651–1715); French writer and archbishop of Cambrai. Tutor of the duke of Burgundy, grandson of Louis XIV and presumed eventual heir. Fénelon wrote *Télémaque* and other works for his pupil's instruction. Fénelon sharply criticized Louis XIV as a despot who had destroyed the political power of the nobility and ruined France by his martial and mercantilist policies.

FERDINAND, V of CASTILLE and LEON, and II of ARAGON – (1452–1516); king who made Spain one of the leading powers of Europe. He and his wife sent Christopher Columbus to America.

FILMER, SIR ROBERT – (d. 1653); a supporter of absolute royal power, he argued that the government of a family by the father is the original form of all government, and that kings derive their authority from the original grant made by God to Adam. Filmer's best known work is *Patriarcha*, published in 1680 after his death. It was the object of lengthy refutations by Algernon Sidney and John Locke.

FLORUS, LUCIUS ANNAEUS – (late 1st–early 2nd century); historian whose works include an *Epitome of Roman History*, which traces the history of Rome from its foundation to the time of Augustus.

GRAVINA, GIAN VINCENZO – (1644–1718); Italian jurist whose major work is the

Origines juris civilis (1701). Its French translation bore the title *Esprit des lois romaines* and was published in London in 1766.

HERODIAN OF ALEXANDRIA – (170–240); Greek historian who compiled a history of his own time from Commodus to Gordian.

HOUSSAYE, AMELOT DE LA – (1634–1706); historian whose work includes the *History of the Government of Venice.*

HUARTE, JUAN DE DAN JUAN – (1529–1588?); author of *Examen de Ingenios*, an important psychological work translated into all European languages.

JUSTINIAN I – (483–565); Byzantine emperor from 527–565. He is best known for his work as a codifier and legislator.

JUSTINUS (JUSTIN), MARCUS JUNIANIUS – (probably 3rd century); a Roman historian who made an epitome in Latin of Pompeius Trogus' *Historiae Phillippicae.*

KIRCHER, ANTHANASIUS – (1601–1680); German physician and Jesuit. Montesquieu referred to his work *Chine illustrée*, published in Latin in 1667 and translated into French in 1670.

LA LOUBERE, SIMON DE – (1642–1729); French diplomat who was the author of *Description du royaume de siam* (1691).

LANGE, LAURENT – (? – ?); Swedish engineer in the service of Peter the Great. He was in Peking between 1719 and 1722. Lange's book *Relation du voyage du Laurent Lange à la chine*, appeared in a collection owned by Montesquieu, *Recueil des voyages au nord* (Amsterdam, 1715).

LAW, JOHN – (1671–1729); Scottish financier who founded the first French bank in 1716, and organized the "Mississippi Scheme," which at its height controlled colonization in Louisiana, absorbed the French East India, China, and African Companies.

LIBANIUS – (314–393); Greek sophist and rhetorician.

LIVY – (59 B.C.–17 A.D.); Greek historian of the Augustan Age.

LYSIAS – (c.459–c.380 B.C.); great orator whom Pericles convinced to settle in Athens.

MACHIAVELLI, NICCOLO – (1469–1527); Italian statesman and writer. His principal works include *The Prince* and *Discourses on the First Decade of Livy.*

MALEBRANCHE, NICOLAS – (1638–1715); French Cartesian philosopher who was a member of the Congregation of the Oratory, the order that operated Juilly, the school Montesquieu attended.

MANDEVILLE, BERNARD DE – (1670–1733); Dutch-English satirist and author of *The Fable of the Bees* (1714).

MARTIAL (MARCUS VALERIUS MARTIALIS) – (c.40–c.104); Latin poet and epigrammatist.

PERRY, JOHN – (1670–1732); English engineer brought to Moscow by Peter the Great; author of *Etat présent de la grande russie*. tr. de l'anglais (1717). The English title is *The State of Russia under the Present Czar* (London, 1716).

PLATO – (c.427–347 B.C.); great Athenian philosopher and student of Socrates whose works include the *Republic* and the *Laws.*

PLUTARCH – (46–after 120); Greek writer best known for his *Lives* and *Moralia.*

POLYBIUS – (203?–120 B.C.); Greek historian of third and second-century Rome. His principal work is the *History* in forty books.

PRIDEAUX, HUMPHREY – (1648–1724); professor of Hebrew at Oxford. Author of *The True Nature of Imposture Fully Displayed in the Life of Mahomet*, 1697 (French translation, 1699).

PRISCUS — (5th century); Greek historian who took part in a mission sent to Attila by Theodosius in 445.

PROCOPIUS — (fl. first half of 6th century); Byzantine historian whose principal work is his *History of the Wars of Justinian* in eight books.

PUFENDORF, SAMUEL — (1632–1694); German jurist best known for his treatises on natural and international law. He was much admired by Montesquieu.

PYRARD, FRANÇOIS — (1570?–1621); French traveler who wrote *Discours de voyage des françois aux indes orientales* followed by *Traité et description des animaux, arbres et fruits des Indes*, 1611.

RETZ, JEAN, PAUL DE GONDI, CARDINAL DE — (1614–1679); French churchman involved in the outbreak of that revolt called the Fronde in 1648.

RYCAUT, PAUL — (1628–1730); English diplomat whose book on the Turkish Empire was twice translated into French (*Histoire de l'état present de l'empire ottoman*, 1648; *Histoire de l'empire ottoman*, 1709). The English title is *The Present State of the Ottoman Empire* (London, 1668).

SAINT-SIMON, LOUIS DE ROUVROY, DUC DE — (1675–1755); French soldier, diplomat, and writer of memoirs of the reign of Louis XIV. Member of the council of the Regency, he, like Fénelon, was a critic of centralized monarchy, and regarded the ancient nobility as entitled to a continuing part in the French Constitution.

SALLUST — (86–34 B.C.); Roman historian. His works include *Bellum Catilinae, Bellum Iugurthinum*, and *Historiae*.

SALVIAN — (390–480); Bishop of Marseilles. He wrote to prove that the barbarians had been sent by God to punish the Romans for their vices and crimes.

SIDNEY, ALGERNON — (1622–1683); English republican theorist most noted for his *Discourses Concerning Government*, published posthumously in 1698.

SPINOZA, BENEDICTIUS DE — (1632–1677); Dutch Jewish philosopher who, in his *Tractatus Theologico-Politicus* (1670), denied the value of Christian revelation, and in his *Ethics* took a pantheist position.

STRABO — (c.64 B.C.–post 21 A.D.); Greek historian and geographer.

SUETONIUS — (c.69–c.140); Roman historian whose biography of Domitian concludes his *De Caesarum*.

TACITUS, CORNELIUS — (c.55–120 B.C.); Roman historian whose work includes the *Annals*.

TOURNEFORT, JOSEPH PITTON DE — (1656–1708); greatest botanist of his time. He was sent abroad by Louis XIV to pursue his research.

VEGETIUS — (late 4th century); Roman writer whose work includes *Epitoma rei militaris*. This book on the military art was dedicated to the emperor Valentian II, and is an important source because of its abundance of detail. Machiavelli made full use of Vegetius in his own *Art of War*.

XENOPHON — (c.430–c.354 B.C.); disciple of Socrates who wrote a memoir of him, as well as important works of history, political theory, and biography.

ZONARAS of CONSTANTINOPLE — (fl. first half of the 12th century); Byzantine historian. His *World History* extends from the Creation to 1118 A.D.

ZOSIMUS — (second half of the 5th century); Byzantine historian who wrote six books on the "Decline of Rome" from Augustus to Alaric's taking of Rome in 400 A.D. Zosimus attributed the decline to Christianity.

Index

MELVIN RICHTER is Professor of Political Science, Hunter College and the Graduate School, City University of New York. He earned the B.A. degree in History and Literature from Harvard College in 1943 and the Ph.D. degree in Political Science from Harvard University in 1953. His publications include the *Politics of Conscience: T. H. Green and His Age,* awarded the Triennial Prize of the Conference for British Studies, 1966; he has edited *Essays in Theory and History,* nominated for the Pulitzer Prize, 1970; and *Political Theory and Political Education* (1980).